CHING

IN TEN MINUTES

Other Avon Books by
R.T. Kaser

AFRICAN ORACLES IN TEN MINUTES
MAYAN ORACLES FOR THE MILLENNIUM
RUNES IN TEN MINUTES
TAROT IN TEN MINUTES

I CHING

IN TEN MINUTES

R . T . K A S E R

AVON BOOKS  NEW YORK

I CHING IN TEN MINUTES is an original publication of Avon Books. This work has never before appeared in book form.

AVON BOOKS
A division of
The Hearst Corporation
1350 Avenue of the Americas
New York, New York 10019

Copyright © 1994 by Richard T. Kaser
Interior desing by Robin Arzt
Published by arrangement with the author
Visit our website at http://www.AvonBooks.com
Library of Congress Catalog Card Number: 93-11886
ISBN: 0-380-77153-5

Library of Congress Cataloging in Publication Data:

Kaser, R. T.
  I Ching in ten minutes / R.T. Kaser.
      p.   cm.
Includes index.
1. I ching. 2. Divination—China. 3. Fortune telling—China.
I. Title. II. Title: I ching in 10 minutes.
BF1773.2.C5K37   1994   93-11886
133.3'3—dc20   CIP

First Avon Books Trade Printing: January 1994

AVON TRADEMARK REG U.S. PAT. OFF. AND IN OTHER COUNTRIES, MARCA REGISTRADA, HECHO EN U.S.A.

Printed in the U.S.A.

OPM 10 9 8 7 6

For the Great Spirit of Potomac Woods
and
With my heart and soul
to Tory

WIND/MIST

Everything changes,
nothing remains without change.

The Teaching of Buddha

PREFACE

I Ching is the ancient Chinese oracle of chance and change. For thousands of years people in the Far East have tossed coins or counted sticks to find the answers to their everyday problems and to gain insight into the meaning of their lives. For Westerners, however, the I Ching method can seem difficult and the guidance of the traditional texts, cryptic . . . but no more.

I Ching in Ten Minutes is a book for beginners . . . and for those who tried I Ching once, but gave up—or for anyone who wants a new perspective on the ancient oracle. **Ten minutes** from now, you yourself will be using the I Ching to ask questions about work, love, money, strategy—whatever you care about, whatever you want to know about—and you'll be getting answers in plain English.

All you need to get started are three coins. Reach into your pocket, fanny pack, or purse right now and dig them out. I'll wait. . . .

In **nine minutes** you will be tossing your coins. You will be looking to see which way they have landed. And—judging by the number of heads and tails that have turned up—you'll be getting a clue to your first answer.

The clue is nothing more, and nothing less, than a line—the kind of line you jot down with your pencil to emphasize a word—a solid line like this: ▬▬▬▬▬, or a broken line like this: ▬▬▬ ▬▬▬.

These lines are like building blocks—they stack up on top of one another. If you toss your coins twice, you'll have two lines . . . and again, three lines . . . and again and again and again, and you'll have six lines. Your resulting I Ching diagrams will look like this:

There's only one last thing you need to know. Some I Ching lines are "changing." Some solid lines are changing into broken lines: ▬▬▬▬ ≫. Some broken lines are changing into solid lines: ▬▬▬ ■ ≫. And this, my friend, is what makes I Ching so unique and dynamic.

Just like you and me and everything else in the Universe, the I Ching is constantly coping . . . constantly adjusting . . . constantly evolving . . .

constantly adapting . . . constantly changing. This perhaps is the very reason the method itself has endured, surviving for over five thousand years.

I Ching in Ten Minutes puts the ancient oracle to the task of doing what it does best: helping you understand and meet the challenge of change . . . helping you think about the changes occurring around you, within you, to you, and through you . . . helping you cope with the fickle finger of fate . . . and most important, helping you realize and achieve the destiny that only you can create for yourself.

In eight minutes, I'll set you loose with it. But first let me give you a couple of pointers on how to use this book.

One way to proceed is to start at the beginning with Reading #1 and just play along with *I Ching in Ten Minutes*. If you choose this route—and the choice, my friend, is yours—you will receive a guided tour of all the I Ching diagrams. And—here's the best part—from the very start you will get to ask specific questions (and get specific answers!) about your love life, home life, work life, or even past lives—whatever you want to know about. You'll start out with simple one-line diagrams and work your way up to classic six-line I Ching hexagrams.

Taken together, the 16 Readings will provide you with a complete and thorough "fortune" and more than a few insights about how you fit into the world and your environment. These Readings can be done time and again, as circumstances change, with many and various results. And you'll be surprised how quickly you can go from start to finish! Whenever you have a big issue to decide, you can run it through the book to see how it computes. But, if you prefer, you can also freestyle your way through *I Ching in Ten Minutes*.

Each Reading is self-contained. Once you get the feel for tossing coins, you are welcome to jump from place to place in the book, as the spirit or the need moves you. Just consult the Contents or the Index for a list of all the questions that are specifically dealt with in the book. These tools will help you zero in on the particular Reading you want to do today.

Yet another way to proceed is to start in the middle. Whenever you decide that you're ready to fly solo, just turn to Reading #16, where you will find complete instructions for conducting Readings on your own. Then, using the Master Answer section on page 176, you can forge your own path with the I Ching.

For those who are familiar with the I Ching, you are welcome to use the method you already know. Once you have cast your diagrams, just look up your answers in the back of the book in the same way you would use a "normal" I Ching book. (Note, however, that I've rearranged the hexagrams for easier look-up.)

Whichever way you choose to go, within **six minutes** you'll be asking questions. To save five minutes, skip the rest of this Preface, and go for it! But if you want to know where *I Ching in Ten Minutes* is coming from and how it is able to do what it does, read on. . . .

The I Ching method used here has come to us across vast language barriers, cultural boundaries, sheer distance, and thousands of years. Legend says that many moons ago, the basic diagrams were revealed to a wise king through the markings on the back of a turtle, which crawled from a sacred river one day . . . a gift from the gods.

Scholars say the I Ching system was developed over thousands of years by successive generations of thinkers, until it has evolved into the system we know today . . . a system so refined, so complete, and so universal that it has been used by ancient soothsayers and modern scientists alike—plus a whole lot of philosophers in between, including Confucius himself.

Most books on the subject, in fact, take their inspiration from the famous Confucian classic, *The Book of Changes*, written about 2,500 years ago. *I Ching in Ten Minutes* comes at it from a slightly different angle, and if you've got **four minutes**, I'll tell you why and how. . . .

First for the why: The first time I tossed my coins, I was simply amazed! My high school buddy[1] decided to read my coins one night. Though I have forgotten exactly what he said 20 years ago, I can't forget the feeling that I had, or how much I understood and believed my answers that night. The point is, it really, really worked . . . at least for us . . . at least that one time. And thus began my quest for the "I Ching Book" that would teach me how to do this on my own.

What I found along the way was a great body of scholarly work . . . various translations, numerous interpretations, broad theories, lots of footnotes, many schools of thought, and even a few software packages. But even after digging into it all—and it was indeed fascinating!—I still had trouble relating to the I Ching diagrams and understanding the answers I was receiving. I was still hunting for that easy "I Ching Book" with the everyday answers.

I never did find the book. But I did eventually learn how to work with the I Ching. How? I guess you could say, I just caught on to the I Ching when I found myself back at the basics. The key came from a book on Chinese history, where I read that—according to the inscriptions on

---

[1]Thank you, Bruce Baldwin, wherever you are.

ancient tortoiseshells—the most frequently asked question of the sooth-sayer had been: "Will it rain tomorrow?"

"Will it rain tomorrow?" All of a sudden it dawned on me. The I Ching did not start out as a Ph.D. thesis. It did not even start out as Chinese philosophy. It did not start out being hard, complex, and inscrutable. It has simpler, more natural roots . . . roots going back to the common past of all peoples.

To make a long story short—for we only have about **three minutes** left—*I Ching in Ten Minutes* takes its inspiration, not from the Chinese philosophers, but from the rich, nature-oriented traditions that predate "civilization" as we know it, and are reflected in the I Ching diagrams themselves. If you want to know how the book works, read on. . . .

Long before Confucius wrote his philosophical treatise on the hexa-grams, people were using simpler one-, two-, and three-line I Ching dia-grams to plan their destinies and ask everyday questions. Most books skip over these basic tools—but not *I Ching in Ten Minutes*.

I Ching in Ten Minutes starts at the very heart and soul of the oracle—with the basic one-line diagram. In Reading #1, you will be tossing your coins just once to ask a popular question from ancient times, "Are Conditions Favorable?" For what? you might ask. And that's just the beauty . . . you get to fill in the blank. Are conditions favorable for: get-ting married this year? . . . landing that new job? . . . selling my house? . . . winning the election? . . . discovering my mission in life? Whatever you ask, you'll find a straight answer on the very next page.

By playing your way through a series of question-and-answer Readings, you will advance quickly through two-line, three-line, and all the way up to the classic six-line diagrams.

Then, in the Master Answer section at the back of the book, you'll find each I Ching hexagram described in terms of work questions, love questions, money questions, and strategy questions. So when you ask a question here, you're going to get an answer that relates directly to the type of question you have asked. This alone makes the book unique, and especially useful to the beginner.

I have also simplified the basic technique of throwing coins and made other modifications, whenever it was possible to simplify without sacri-ficing performance. I have borrowed liberally from other methods of for-tune-telling to expand the number of things you can do with the I Ching. And I have also introduced a couple of new methods for con-structing the diagrams.

In less than **one minute**, I'll let you go. But just let me say this. . . .

This book will let you experience the sheer beauty of I Ching and feel the magical way that this method works, without having to study it a lifetime. But even though it is easy to use, this is also a serious book for people who want to know what's going on in their lives, who want to be prepared for the things to expect, and who want to manage change in an ever-changing environment.

So in the hopes that this method will give you fresh insights and help you make your own way through life—and with apologies to Confucius—I give you my humble attempt at writing the easy "I Ching Book" with the down-to-earth answers.

CONTENTS

The Readings

Contents

Contents

The Readings

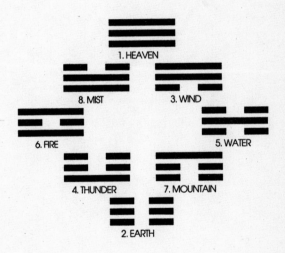

1. HEAVEN

8. MIST   3. WIND

6. FIRE   5. WATER

4. THUNDER   7. MOUNTAIN

2. EARTH

Reading #1

ARE CONDITIONS FAVORABLE?
(Yes/No)

In this Reading, you will use the basic I Ching building blocks—the solid and the broken lines—to get a quick assessment of your current situation. This Reading is particularly good at determining whether the time is right to make a move, to act on your instincts, or to reach a big decision. And in order to warm up with your coins, it's a good way to begin every session.

I CHING TOOLS

Throughout this book, the only equipment you will need are three coins, which you can get from your pocket or purse. The method is really quite simple: Just think of your question, toss your coins, and translate the results into an I Ching symbol.

There are only two symbols to learn:

The solid (or unbroken) line, which looks like this: ▬▬▬▬

The broken line, which looks like this: ▬▬ ▬▬

The How To section will walk you through the process. May good luck go with you.

HOW TO

❶ To conduct this Reading, you will need three plain, old, ordinary coins. The Chinese used bronze coins, but copper is also lucky. So Lincoln pennies will do nicely. Any coin will do fine. For extra luck, use coins minted in the year you were born or those minted in any leap year (. . . 1968, 1972, 1976, 1980, 1984, 1988, 1992, 1996, 2000 . . .).

❷ Clasp the coins between the palms of your hands (or clench them in your fist . . . or hold them loosely and shake them up and down). You can't hold them wrong. As you hold them in your hands, think about your question: **Are conditions favorable right now?** To ask for a raise? To pop the question? **Is the timing right for making love?** Money? A career move? **Is this the right time to act on my plans?** Instincts? Dreams? **Should I go ahead with _____ right now? Is this a good time to consult the I Ching?**

❸ With your question fully in mind, toss the coins onto a table or any flat surface. Whether the coins turn up heads or tails determines your answer. If two or three heads turn up, call it heads. If two or three tails, call it tails.

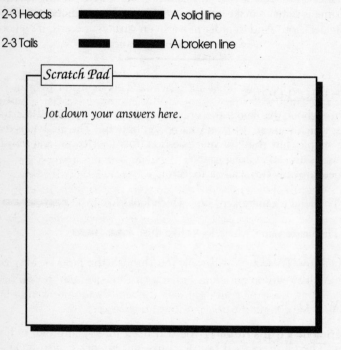

2-3 Heads   ▬▬▬▬▬▬▬   A solid line

2-3 Tails   ▬▬ ▬▬   A broken line

Scratch Pad

Jot down your answers here.

Look up the line you have cast in the Answer section immediately following.

THE ANSWERS

Go! Even if you don't fully appreciate it, your situation right now is one that favors action, for the line you have cast is unbroken. All systems are go. You are in the driver's seat. You have the green light. But . . . what are you waiting for? In love, don't hesitate to make the first move. At work, display some initiative. Money matters of all kinds are supported. Activities of all types are encouraged. Now is the time to make progress in the matter that concerns you most. *The answer to your question is YES! YES! YES! Now is the time. The time is now. Go for it.*

No Go! You may not be aware of it, but your position right at this moment is one that favors waiting, for the line you have cast is broken. This is not the best time for attempting great strides forward or for making important moves. In love, play it cool and listen to your heart. At work, follow your hunches and keep a low profile. For the time being, put your nest egg in a safe place. Speculative or daring attempts are a no-no. Efforts to get ahead quick are likely to progress slow. It's best to lie low for a while. But watch for conditions to change. Plan possible scenarios. Be ready when the opportunity presents itself. *The answer to your question is no, at least not right now. You are in a no-go situation. Make the best of the status quo.*

EXTRA CREDIT

To ask any yes/no question, gather your three pennies in your hand and ask away. Cast the coins, translate the result into unbroken or broken lines, and consult the *italic* portion of the answers.

EXTRA, EXTRA CREDIT!

As a more traditional alternative to coins, make a set of I Ching sticks. All you need is a black marker and 16 wooden toothpicks—or 16 chopsticks, pick-up sticks, or dowel sticks cut to a common length (let's say four or five inches). Just draw a black line around the middle of eight of your sticks to indicate that these are "broken lines." Then place all 16 sticks into any kind of bowl or other container. To answer yes/no questions, just close your eyes, ask your question, reach in, and select one stick at random. If it has a black line, read it as broken: ▬▬ ▬▬. If it has no line, read it as solid: ▬▬▬▬▬. Consult the answers as before.

Go on to the next Reading whenever you are ready to continue.

Reading #2

IS THE FORCE WITH ME?
(Will I be lucky?)

The Chinese believe that two kinds of energy are operating in the Universe—male and female . . . YANG and YIN . . . plus and minus. Is your energy positive or negative today? Is the atmosphere around you charged up or neutralized? Are the Forces of Nature pushing you or yielding to you? In this Reading, you will use your coins to find out what kind of energy surrounds you today, and how your luck can be expected to hold up in the days ahead. . . . All power to you.

I CHING TOOLS

Things are constantly changing in this Universe of ours, and so is the I Ching. In Reading #1, you learned how to toss your coins and read the answers as broken and solid lines. But there's one more trick you need to know: I Ching lines are in constant motion! Some of them are actually changing!

Some broken (YIN) lines ▬▬ ▬▬ are firming up ▬▬▬ ▬▸▸ into solid lines ▬▬▬▬▬.

And some solid (YANG) lines ▬▬▬▬▬ are breaking down ▬▬▬▬ ▸▸ into broken lines ▬▬ ▬▬.

Ah! The plot thickens. The possibilities double.

To tell whether your lines are changing or holding constant, just look at how your coins have landed—heads or tails. If you've got three of either, the line is changing into its opposite sign. Just note it as such in your diagram. The How To section will give you the step-by-step details.

HOW TO

❶ Conduct this Reading just like you did in Reading #1. Clasp your three coins between the palms of your hands as you think about your question: **What forces are at work in my life right now?** In my love life? My home life? On the job? **What kind of energy surrounds me right now?** At home? At school? On the road? **What kind of energy do I need to tap into? What kind of vibrations am I picking up on?**

7

Sending? Encouraging? **What forces are coming into play? How fortunate will I be this week?**

❷ With your question fully in mind, toss the coins onto a table like you did in Reading #1. But this time there are four possible answers:

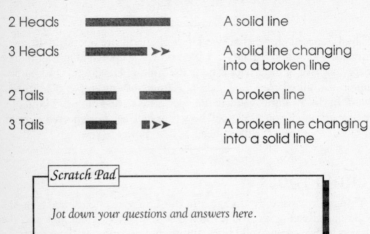

2 Heads		A solid line
3 Heads		A solid line changing into a broken line
2 Tails		A broken line
3 Tails		A broken line changing into a solid line

Scratch Pad

Jot down your questions and answers here.

Look up the line you have cast in the Answer section.

THE ANSWERS

Yang. The two primary forces of nature—YANG and YIN—are at all times and in all places operating from you, within you, and around you. But right now YANG's constructive male energy is building up in your life. **Under a YANG influence,** there will be physical activities and physical efforts of all kinds. You are surrounded by much coming and going as YANG forces attempt to bring change into your life. The key is to channel your male energy <u>outward</u> . . . and <u>into</u> the things you want to accomplish. Now is the time to make your mark. *In the days ahead, you will feel as lucky as you are. In any event, be sure to keep your fingers crossed.*

Yang Changing into Yin. The two primary forces of nature—YANG and YIN—are at all times and in all places operating from you, within you, and through you. But right now YANG's creative male energy is building up in your life to the point of distraction . . . and discharge. **Under a YANG/YIN influence,** there will be physical attractions, physical contacts, and physical unions. Sparks will fly. In one way or another, you will feel moved to express yourself. The key is to release your tension and alleviate your stress. Watch out for a burst of creativity in the process. Focus on artistic pursuits. *In the days ahead, you will be more lucky at love than at cards. In either case, be sure to wear your lucky socks.*

Yin. Both primary forces of nature—YIN and YANG—are at all times and in all places operating upon you, within you, and around you. But right now, YIN's receptive female energy is opening up in you. **Under a YIN influence,** things have a way of needing to be responded to. As you go about your duties, you will be guided by your inner voices as YIN's female energy attempts to create stability in your life. The key is to tune into the YIN forces within you and to open yourself up to the possibilities that present themselves. The emphasis is on practicing common sense. Go with your hunches, intuition, instincts, and gut feelings. *In the days ahead, your luck will find you. To attract it, be sure to wear your lucky charm.*

Yin Changing into Yang. Both primary forces of nature—YIN and YANG—are at all times and in all places operating upon you, within you, and through you. But right now, YIN's receptive female energy is operating at maximum strength. **Under a YIN/YANG influence**, there will be warm feelings, tender emotions, and caring thoughts. The emphasis is on home, family, friends . . . and the love in your life. The key at this time is to express the YIN forces within you. You need to let your feelings show. And don't be afraid to gush. *In the days ahead, you will be more lucky at love than at money. At any rate, be sure to carry a lucky coin in your left pocket.*

EXTRA CREDIT

To find out quickly how you can expect your luck to hold up this week, gather your three coins in your hand and ask: **What kind of luck can I expect in the days ahead?** Cast the coins, translate the result into solid or broken lines, and note whether they are changing or not. Consult the *italic* portion of the answers.

EXTRA, EXTRA CREDIT!

For a more traditional method, use the I Ching sticks you made in Reading #1, but first add red dots to <u>three</u> of the sticks that are not already marked. Also add a red dot to <u>one</u> of the sticks that already has a black line across its middle. These red dots will indicate which sticks represent changing lines. Now just ask any of the questions listed in the How To section, and draw one stick at random:

no mark at all	solid	[5 of 16 sticks]
red dot only	solid changing into broken	[3 of 16 sticks]
black line only	broken	[7 of 16 sticks]
black line, red dot	broken changing into solid	[1 of 16 sticks]

Consult the answers.

Note: *Your 16 sticks will produce very similar results to the oldest known method of consulting the I Ching. The ancient method uses 50 sticks and many repetitive steps to arrive at solid, broken, and changing lines. Who has the time? Your 16 sticks will work just as well.*[1]

Go on to the next Reading whenever you are ready to continue.

---

[1] Thanks to Larry Schoenholz, *New Directions in the I Ching*, University Books, 1975.

Reading #3

WHAT'S MY SIGN?
(Who am I looking for?)

Are you a YIN person or a YANG person? In this Reading, you'll learn how you are naturally connected to the I Ching as a result of the numbers in your birthday. Depending on these dates, your I Ching "sign" is a solid, a broken, or a changing line. This Reading will tell you which sign you are, and what it means to you.

I CHING TOOLS

There are some things you can do with the I Ching that are so easy, you don't even need your coins! Any lucky number can be easily translated into an I Ching diagram:

Odd number   ██████████████
                      YANG

Even number   ██████   ██████
                    YIN

In this Reading, you'll use the lucky numbers in your birthday to find out what kind of character you are.

HOW TO

All you need to know to do this Reading is the day and year you were born. First, we're going to note whether each of these things has a YANG or a YIN influence. Then we'll translate these influences into solid, broken, or changing lines.

❶ What day were you born? If it's an odd number (1, 3, 5, 7, 9, 11, 13, 15, 17, 19, 21, 23, 25, 27, 29, 31), you were born on a YANG day. If it's an even number (2, 4, 6, 8, 10, 12, 14, 16, 18, 20, 22, 24, 26, 28, 30), you were born on a YIN day. So if you were born on November 4—and since 4 is an even number—you were born on a YIN day.

❷ What year were you born? If the year you were born in ends in an even number or a zero, you were born in a YIN year. If it ends with an odd number, you were born in a YANG year. Say you were born in 1979. Since 1979 ends in a 9—which is an odd number—you were born in a YANG year.

❸ To determine which I Ching sign is yours, use this table.

Day of Birth	Year of Birth	I Ching Sign
YANG	YANG	▬▬▬▬ **YANG**
YANG	YIN	▬▬ ▶▶ **YANG Changing**
YIN	YIN	▬ ▬ **YIN**
YIN	YANG	▬ ▬▶▶ **YIN Changing**

Scratch Pad

Note your dates and signs here.

Look up your sign in the Answer Section. In this Reading, there are separate answers for men and women.

THE ANSWERS
FOR MEN ONLY

Yang. As a man born on a YANG day in a YANG year, you direct male energy into your work. Your sign is the unbroken line, solid as rock and straight as an arrow. On the surface you are firm. And to the core, you are strong. All in all, you are a family man. As such, you are inclined to put your shoulder to the task and to hold up your end of the bargain. You work hard, play hard . . . gravitate to power, and tend to attract money. You usually get exactly what you want, if not what you necessarily deserve. You see yourself as a provider. You view sex as a right and a responsibility. *In general, you relate better to women than to men, but you will never be at a loss for bosom buddies. You need a wife for a mate, as well as a mother for yourself. You have an eye for a woman who really cooks.*

Yang Changing into Yin. As a man born on a YANG day in a YIN year, you pulse with male energy. Your sign is the changing solid line, strong as a heartbeat and sharp as a knife. On the surface you are smooth. And to the core, you are tough. All in all, you are a man's man. As such, you are inclined to go after the things you want and to conquer them in the process. You work out, play rough . . . gravitate to conflict, and attract rivals. Money burns a hole through your pocket. You usually get whatever you shoot for, but it may take practice or come at a high price. You see yourself as a hero. You think of sex as a reward. *In general, you relate better to men than to women, but you will never be at a loss for either female companionship or teammates. You require a woman to be your mistress as well as your wife. You have an eye for anything in a skirt.*

Yin. As a man born on a YIN day in a YIN year, you temper male energy. Your sign is the broken line—all things being equal. On the surface you are cool, calm, and refined. But at the core, you are hot, tense, and calculating. All in all, you are a gentleman . . . and a politician. As such, you are inclined to charm your way through life and strike sweet deals along the way. At work, you define your turf. At home, you mark your territory. And in love, you stake your claim. You gravitate to land and real estate on wheels. You attract regular Joes and sweet Janes (who vote for you?). You see yourself as the prime example and the perfect case in point. But in the end, you measure your success on the basis of how much you can pull off. You view sex as a strategic weapon. *Since you make an effort to relate equally well to men and women, they relate equally well to you (as long as you play your cards right). You require a woman who is above reproach to be your bride and a caring lover (perhaps on the side). You have an eye for the profile of a well-endowed woman.*

Yin Changing into Yang. As a man born on a YIN day in a YANG year, you exude male energy. Your sign is the changing broken line, open and sensitive and split down the middle. On the surface you are strong and silent. But inside you are soft, gentle, and kind. All in all, you are one of the good guys. As such you are inclined to come to the rescue of others or fight for a good cause. You work more than you rest . . . you play even less, for even when you relax the wheels inside you are spinning. Love, friendship, and money have a way of finding you out . . . at just the right moment, and in amounts just equal to what you need. You gravitate to causes. You attract funny coincidences. You think of yourself as a martyr. But in the end, you define your success in terms of what you have learned about yourself. You view sex as both a spiritual thing and a religious challenge. *Though you relate equally well to men and women—and will never be at a loss for friends—you actually prefer to be alone with your own thoughts. You need a woman who believes in you . . . and who can read your mind from a safe distance. You have an eye for the figure of a receding woman.*[1]

FOR WOMEN ONLY

Yin. As a woman born on a YIN day in a YIN year, you devote your female energy to those around you. Your sign is the broken line, open and caring . . . calm and receptive. On the surface, you are mellow and soft to the touch. But to the core, you are wise beyond your years—deep, sincere, and honest in your beliefs. All in all, you are an Earth Mother . . . and the salt of the earth. As such, you are inclined to handle things, take care of things, and watch over those who cannot yet fend for themselves

---

[1]Thanks to Agatha Christie's *Murder on the Orient Express*, Paramount Pictures, 1974.

(including those who ought!). At work, you build communities. From home, you form networks. And when it comes to money, you can always make ends meet. You gravitate to responsible positions. You attract sincere friends. You tend to get repaid in small ways. And in the end, you count your successes in terms your grandchildren can understand. You view yourself as someone to come to. Sex for you is doing what comes naturally. *In general you relate better to women than to men, but when it comes to children, you favor neither gender and care equally for both. You need a husband, father, and provider for a mate. You have an eye for an honest face.*

Yin Changing into Yang. As a woman born on a YIN day in a YANG year, you surge with female energy. Your sign is the changing broken line, open to the possibilities and flowing like a current. On the surface you are charming, coy, and polished. But beneath that calm exterior lies a pounding heart. All in all, you are a sensuous woman. As such, you are inclined to feel your way along, modifying your approach to fit the mood. At work, you adopt your own technique. And at home, you create your own mood, style, and ambiance. You tend to get whatever you have your heart set on . . . or your mind put to. And in the end, you count your many blessings as if they were assets. (In love it is no different.) You view yourself as desirable. And sex for you is a moving experience. *In general, you relate better to men than to women, but there is also room in your heart for a close friend. You require a man who makes you feel like a woman. You have an eye for a great pair of jeans.*

Yang. As a woman born on a YANG day in a YANG year, you crystallize female energy. Your sign is the unbroken line, strong and directed and true to its purpose. On the surface you are tough as diamonds. And at the core you are bright as stardust. All in all you are a wonder woman. As such you are inclined to overcome the things that get in the way of progress. At work you are a whirlwind. At home you are a tornado. Your candle burns at both ends. You gravitate to burning issues and bright lights. You attract causes. And in the end, you leave your mark on the world in one way or another. You view yourself as a force for good. Sex for you is an emotional release. *Though you relate equally well to men and women, you have a hard time understanding either. You find a friend in a like-*

minded woman. *You need a man who will uphold his end of the deal. You have an eye for big hands and feet.*

Yang Changing into Yin. As a woman born on a YANG day in a YIN year, you project female energy. Your sign is the changing solid line, constantly in flux. On the surface you are hard to read—deep, dark, and mysterious. For at your core, you hold the riddle for us all. All in all you are a spiritual woman . . . a dreamer and a seer. As such, you are inclined to tap into—or connect to—things. At work you provide guidance and insight. From home, you lend advice. And in return, you earn the trust and respect of others . . . as well as a decent income for yourself. You gravitate to secret places. You attract mystical experiences. And in the end, you find the answer you are looking for . . . inside yourself. You see yourself as an instrument for some greater good. Sex for you is a religious experience. *Though you relate equally well to both women and men, it all depends on your mood. Friends need to be people you can empathize with. You need a man who gives you the respect, privacy, and sympathy you deserve. You have an eye for the aura of decency.*

EXTRA CREDIT

To find out about others in your life, conduct this Reading for your friends and associates. If you don't know their birth dates (or they won't tell you), not to worry. Just cast your coins and consult the appropriate sections in the answers—men for men, women for women. **To consider what you're looking for in a partner or mate,** toss the coins and consult the italic portion of the answers.

EXTRA, EXTRA CREDIT!

How do others see you? To find out, toss your coins. Or use the sticks you finished making for yourself in Reading #2 to pick a stick at random. Consult the appropriate section of the answers for your sexual condition and read for the appropriate line that you have cast.

2 Heads ▬▬▬▬▬ A stick with no mark

3 Heads ▬▬▬ ➤➤ A stick with a red dot only

2 Tails ▬▬ ▬▬ A stick with a black line

3 Tails ━━━ ■➤➤ A stick with a line and a dot.

To customize this Reading, insert the name of any particular person: **How does _____ see me?**

Go on to the next Reading whenever you are ready to continue.

Reading #4

In this Reading, you will use your coins to cast two lines in order to forecast the likely outcome of any matter that concerns or interests you. This Reading is especially good at forecasting the probability or likelihood of a particular event taking place as planned. Ask as many questions as you please. You can compute the odds for anything and everything.

I CHING TOOLS

In learning how to read your coins as solid ▬▬▬▬ , broken ▬▬ ▬▬, and changing ▬▬ ▬ ≫ / ▬▬▬▬ ≫ lines, you have already mastered the basic I Ching method. These lines are all there is to it! But there is one last thing you need to know. These lines can be stacked on top of one another!

To get a two-line I Ching diagram, just toss your coins twice. The How To section walks you through the process, but there's really nothing to it. Just remember, your diagram always builds from the bottom up. It's like a building you're putting up. The first line you toss is the foundation. And the second line is the first floor.

By casting two lines instead of one, the number of possible outcomes quadruples! There are 16 possible combinations, giving you 16 potential answers.

HOW TO

Just as in all the previous Readings, you will need your three coins.

❶ Clasp the coins between the palms of your hands as you think about your question: **What are the odds?** That I will get ahead? That my plans for _____ will succeed? **What are the prospects for _____?** Increasing my income? Falling in love? Buying a new car? Getting my point across? Convincing so-and-so? **How likely is it that _(you name it!)_ will happen?** This Reading covers just about any subject.

❷ With your question fully in mind, toss your coins onto the table. The rules for interpreting your answers are the same as those described in Readings #2 and #3: 2 heads = a solid line; 2 tails = a broken line; 3 heads = a solid line changing into a broken line; and 3 tails = a broken line changing into a solid line.

Use the Scratch Pad to jot down your answer as line 1 of your two-line I Ching diagram.

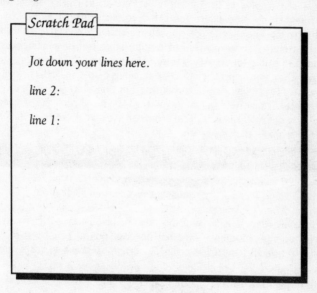

> **Scratch Pad**
>
> *Jot down your lines here.*
>
> *line 2:*
>
> *line 1:*

❸ Next, repeat the process: Think of your question again. Recast your coins. Translate your second answer into a solid, broken, or changing line. And write it <u>above</u> the line you drew before.

❹ At first, ignore your changing lines and look up your diagram, which will be one of these four:

If your diagram has no changing lines in it, just read the main description provided. If there <u>are</u> changing lines, you may want to consult the main description as well, but focus on the bonus answer included for your special situation.

19

THE ANSWERS

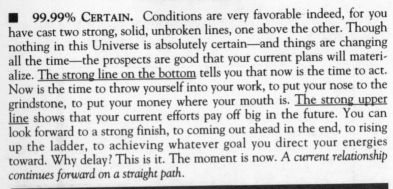

■ **99.99% Certain.** Conditions are very favorable indeed, for you have cast two strong, solid, unbroken lines, one above the other. Though nothing in this Universe is absolutely certain—and things are changing all the time—the prospects are good that your current plans will materialize. The strong line on the bottom tells you that now is the time to act. Now is the time to throw yourself into your work, to put your nose to the grindstone, to put your money where your mouth is. The strong upper line shows that your current efforts pay off big in the future. You can look forward to a strong finish, to coming out ahead in the end, to rising up the ladder, to achieving whatever goal you direct your energies toward. Why delay? This is it. The moment is now. *A current relationship continues forward on a straight path.*

BONUS ANSWERS FOR CHANGING LINES

■ **25% Chance.** The weakening bottom line is a sign that you may not get up enough momentum to realize your goals. You need to overcome your tendency toward inertia. *A current relationship is spinning its wheels.*

■ **75% Chance.** The weakening upper line indicates that though your current position is quite strong, you could still change your mind at the last moment. *A good relationship could peter out right at the end or peak too early.*

■ **00.01% Chance.** Both solid lines weakening is a sign that you do not have a prayer of succeeding on this one. There isn't any spark here, let alone follow-through. *A current relationship is disintegrating fast.*

■ **50/50 SPLIT.** Any way you look at it, your diagram is split down the middle. All things considered, you have a 50/50 chance of succeeding in your current plans, for you have cast two broken lines, one above the other. Bear in mind, however, that the world is subject to change without notice, and things can go either way for you right now. _The weak lower line_ tells you that your current situation is more conducive to making incremental progress than to taking great strides. Put one foot before the other. Take things one day at a time. Keep your nose to the grindstone. _The weak upper line_ tells you that in the future you can anticipate more of the same. Keep doing what you are doing. Keep on carrying on. In the long run, you can expect things to even out. You can expect to break even. Hang in there. A *current relationship runs its natural course.*

BONUS ANSWERS FOR CHANGING LINES

■ **60% CHANCE.** A strengthening bottom line is a sure sign that you will give this your best shot. If you're going to go for it, you might as well make it a strong attempt. A *current relationship increases in intensity.*

■ **80% CHANCE.** A strengthening upper line indicates that you will come out stronger in the end. Sit tight and remain patient. A *current relationship makes steady forward progress.*

■ **110% CHANCE.** With both weak lines strengthening, the signs are very good indeed that you will be successful. Gather your strength, for you are going to need it. A *current relationship sweeps you off your feet.*

1 in 3, Against You. Your current plans or desires would appear to be something of a long shot, for you have cast a strong, solid line above a weaker, broken one. Right now, the odds are against you. <u>The weak lower line</u> tells you that your current situation is at best limiting, if not downright ludicrous. You appear to be vulnerable, overpowered, and out-numbered. The first order of business is to put your own house in order: Identify your strengths. Minimize your weaknesses. Get ready to break out when conditions change. <u>The strong upper line</u> tells you that something or someone is coming between you and the progress you would like to make. Still, the world is changeable, and things are changing all the time. Plan now so that you are ready to seize the moment of opportunity when it comes. *A current relationship has a long, rough road to travel.*

BONUS ANSWERS FOR CHANGING LINES

■ **40% CHANCE.** The strengthening bottom line is a sign that you are putting up resistance. You are a squeaky wheel at present. But it will not make much difference in the long run. *A current relationship requires two equal partners. There is a distinct possibility this will all end in stalemate.*

■ **66% CHANCE.** The weakening upper line indicates that there will be a softening toward you, which is sure to improve your position. Be patient. *A current relationship improves.*

■ **90% CHANCE.** With both lines changing, it is clear that you are strengthening your position, while at the same time the resistance weakens. Nothing could be more opportune. *A current relationship turns around once the parties swap roles.*

70/30, Your Favor. The odds are strongly tilted in your favor, for you have cast a broken line above a solid one. Very little stands in your way. You have a window of opportunity. Conditions favor your upward progress at this time. But since things could change suddenly, you need to act fast, before this moment passes you by. <u>The strong lower line</u> tells you that you are currently operating from a position of strength, and that bold, decisive actions are encouraged. This is a time for acting on your impulses and letting your feelings be known. <u>The weak upper line</u> tells you that you will meet with little opposition or resistance. You should be able to make rapid forward progress at this time. Since the odds are 7:3 (or 70/30) that you will succeed, the outcome depends on your taking advantage of the current situation. *A current relationship is on a sure path.*

BONUS ANSWERS FOR CHANGING LINES

■ **30% CHANCE.** The weakening lower line is a sign that you are inclined to give up before you even start the race. Are you sure this is what you really want for yourself? *A current relationship won't get off the ground unless you really want it to.*

■ **20% CHANCE.** The strengthening upper line indicates that the moment of opportunity is passing you by quickly. Somebody is putting up roadblocks even as we speak. *A current relationship meets with resistance.*

■ **10% CHANCE.** With both lines changing, it seems very likely that things will break down suddenly—or come apart at the seams—just at the last minute . . . and perhaps, just in the nick of time. *A current relationship suddenly takes a 180-degree turn.*

EXTRA CREDIT

For a quick reading of how any current relationship is going, think of the other person and ask, **How are our chances?** For getting together? Staying together? Working things out? Getting back together again? With your question in mind, toss your coins. As in the main Reading, toss your coins twice, translating the results into a two-line I Ching diagram. (Remember to place the second line above the first.) Consult the *italic* portion of the answers.

EXTRA, EXTRA CREDIT!

Loves me/loves me not? To find out how strongly someone special feels about you, use the I Ching sticks you made in Readings #1 and #2 to cast a two-line diagram. Just think of your question (How much does so-and-so love me? Want me? Need me?). Select one stick at random from your bag or bowl and note the kind of stick it is (black line = broken; red dot = changing). Next—and this is very important—return the stick to your container. Now think of your question again, and draw a second stick at random. Jot down the line it represents above the first line you drew. Then look up your diagram in the answers. It's that simple.

Scratch Pad

Jot down your questions and answers here.

line 2:

line 1:

line 2:

line 1:

line 2:

line 1:

Go on to the next Reading whenever you are ready to continue.

Reading #5

WHICH WAY (AM I HEADED)?
(What will tomorrow bring?)

———————

Which way are the winds of change blowing through your life right now? Which direction are you being pushed in? Which way should you head? In this Reading, you will use your coins like a compass to get your bearings and set your sights. Some people feel they should face west when consulting the I Ching. Use this Reading to choose your own direction in life.

———————

I CHING TOOLS

One of the traditional uses of the I Ching was for establishing the direction in which a hunt needed to proceed, an army needed to march, or a wedding party needed to travel for the best luck. In this Reading, we will be using the two-line I Ching diagrams as compass points.

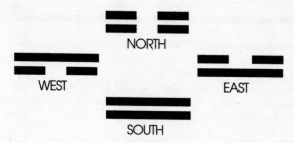

HOW TO

Just as in Reading #4, we will be casting a two-line I Ching diagram here.

❶ You will need your three coins. Clasp the coins between the palms of your hands as you think about your question: **Which way am I headed?** In this relationship? With this job? On this investment? **Which direction am I being pulled in?** Pushed? **Which way should I go?** To find true love? To locate work? To seek my fortune? To have a good time?

❷ With your question fully in mind, toss your coins onto the table. Note how they land. As always, two heads represent solid lines, and two tails are broken lines. When all three coins turn up the same, the line is changing. Make note of your answer, as line 1:

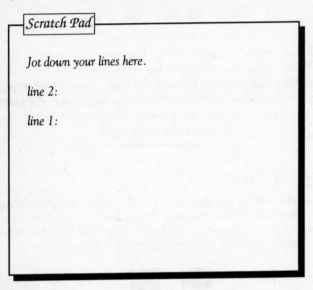

Scratch Pad

Jot down your lines here.

line 2:

line 1:

❸ Next, repeat the process: Think of your question again. Retoss your coins. Translate your second answer into a solid or a broken line. And write it <u>above</u> the line you drew before.

There are four possible main answers, and 12 variations for changing lines. Consult the Answer section for the main diagram and read your bonus answer for changing lines.

THE ANSWERS

North. Like a guiding star, north is the direction that steers you now. The changes that are approaching require you to line up your sights or get your bearings. The thing you must do involves holding your direction. Fortunately, you are not alone in all of this. You will know when things are right, because you will feel the spirit move you. The signs are these: The last word on a matter comes from out of the north. To prove yourself, go north. To pass a test, come to the place via the north. For inspiration, face north. In relationships, you will know it is right when you feel it click inside you. At work, something is going around and around. The truth emerges under a Quarter Moon. *You can expect to make forward progress tomorrow by calling on your past experience. Seek guidance from people who have been there before. Apply what you have learned.*

BONUS ANSWERS FOR CHANGING LINES

■ **N BY NE.** A strong tail wind pushes you in the direction you wanted to go anyway. You make swift progress now. *Tomorrow, you recover lost time spent waiting for takeoff. You may actually arrive at your destination a little early! Count your lucky stars.*

■ **N BY NW.** A stiff head wind prevents you from making sure, swift progress. Better cool your heels and wait out the added flight time. *Tomorrow you can expect a few delays. Work around the unexpected—and don't tamper with those lavatory smoke detectors.*

■ **DOWN SOUTH.** Change comes on the heels of the past, undoing the good with the bad and dragging everything forward with it. *Tomorrow brings a radical change of pace, but you shall overcome, my friend, you shall overcome.*

South. At this time in your life, south is the direction that has the biggest influence on you. The changes that are coming into your life require you to keep taking action until everything is lined up, worked out, or completed. Keep an eye open and an ear cocked for details. The signs are these: Expect news of a professional nature from out of the south. Whenever the need calls, travel south. To improve your performance, approach things from the south. For inspiration, face south. In relationships, you will know when it is right, because you are able to make things click. At work, you are directed. *You can expect to make forward progress tomorrow by imitation combined with innovation. Break with the past. Prepare to forge ahead. Be creative.*

BONUS ANSWERS FOR CHANGING LINES

■ **S BY SW.** A desert wind kicks up in your life . . . and with it, dust from out of the past. You cover your face and rub your eyes against this day of reckoning with the Powers that Be. *Tomorrow is a good day to worship the moon and count your lucky stars. Father Time really knows what he's doing.*

■ **S BY SE.** A gulf breeze blows into your life . . . and with it, spume and spray. The sand gets in your shoes and the salt gets in your hair— and you deserve the breather. *Tomorrow is a good day to worship the sun and thank your lucky stars. Mother Nature sure knows what she's doing.*

■ **UP NORTH.** Change plays no favorites, and the only thing for certain is that nothing remains the same for very long. In the great march forward, the way things always were gets left behind. *Tomorrow brings changes of the basic, fundamental kind. But the Powers that Be sure know what they're doing!*

East. East is the direction of highest importance to you now, the direction from which your guiding light comes. Like the sun rising above the horizon, the right thing to do suddenly dawns on you. At last a light goes off in your head. And the path in front of you becomes clear. Looking back in the direction from which you have come, you will see now how it could have been no other way. The future is up to you. The signs are these: Watch for word from the east. For a getaway, take a trip east. For good luck, come at things from the east. For inspiration, face east. In relationships, you will know it is right if you feel radiant...when you feel the light inside you glow. In a business undertaking, the options available become clear. *Things go like clockwork tomorrow. The day favors plans and progress in important pursuits. Be direct and aggressive.*

BONUS ANSWERS FOR CHANGING LINES

■ **NE.** A cold wind dampens the spirit and sends a chill down the spine. You'd best lay up and put in until this storm passes. *Tomorrow things will take a sudden turn for the better. Everything will all blow over soon.*

■ **SE.** A warm breeze blows into your life, and there's excitement in the air. Something stirs within you, and it feels like Spring fever. *Tomorrow may well be another day, but frankly, my dear . . . you'd best embrace this one while it lasts. Savor the moment.*

■ **FAR EAST.** Change comes from out of left field, and you are challenged to defend your old ways, values, and habits. *Tomorrow finds you eating humble pie or playing by somebody else's rules. What good is resistance? As everything around you changes, you, too, must alter your behavior or be altered by others.*

■ **WEST**. West is the direction of deepest significance to you now, the direction from which a voice calls. The changes that are approaching require you to be open and receptive to the forces within you . . . to the things that act upon you from the top down, and from the outside in. Listen to the sound of your own instincts. The message that you seek comes from the west. To seek your fortune, go west (young man, go west). To show a little respect, approach things from the west. For inspiration, face west. In a business matter, a new era begins. In relationships: You will know it is right when you feel the silence deep inside—empty and full at the same time, like the old moon in the New Moon's arms. *Things are inclined to happen in slow-mo tomorrow—and there may be a few steps backward to take—but by the end of the day, you will receive a sign.*

BONUS ANSWERS FOR CHANGING LINES

■ **SW.** An acrid breeze is blowing into your life. It will serve to clear your head, and you will be able to decide things for yourself . . . at last. *Tomorrow, take the bull by the horns and fly by the seat of your pants. Yip-e-i-o-ki-a, pal!*

■ **NW.** A moist wind clips into your life, bringing a period of wet weather. You'd best get in out of the cold and damp for a while . . . and under the covers. *Tomorrow finds you a bit under the weather, a tad down in the dumps, or a little preoccupied. Go on, you deserve it . . . pamper yourself.*

■ **FAR WEST.** Change comes from out of your own backyard and from the spirit that moves you into action and reaction. *Tomorrow finds you picking yourself up by your roots and replanting yourself. Write your own ticket. Build a new life.*

EXTRA CREDIT

For a quick Reading on what's in store for you tomorrow, ask your question: **What will tomorrow bring?** Cast your coins twice to draw two lines—placing the second above the first. Then consult the *italic* portion of the answers.

EXTRA, EXTRA CREDIT!

Which direction should you face to consult the I Ching? Some say it makes a difference. To find out which direction is right for you, why not ask your sticks? Just pick one at random from your pile. Note it. Put it back. Pick another. Or try this technique that will introduce you to the more traditional method of I Ching—counting sticks:

a.   Take your 16 sticks out of their container and mix them up. Concentrate on your question.

b.   Divide your sticks into three groups (however you feel like doing it).

c   Remove one stick from each group (your choice.)

d.   Combine and count off the remaining sticks by fours.

e.   The stick you have left at the end is the answer for your first line.

Repeat the process for your second line, then consult the **boldfaced** direction with your answer. (Remember, red dots indicate changing lines; black marks indicate broken lines.)

This Reading also works with questions like, **Which way should my bed face? Which way should I face to do my best work?**

Go on to the next Reading whenever you are ready to continue.

Reading #6

What kind of year will this one be for you? In this Reading, a single, two-line I Ching diagram provides the clue. Using the I Ching like a calendar, you will identify the "season" and "month" that you are passing through in this year of your personal growth cycle. This Reading also works with many other types of time-dependent questions, if you use it like a calendar, to anticipate when things are going to happen. Plan your own life accordingly . . . and in advance.

I CHING TOOLS

In this Reading, the two-line I Ching diagrams have been assigned to the seasons according to a 5,000-year-old tradition.

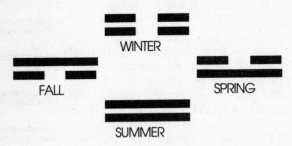

This system was quite possibly based on the positions of the sun and moon on the horizon at various times of the year. If you're not into astronomy, not to worry. As always, the text will tell you what to look for.

HOW TO

Just as in Readings #4 and #5, we will be working with two-line I Ching diagrams. But you will <u>not</u> need your coins to get an answer here.

❶ To do this Reading, all you need to know is your age in years. (In other words, just how old are you? . . . really?)

❷ Look up your age in this table, and follow it across to your diagram. If you have a birthday coming up, read for your new age, too. And what about last year?

YOUR AGE IN I CHING YEARS

Your actual age in years	Your Season	Your Month	Your Diagram
1 13 25 37 49 61 73 85	Winter	February	[diagram]
2 14 26 38 50 62 74 86	Spring	March	[diagram]
3 15 27 39 51 63 75 87	Spring	April	[diagram]
4 16 28 40 52 64 76 88	Spring	May	[diagram]
5 17 29 41 53 65 77 89	Summer	June	[diagram]
6 18 30 42 54 66 78 90	Summer	July	[diagram]
7 19 31 43 55 67 79 91	Summer	August	[diagram]
8 20 32 44 56 68 80 92	Fall	September	[diagram]
9 21 33 45 57 69 81 93	Fall	October	[diagram]
10 22 34 46 58 70 82 94	Fall	November	[diagram]
11 23 35 47 59 71 83 95	Winter	December	[diagram]
12 24 36 48 60 72 84 96	Winter	January	[diagram]

Scratch Pad

Copy your sign down.

line 2:

line 1:

❸ Look up your diagram in the Answer section, by first ignoring any changing lines. This will give you your I Ching "season." But also read for the changing lines, which will tell you about your I Ching month, as well.

THE ANSWERS

Winter. The moon rides high in your sky, and the sun lies low. The nights now are silent and brittle . . . and the days are endlessly slow. For this, my friend, is the chilling season, and you are in an incubation period. This is a time for turning inward, withdrawing, and working on the insides of things. There are many things to review and many books to catch up on . . . old friends to get in touch with and past wrongs to make up for. Things need to be mended and fixed now, especially the things close to the heart. The poor, old soul stands staring out the window at the waning light. *You are involved in something bigger than a single lifetime. That which goes on and on forever is in no hurry and has not need of time. Whether today, tomorrow, or the day after, makes no difference.*

■ **DECEMBER.** Everything has come full circle again. For this, my friend, is the beginning of the dark season, and you are at the end of another year in the sun. It is a time for giving and accepting . . . for coming and for going . . . for forgiving and for taking back. Everything happens all at once, it seems, in a tide of high emotions. There are never such heights . . . and there were never such lows. *It won't be long now until you get to open your presents. Make a wish on the 25th . . . another on the 26th.*

■ **JANUARY.** The wind comes, bringing the arctic with it. For this, my friend, is the height of this bitter season. And you are about to pass the test of time again. This is a time for renewing your convictions . . . for making lists and taking stock of things. You stay in, rather than going out . . . you wait alone with a candle in the window for the car that can't get through. *Soon you will learn who your true friends are. It all goes down at midnight. Make a fresh start on the 1st.*

■ **FEBRUARY.** As the light lengthens, things lie silent and waiting beneath a glare of ice. For this, my friend, is the last stretch of the chilling season, and you are about ready to thaw out. This is a time for leaning out . . . for sticking your neck out . . . or for coming out all the way. As the first invisible stirrings of spring fill the air, you long for company. *Prepare yourself for both possible outcomes. Soon you will receive a sign. Look for it by the 29th.*

Summer. A summer sun is high in your sky. The days are long now . . . and the nights, alive. For this, my friend, is the growing season, and you are in a growth situation. At this time, things have a way of developing rapidly . . . even overnight. But how far you can go depends on prevailing conditions. In light of adverse weather, do your best to stay deeply rooted and firm in your convictions. There are many things beyond your control right now. And there are many others who are vying with you for their rightful place in the sun. To achieve the full potential that this season brings, you must learn the lessons of past seasons. *You are involved in something that lasts a lifetime. Give it the time it needs, and it will happen in its own time. Tomorrow will be here before you know it.*

■ JUNE. Your longest day approaches . . . and your shortest night. For this, my friend, is the start of a growing season for you. This is a time for sending out feelers and establishing ties . . . for setting up house and putting down roots. The changes ahead are so big that you could hardly prepare for them; but what the heck, feeling your way along often works too. *The how, where, and when are pretty much up to you. Look for a change around the 21st of this month.*

■ JULY. Subtly, slowly, imperceptibly, the days are getting shorter . . . but you'd never know it. For this, my friend, is the height of the growing season. And you are having a growth spurt. This is a time for stretching and reaching . . . winding around and rising above. Everything happens suddenly . . . even the storms that blow through your life blow just as quickly off to sea. And you never felt so alive. *It won't be long now until you come to terms. Look for some excitement around the 4th of this month.*

■ AUGUST. All of a sudden the late evenings are over . . . and the early mornings, too. For this, my friend, is the waning of another growing season for you. And—at last—you are coming into your own. This is a time for letting up a bit, for cutting off and thinning out, for scaling back and easing down. It all seems now to have come easily in the end. But you have worked hard for your day in the sun. *The time is near, for the effort you invested in the past is about to pay off. You will know for sure by the end of the day.*

Spring. A spring sun rises due east now, and the Egg Moon sets due west. There is equal day and equal night again . . . and everything that was at odds gets back together. For this, my friend, is the rainy season, and you are having an emotional outpouring. At this time things have a way of developing slowly—yet steadily, surely. You must look carefully for the first timid signs of great things to come. Your own feelings push themselves to the surface now like thin sprouts. You wear your heart on your sleeve . . . and the future rests in the palm of your own hand. It all depends—as always—on prevailing conditions. But it would be futile to worry now about what might go wrong. All you can do is hope. Reach for the sun. Bend in the rain. *You are involved in something that leads to a lifetime of adventure . . . starting right about now. This is the day.*

■ MARCH. The signs are changing daily now. Soon the equal and opposite will cross paths again. For you, my friend, are at the start of another spring, and you have come to a crossroads in your life. This is a time for wiping the slate clean again . . . for cleaning up and clearing out . . . and swearing off your evil ways. Only after the weight of the past has been lifted can you actually move on. *The moment is at hand. But you will have to make the choice for yourself. Take care, especially on the 15th of this month.*

■ APRIL. There is a restless feeling in the air now as things start to stir in the dark earth and the lengthening light. For this, my friend, is the start of another planting season, and you are growing restive to get things started. This is a time for digging things up . . . for turning things over . . . and for setting things in. Plant seeds. Try out new ideas. Dye eggs. Put on new clothes. *It will be but a little while longer until you cast off this cocoon of yours. Get ready for the next Full Moon.*

■ **MAY.** In the dawn there is dew on the scattered blossoms. For this, my friend, is the end of the rainy season, and everything old is new again. . . including you. This is a time for breathing in the night air . . . for hungering and yearning . . . and for feeling rarin' to go. The world lies open at your feet like a great expanse of possibilities, probabilities, and potentials. No wonder a restless feeling has crept into your bones. There are people to see, places to go, and things to do, do, do. *Everything has its time and place, if you can only work it in. Do something special over the long weekend.*

Fall. An autumn sun sets due west, as the Harvest Moon rises in the east. There is equal day and equal night . . . and no extremes. For this, my friend, is the harvest season, and you are in the time of self-realization. At this time, things have a way of being counted and tallied . . . understood and decided—one way or the other—and there is no denying the facts and figures. In this time of reckoning, everything you did in the past and everything that was done to you in the process are now measured by the results that fill the scales. And suddenly you see what it all adds up to. You are involved in something that has required the work of a lifetime. *The time is upon you, and there is no more need for waiting. Yesterday is behind you. At last you know.*

■ **SEPTEMBER.** It is the equinox. Things are evening out. Things are turning in upon themselves. For you, my friend, are at the start of another harvest season. And now you must bring the things of the past to closure. This is a time for wrapping up and putting away . . . for cutting down and clearing out. A chapter in your life comes to its natural end. At last, you can breathe a sigh of relief. *The moment is now, and this is as good as it gets. Make plans for early in the week. (What are you doing Monday?)*

■ **OCTOBER.** The nights fall early to spectacular sunsets and glorious moonrises. For this, my friend, is the height of the harvest season, and you are involved in preparations. This is a time for putting up and laying in . . . for squirreling away and setting aside for a snowy day. What you feared would never be enough suddenly overwhelms you with how much it has turned out to be . . . and how much it now involves. *It will take some time yet to sink in, but everything that could have been, already is. Look for a change of pace on the 31st of this month.*

■ **NOVEMBER.** These are the last days for taking something from the year and making something of yourself. For you, my friend, have come through another planting, growing, and gleaning cycle, and what you see now is what you get . . . at least this time around. Now is a time for paying back what you have borrowed, for giving away what you no longer need, and for sharing any surplus with others. *It is never too late to be thankful for what you have received . . . and for what you have been spared. Get together at the end of the week. (Is Thursday good for you?)*

EXTRA CREDIT

Conduct this Reading for your friends and associates (if they'll tell you how old they are!—if not, just toss your coins and see what you get). Or, to find out when something of importance to you will take place, simply ask, **When's it going to happen?** To be more specific: **When is _____ going to happen?** Toss your coins twice to cast a double line. Read the *italic* portion of the answers or note the **boldface** title of your diagram, whichever seems more appropriate to your specific question.

EXTRA, EXTRA CREDIT!

To use your sticks to ask the Extra Credit questions, draw two sticks— one at a time—and jot down your two-line diagram. (Remember, broken lines are sticks with a black mark, and changing lines are sticks with a red dot.) Or count your sticks using the method you learned in Reading #5's Extra, Extra Credit! section.

Go on to the next Reading whenever you are ready to continue.

Reading #7

In this Reading you will use your coins to cast three lines. When you read them all together, these three will describe the position you occupy in any situation—you name it. You can also use this Reading to identify your strengths and weaknesses with regard to the other people in your life. In soul-searching, use it to consider where you're coming from.

I CHING TOOLS

In the last several Readings, you have been tossing your coins twice in order to build two-line I Ching diagrams. But why stop with two lines? By this time, it should come as no surprise that you can continue to toss coins, building your diagram up as you go.

In this Reading you will toss your coins three times to build a three-line I Ching diagram. These three-liners—or "trigrams," as they are known to I Ching enthusiasts—are the cornerstone of the I Ching method of fortune-telling. Once you get a feeling for what these three-line figures mean, you will be well on your way to making full use of the I Ching.

By adding the third line, we have again multiplied the possible number of answers you can receive. There are eight primary three-line diagrams:

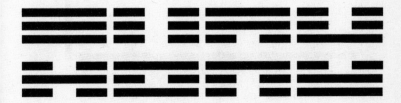

. . . with 56 possible variations for changing lines!

HOW TO

❶ Just as in all the previous Readings, cup your three coins in the palm of your hand, while you concentrate on your question: **Where do I stand in my love life?** In my career? In money matters? In my relationship with _____? **How do I relate?** To others? To my environment? **What role do I play?** At work? At home? At school? **Where do I fit in?**

❷ With your question firmly in mind, cast your coins, and note how they land. (2 or more heads = a solid line; 2 or more tails = a broken line; 3 of a kind = changing.)

❸ Cast the coins again, and write your second line above the first.

❹ Cast the coins a third time, and write your third line above the second.

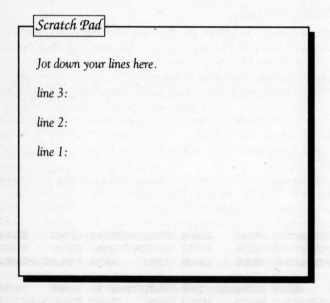

Scratch Pad

Jot down your lines here.

line 3:

line 2:

line 1:

❺ Ignoring any changing lines for now, read the answer for your three-line diagram. This primary diagram describes your current situation. Then the "See Also" references will guide you to the diagram that answers your changing lines. Read also for this resulting diagram, which will show you how your situation is evolving.

THE ANSWERS

HEAVEN

Two Steps Above. Your standing couldn't be better right now, if power is what you wanted. With three solid lines going for you, you are in command. Position, security, and power are yours. You are on top of your game. You are at center stage. You are in grace. You come out on top of the heap. Your situation is like the sky—endless and limitless. This is a time to shine like a star. Be active rather than passive. Show them what you can do. Flex some muscle if you have to. Give others something to believe in . . . something to look up to . . . maybe even a little something to worry about. But know this: Some want something from you. Some hide from you. A few admire you. And one adores you. *All in all, you have it all, and there is nothing to fear.*

BONUS ANSWERS FOR CHANGING LINES

Your diagram ...	SEE ALSO ...	Your diagram ...	SEE ALSO ...

EARTH

Two Rungs Down. Your standing couldn't be better, if being of help to others is what you had in mind. With these three broken lines on your side, you find yourself playing a supportive part in somebody else's life. You tend to things. You tend to others. Your situation is like earth. You nurture the growing. You comfort the dying. You take care of those who cannot care for themselves. And in this situation, your work must serve as its own reward. Be humble rather than bold. Be gentle rather than abrasive. Give way, rather than giving under. Your intuition will see you through in the end. But know this: Some will respect you. Some will fear you. Some walk all over you. And one appreciates you. *All in all, you have things tucked under your wing, and thus you control everything.*

BONUS ANSWERS FOR CHANGING LINES

| Your diagram ... | SEE ALSO ... | Your diagram ... | SEE ALSO ... |

WIND

On the Bottom Rung. Your standing couldn't be better right now, if you don't mind entry-level positions and ground-floor opportunities. With two solid lines above you, you are under the thumb of a higher authority. You are living in somebody else's shadow. You are deferring to someone's judgment. You are like branches in the storm. You must submit, rather than putting up resistance right now. You must attempt to fit into the scheme of these things. You are like chimes in the wind—you are dependent on circumstances. Form alliances with your superiors, if you can. Become indispensable to them, if you wish. But know this: Some use you. Some abuse you. Some count on you. A few take you for granted. And one repays you. *All in all, it is a comfortable position, once you learn the ropes.*

BONUS ANSWERS FOR CHANGING LINES

YOUR DIAGRAM ...	SEE ALSO ...	YOUR DIAGRAM ...	SEE ALSO ...

THUNDER

Climbing the Ladder. Your standing couldn't be better right now, if you were planning on getting ahead. With two broken lines above you, this may be your chance. This may be your lucky day. This may be your big break. Right now, conditions are simply right. Nothing blocks your path. Nobody stands in your way. You've got the energy. You've got the drive. You've got the ambition. All you need now is that one last leap of faith. You are like lightning and thunder. You need to break loose . . . and let the chips fall where they may. This is the time to come out in the open. This is the time to announce your intentions to the world. But know this in advance: Some will cheer you along. Some will jeer you. Some intend to hold you back. A few will wish you well. And one believes in you. *All in all, you have the tiger by the tail, and nowhere to go but up.*

BONUS ANSWERS FOR CHANGING LINES

YOUR DIAGRAM ...	SEE ALSO ...	YOUR DIAGRAM ...	SEE ALSO ...

WATER

Caught in the Middle. Your standing couldn't be better right now, as long as you like to live life on the edge. With broken lines above and below you, you totter on the brink. You walk the tightrope. Trouble brews on either side. But is it danger, or excitement? It is like the tides—it's difficult to tell sometimes which way these waters flow. There is swaying to and fro. Like the moon, you go back and forth. This is a time to choose carefully, tread softly, and go with the flow. You can change your mind up until the very last moment, if you choose. Or you can live for the thrill of the moment, if you dare. But know this: Some need you. Some want you. Some help you. A few are out to get you. And one tempts you. *All in all, these are some pretty exciting times, even if you feel a little vulnerable and confused.*

BONUS ANSWERS FOR CHANGING LINES

YOUR DIAGRAM ...	SEE ALSO ...	YOUR DIAGRAM ...	SEE ALSO ...

FIRE

At the Center of Attention. Your position couldn't be better right now, as long as you like being where the action is. With a solid line above and below you, you are smack dab in the middle of things. You are in the spotlight. You are the focus of attention. Heads turn when you enter a room. Looks and smiles greet you. And when you talk, there is silence. You are like the sun—you are golden. You are like flame—you are glowing. This is a time for putting on your best face. Focus on what shows. Tend to your mirror. Wash. Brush. Trim. Manicure. But know this: Some want you. Some need you. Some lust after you. Some eat out their hearts for you. A few are drawn like moths to the flame. And one lives and dies for you. *All in all, this is a rare and perfect moment, when everything in the world seems to be going your way.*

BONUS ANSWERS FOR CHANGING LINES

YOUR DIAGRAM ...   SEE ALSO ...   YOUR DIAGRAM ...   SEE ALSO ...

MOUNTAIN

About as Far as You Can Go. Your standing couldn't be better right now, as long as you are happy with the status quo. With two broken lines beneath you, you have come to a plateau. You have reached a climax. You have peaked. You are like mountains—you have gone about as high as you can go, and any further progress would only be downhill from here. You might as well take a load off your feet for now. You might as well remove the burden from your back. You might as well enjoy the view from up here. For this, my friend, is what it all adds up to. Your past comes down to this. It's time now to appreciate it for what it is. It's time for a moment of silence. Know this: Some are above you. Some are below you. A few are your equals. And one is your peer. *All in all, if this is as good as it gets, it's not half-bad, is it?*

BONUS ANSWERS FOR CHANGING LINES

YOUR DIAGRAM ...	SEE ALSO ...	YOUR DIAGRAM ...	SEE ALSO ...

MIST

On the Top Rung. Your standing couldn't be better, as long as you don't mind being placed on a pedestal. With two solid lines beneath you, you are being set apart. Someone elevates you. Someone places you head and shoulders above the rest. Someone holds you up as a perfect example. You are like grass in the marshes—you make it seem possible to walk on water. This is not exactly the time to be modest. This is not exactly the time to be timid or shy. Stand tall, my friend. Take pleasure in this moment of glory. Walk proudly into your good fortune. And know this: Some pamper you. Some humor you. Most would like to be in your shoes. A few attempt to undermine you. And one worships the ground you walk on. *All in all, you have it pretty good, for as far as it goes and as long as it lasts.*

BONUS ANSWERS FOR CHANGING LINES

Your diagram ...	SEE ALSO ...	Your diagram ...	SEE ALSO ...

EXTRA CREDIT

For a quicker Reading about how something in particular is going, ask, **How am I doing today with regard to _____ ?** Cast your coins three times, noting whether each toss has produced a solid, a broken, or a changing line of either kind. Write them down one above the other, and read the *italic* portion of the answers.

EXTRA, EXTRA CREDIT!

Use your I Ching sticks to conduct this Reading. One at a time, select three sticks from your bag or bowl. Note each time whether you have selected a solid, a broken, or a changing line, then replace the stick before selecting the next one. Write your lines down in order, one above the next, until you have drawn three lines in all. Look up your answers.

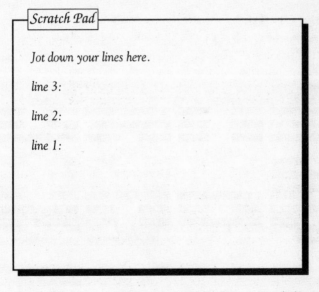

Scratch Pad
Jot down your lines here.
line 3:
line 2:
line 1:

If you'd like to count your sticks instead, use the method you learned in Reading #5's Extra, Extra Credit! section. Count separately for each of the three lines.

Go on to the next Reading whenever you are ready to continue.

Reading #8

WHAT IS THE NATURE OF THIS RELATIONSHIP?
(How should I handle it?)

In this Reading you will toss your coins three times in order to learn the true nature of any personal, professional, or physical relationship. This is also a fine Reading for evaluating business associates or for assessing the prospects for any kind of legal partnership. In soul-searching, use it to figure out how you relate to the Forces of Nature.

I CHING TOOLS

In Reading #7 you started to work with the 8 three-line I Ching diagrams (the trigrams). These same trigrams have been in continuous use for over five millennia. In this Reading you will learn their 5,000-year-old names:

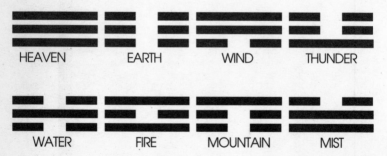

HEAVEN   EARTH   WIND   THUNDER

WATER   FIRE   MOUNTAIN   MIST

Everything else you do in this book will be expressed in terms of these names.

Since, by ancient tradition, these trigrams stand for the Forces of Nature, they can help us understand the nature of things going on in our lives. In this Reading, you will use them to get a handle on your personal relationships. But once you get a feeling for their meanings, you will see that they are useful in understanding just about anything.

HOW TO

❶ Clasp your three coins in the palm of your hand, while you concentrate on your question: **What is the nature of my relationship with _____ ?** This company? This firm? This partner? My significant other? **What can I expect from this relationship?** With my friend? Boss? Lover? **How will this relationship turn out?** By the end of next week? Next month? Next year? Ultimately? **How do I relate to _____ ?**

❷ With your question firmly in mind, cast your coins, and note how they land. (It's the same drill: 2 heads = solid; 2 tails = broken; and 3 of either kind = a changing line.)

❸ Cast the coins twice more. Write your second line above the first. Write your third line above the second.

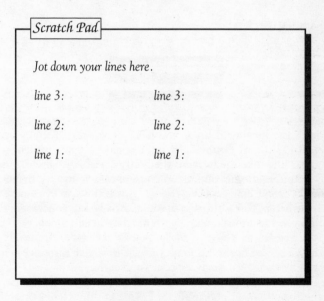

Scratch Pad

Jot down your lines here.

line 3:   line 3:

line 2:   line 2:

line 1:   line 1:

❹ Look up your trigram in the answers below. Read first for your *primary* trigram—by ignoring any changing lines. If no lines are changing, this is your entire answer. If lines are changing, convert them into their opposites. Convert solid changing lines into broken lines; convert broken changing lines into solid lines. This will produce your *resulting* trigram. Consult the answer for this second trigram to see how your current situation is changing. For example,

If you cast:	read for:	also read for:

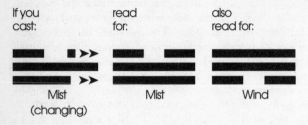

Mist (changing)	Mist	Wind

If you need help figuring out what trigram has resulted from your changing lines, consult the "SEE ALSO" tables in Reading #7's Answer section.

THE ANSWERS

HEAVEN

Having cast three solid lines, you have drawn the I Ching sign for Heaven. And this, my fortunate friend, is a most auspicious sign—three strong YANG lines like the heavens themselves, deep, distant, and unbroken. By tradition, the sun and moon and stars are yours. . . . By point of fact, the sky's your limit. Among friends, this is the sign of blood brothers. Among lovers, this is the sign of soul mates. For all concerned, this is a true and good relationship, one with a strong male influence. *This is a relationship that has the power to change you for the better. Act swiftly on a sudden impulse. Someone wants to play rough. Be a little aggressive yourself. Take things into your own hands, especially at New Moon.*

EARTH

You have drawn the I Ching sign for Earth—three broken lines, like the furrows in a freshly plowed field. As Earth brings forth new things, so, too, does this relationship bring you a new reason for living, a fresh start, a new opportunity, or a second chance at a new beginning. You are most fortunate, my lucky friend, to have someone who supports, defends, and encourages you so much. Between close friends there is unquestioning acceptance and devotion. Between man and woman, there is a silent understanding and an unspoken trust. Among colleagues there is mutual respect. For all concerned, this is a beneficial relationship, especially if it involves a gentle woman's touch. *This is the kind of relationship that gives you back as much—or quite possibly more—than you put into it. Someone wants you to be more responsive. Consider the consequences of disobedience. Learn to adapt. Let loose when the moon is full.*

WIND

You have cast two solid lines above a broken one—like the wind below the heavens. This is the I Ching symbol for the invisible and ever-changing Wind. This means, my friend, the signs are mixed. For the time being at least, and in the here and now, this gentle, simple relationship serves a useful, rewarding, and mutually beneficial purpose. It is like a breath of fresh air. It is a boon to your spirit. It warms the cockles of your heart. Though in its time this love may yet prove false and these friends may still drift apart, there are at least these balmy days and tranquil nights. Tomorrow, who knows what the winds will bring? Changing conditions are always prevailing. For now at least, you are involved in a relationship whose time has come. Enjoy it while it lasts. *This relationship exists in, by, and for the moment. Someone wants to join forces with you. Anything you do now will be of an ephemeral and transitory nature. When you see the Crescent Moon at dawn, it is a good time to break free from a bad habit.*

THUNDER

You have cast a strong solid line beneath two weaker, broken lines—like thunderheads towering in the sky—to form the I Ching symbol for Thunder. This is a sure sign, my friend, that a deep passion underscores the otherwise stormy relationship you find yourself in. Yes, there is something provocative, arousing, and exciting here, like the rumble of a distant storm. But there is also something rather disturbing, unpredictable, volatile, and even explosive about this scene. As friends, you no doubt pick up on—and play off of—each other's energy. As lovers, there is no question but that the sparks really fly between you. But there are moments, too, when you simply rub each other the wrong way. *Though volatile at times, in general this is a spontaneous and exciting relationship. Accept a spur-of-the-moment invitation. Dress for both the shock value and the occasion. As the moon waxes, act out your fantasies, but take all necessary precautions and due considerations.*

WATER

You have cast a solid line between two broken lines. Like the river flowing between its banks, the solid YANG line in the middle distinguishes this figure as the I Ching symbol for Water. And you, my friend, are involved in a relationship of the watery kind. In general this is the sort of relationship that flows right along and remains on its due course. Lovers stay together and remain true. Friends hang around and remain loyal. Everything is more or less okay for the time being. But this sign can also indicate a period of turbulence or danger up ahead. Quite possibly there is a bit of trouble to get through, a bridge to be crossed, or some rite of passage to make it through together—perhaps the birth of a child or some equally difficult labor of love or act of deliverance. Whatever the situation, the forces of life are intimately involved and intermingled here. *This is a vital, deep, and mysterious relationship you are involved in. Remain open to all the possibilities. Get prepared. When you see the Quarter Moon in the morning, be ready for action.*

FIRE

You have cast a broken YIN line between two solid lines. This is the I Ching symbol for Fire—an ember glowing in the heart of a log. And having drawn it, it is clear that you, my friend, are involved in a relationship of a fiery nature. Among friends, there is a sure and certain warmth. Between lovers, there is a glowing radiance. All in all, your present arrangement is both enlightened and illuminating, and what you see is pretty much what you get. But these fires of the heart can also rage out of control. There is the possibility for jealousy and for heated words. You may need to rise above your own emotional involvement and make a conscious decision to throw a little water on this relationship. Alternatively, you might want to heap on a few extra coals. *All in all, this is a relationship based more on actions than on words—perhaps more on appearances than on substance. At any rate, try to remain aware of what's really going on. Make an effort to communicate your feelings under a Quarter Moon.*

MOUNTAIN

You have cast a solid line above two broken ones. This is the I Ching symbol for Mountain—the hills peaking to the sky. And having drawn it, it is clear, my friend, that you are involved in a substantial and long-lasting relationship. Among friends, there is an unspoken understanding. Between lovers, there is a true bond. For companions, there is a sense of endurance. The going may be difficult from time to time, and the uphill way may prove slow and steep. But your joint efforts and shared experiences weave themselves into a solid, lasting experience. *This relationship is of an enduring nature. Be neither modest nor perverse. When in doubt, keep still, remain silent. Meditate on the nights when the moon begins to wane.*

MIST

You have cast a broken line above two solid lines—just like the fog lingering on the land or above the waters—and in so doing, you have drawn the I Ching symbol for Mist. It is a sign, my friend, that you have a relationship of a most private and sensuous kind on your hands. It is hard to define this one. There is something intangible and magical about how you feel toward each other. These friends keep their true feelings hidden. These lovers keep their true relationship under wraps. Some aspects of this arrangement may prove to be insubstantial in the end. And even now you may feel fragile, tentative, or uncertain about what you are doing. But mostly you will be drawn in by the deep sensuality and romance of this fog-drenched situation. *This is a relationship that envelopes you completely. Make a secret pledge to each other when you see the Crescent Moon at sunset. Say a prayer of thankfulness for your deliverance.*

EXTRA CREDIT

For a quicker Reading about how a current relationship should be managed, ask, **How should I handle my relationship with _____ ?** Toss your coins three times, noting whether each toss has produced a solid, a broken, or a changing line. Write down your three lines one above the other, and read the *italic* portion of the answers for your primary trigram, as well as for the one resulting from changing lines. The first answer tells you how the situation stands right now, the second tells you how the relationship is changing.

EXTRA, EXTRA CREDIT!

To trace a relationship over time, use the I Ching sticks you made in Reading #2—or your coins—to construct three trigrams. The first trigram represents your relationship as it existed one month ago. The second trigram represents the relationship as it now stands. And finally, the third trigram represents the relationship as it will exist one month from now. To find your answer, read the *italic* portion of the answers for both your primary and resulting trigrams.

As long as you decide to do so in advance, you can "set" the time frame however you like for this Reading. (For example: first trigram = last year, second trigram = this year, and third trigram = next year . . . or last week, this week, next week.) Play around with it. See what works for you.

Go on to the next Reading whenever you are ready to continue.

Reading #9

WHO CAN I TURN TO?
(Who should I watch out for?)

Who can you trust? Who can you count on? Who can you turn to? Who can you tell? In this Reading, you will cast three I Ching lines to find out who your true friends are right now. This Reading also provides you with an excellent way to find out if a mysterious stranger is about to enter your life . . . and if so, who. For soul-searching, use this Reading to discover the source of your soul's inspiration.

I CHING TOOLS

As we've seen in the previous Readings, I Ching diagrams can be interpreted in many different ways. By ancient tradition, one of the things the three-line trigrams stand for is the people in our lives. In this Reading you will meet them:

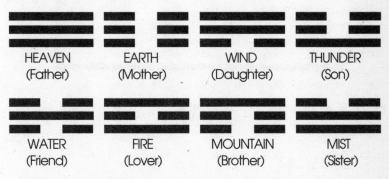

| HEAVEN | EARTH | WIND | THUNDER |
| (Father) | (Mother) | (Daughter) | (Son) |

| WATER | FIRE | MOUNTAIN | MIST |
| (Friend) | (Lover) | (Brother) | (Sister) |

This system of assigning types of people to the trigrams is based on a very old method, but has been updated to more accurately reflect the full range of relationships we must manage in this day and age.

HOW TO

❶ Clasp your three coins in the palm of your hand, while you concentrate on your question: **Who can I turn to?** For help with my problems?

For hope? For consolation? For support? For love and comfort? **Who can I trust?** In business dealings? With my money? With my secrets? **Who can I believe? Who can I lean on?**

❷ With your question firmly in mind, cast your coins three times, and note how they land each time. (2 heads = solid; 2 tails = broken; 3 of either kind = changing.)

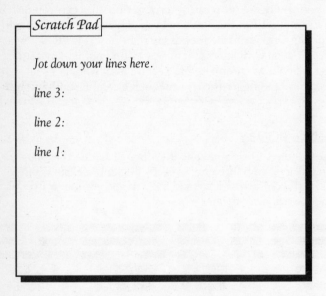

Scratch Pad

Jot down your lines here.

line 3:

line 2:

line 1:

❸ Look up your trigram in the answers. Be sure to consult the full answer, but pay special attention to the Bonus Answers for your particular changing lines.

THE ANSWERS

HEAVEN

Father. You have drawn three solid YANG lines—the I Ching sign for

Heaven. So it is clear as the blue sky above your head that you have friends in high places. Now is the time to turn to them for the answers to your questions or to address your needs and concerns. Place your trust in those who have earned your respect in the past . . . someone older and wiser—a parent, perhaps a strong father figure. (In fact, your old man himself is not a bad place to start.) When in trouble, turn to those in authority, but be ready for a lesson in politics. At school, go to the dean. At work, go to the boss. *A mature man is coming into your life. Be careful that his desire is not simply to control or possess. Your inspiration comes from out of the blue. Gaze upward for a sign. Look to the clouds and the stars when you need a clue. Rainbows are lucky for you.*

BONUS ANSWERS FOR CHANGING LINES

■ BOTTOM LINE CHANGING: Turn to a trusted peer or close male friend. *A breezy character is coming into your life. Watch out for the B.S.*

■ MIDDLE LINE CHANGING: Turn to an immediate superior or role model. *A fiery character is about to descend on you. Watch out you don't get singed.*

■ TOP LINE CHANGING: Turn to a leader or manager. *A mysterious character is going to attract your curiosity. Watch out you don't get taken in.*

EARTH

Mother. You have drawn three broken YIN lines—the I Ching sign for Earth. Just as the Earth provides a home for all living things, it is certain that you will find your best friends already living under your own roof, or at least in the general vicinity—perhaps even in the house next door. A strong mother figure is definitely involved. Now is a good time to consult her for some advice, a little encouragement, or a good dose of consolation. (If you are all grown up and moved away, don't forget to call your mother!) When in trouble, turn to the woman in charge for the answers, but be ready for a lesson in morality. At school, go to the guidance counselor. At work, go to Personnel. *A mature woman is actively involved in your life. Be careful that her desire is not simply to mother. Your inspiration* comes from keeping both feet planted firmly on the ground. *Watch where you are going. Look down for a sign—something you find lying around will inform you of what you need to know. Stones work wonders for you.*

BONUS ANSWERS FOR CHANGING LINES

■ **BOTTOM LINE CHANGING:** Turn to an outspoken woman or a powerful ally . . . someone who will stand up for you through thick or thin. *A loud character is coming into your life. Watch out what you reveal about yourself.*

■ **MIDDLE LINE CHANGING:** Turn to an even-tempered woman or any close contact on the same wavelength as you. *A slippery character is coming into your life. Watch out you don't get drawn in by appearances.*

■ **TOP LINE CHANGING:** Turn to a strong-willed woman or anyone in a well-established position. *A rigid character is coming into your life. Watch out you don't run up against a brick wall.*

WIND

Daughter. You have drawn two solid YANG lines above a broken YIN line—the I Ching sign for Wind. Just as the wind surrounds us at all times, it is clear that you walk in a circle of friends and acquaintances. Still, it may be difficult to say who among them is your best friend of all right now. A big sister proves to know the answers . . . or an older woman who is like a sister to you. At any rate, place your trust in those who can keep a secret and have no interest in steering you wrong. When considering how best to proceed, turn to someone who has been there before. A role model plays an important part in your life. At school, learn from those you admire. At work, turn to a trusted colleague for advice. *A new sensuous woman is emerging in your life. Mind that your intentions remain honorable. Your inspiration comes from scents. A sign comes to you on the breeze. Pay special attention to aromas, flavors, and fragrances. Choose carefully among perfumes. Fresh air is good for you.*

BONUS ANSWERS FOR CHANGING LINES

■ **BOTTOM LINE CHANGING:** Turn to the female head of household or someone else in authority. *An elusive character is coming into your life. Don't let this one out of your sight.*

■ **MIDDLE LINE CHANGING:** Turn to a self-made woman or someone else who has worked their way to the top. *An oppressive character is coming into your life. Don't let yourself get tied down.*

■ **TOP LINE CHANGING:** Turn to a woman who has given birth or someone who has gone through it all before. *A meandering character is coming into your life. Don't expect the straight and narrow.*

THUNDER

Son. You have drawn two broken YIN lines above a solid YANG line—the I Ching sign for Thunder. As such, your relationships with others are sure to be rather stormy and tumultuous . . . electric and spontaneous. You will know your friends by those who touch—or are touched by— you. There will be a magnetic attraction between you and your closest friends. Your best relationships are based on plenty of physical contact. An older brother is the best one to consult on the immediate problem you face . . . or someone who plays the role of a big brother in your life. Put your trust in those you can look up to. At school, consult with a hero. At work, turn to a visionary for advice. *A strong male influence is at work in your life. A young man may want to get physical with you. If you decide to follow your impulses, be sure to think at least twice. Your inspiration comes from the dark of the storm or from coming through some personal crisis. When you least expect it, the sign you are seeking will come to you in a sudden, blinding flash of light. Smoke is lucky for you.*

BONUS ANSWERS FOR CHANGING LINES

■ **BOTTOM LINE CHANGING:** Turn to a married man or someone else who has experience with women. *A soft-spoken character is coming into your life. Watch out for deeper emotions.*

■ **MIDDLE LINE CHANGING:** Turn to a religious man or someone else who tries to understand. *A creepy character is coming into your life. Approach this one only from a distance.*

■ **TOP LINE CHANGING:** Turn to a passionate man or someone else who is capable of sharing your deepest feelings. *A reckless character is coming into your life. Be sure to wear your seat belt.*

WATER

Friend. You have drawn a solid YANG line between two broken lines—the I Ching sign for Water. Just as the river flows between its banks, you are accompanied through this life by two very near and dear friends. These two may be your actual biological brothers or sisters or quite possibly cousins or other close relatives. But they could also be people so close to you that they feel like blood relations, when in fact they are not. In general, place your trust in those who will stand by you come hell or high water. In an emergency, call on them to rescue you. At school, take the word of a pal. At work, listen to a little friendly advice from a peer. *A deep or mysterious man—or a changeable woman—is getting close to you. Be careful you don't get into trouble as a result of your acquaintance. Your inspiration comes from gazing into liquids. Cold showers invigorate you. A body of flowing water will surely bring you a sign.*

BONUS ANSWERS FOR CHANGING LINES

■ **BOTTOM LINE CHANGING:** Turn to a young man or someone else who has recently gone through a physical change. *A magical character is coming into your life. Watch out for sleight of hand.*

■ **MIDDLE LINE CHANGING:** Turn to a middle-aged man or someone else who has softened toward the world. *An earthy character is coming into your life. Watch out for your burning ears.*

■ **TOP LINE CHANGING:** Turn to an old man or someone else who wants to shoot the breeze. *A fascinating character is coming into your life. Watch out for tall tales.*

FIRE

Lover. You have drawn a broken YIN line between two solid YANG lines—the I Ching sign for Fire. So it would seem you are inclined to have relationships of a fiery nature . . . hot and heated, perhaps . . . steamy and sultry, no doubt. For it takes sparks to make a flame, and your best friends are those who are inclined to hit it off with you right from the start. Many are naturally drawn to you—like moths to the flame, perhaps—but trust only those whom you feel equally attracted to. There is magic between you. At school, take the advice of someone bright and energetic. At work, talk to someone who is in a position to shed some light on the subject. *A spirited young woman—or an aggressive someone—is trying to tell you something. Listen completely and decide carefully. Your inspiration comes from the flickering candlelight. Stare into the embers of a fire and you will see the sign you seek. Sunlight works wonders.*

BONUS ANSWERS FOR CHANGING LINES

■ **BOTTOM LINE CHANGING:** Turn to a dynamic woman or someone else who knows how to get things done. *A towering character is coming into your life. Be careful not to get lost in the shadows.*

■ **MIDDLE LINE CHANGING:** Turn to a spiritual woman or someone else who has special powers. *A down-to-earth character is coming into your life. This is one you can trust.*

■ **TOP LINE CHANGING:** Turn to an energetic woman or someone else who sparks and sparkles with energy. *An electric character is coming into your life. Watch out you don't get shocked.*

MOUNTAIN

Brother. You have drawn a solid YANG line over two broken YIN lines—the I Ching sign for Mountain. So, just as the mountain remains solidly in the place where it began, your relationships tend to be cemented early in life. Your best friends will be lifelong acquaintances, family members, and others you have known for a long time—or those who, for whatever reason, do not need to be kept at a safe distance. Trust only those relationships that have endured long enough to warrant your trust. At school, hang out with the old gang. At work, consult the ones you started out with. *A strong, silent male is at work in your life. Make sure to leave him plenty of room for comfort and personal expression. Take your inspiration from the hills. If you are looking for a sign, the mountains will lead you to it in their own good time. High places are lucky for you.*

BONUS ANSWERS FOR CHANGING LINES

■ **BOTTOM LINE CHANGING:** Turn to an idealistic young man or someone else who has been to the mountaintop. *A free-spirited character is coming into your life. Be careful you don't get caught up in somebody else's dream.*

■ **MIDDLE LINE CHANGING:** Turn to a weathered man or someone else who knows how to navigate rough terrain. *An unassuming character is coming into your life. Be careful to look below the surface before you judge.*

■ **TOP LINE CHANGING:** Turn to a humble man or someone else who has learned the lessons of a lifetime. *A sincere character is coming into your life. Be careful about doubting a good thing.*

MIST

Sister. You have drawn a broken YIN line above two solid YANG lines—

the I Ching sign for Mist. So, just as the undulating mists that rise from the smooth waters of the lake are tranquil and serene, you tend to form discreet, quiet relationships with others. Since your meetings often are clandestine, trust only those who bring magic into your life. Your best friends will be up-front, open, and honest with you . . . caring and sensitive. They will honor your wishes. At school, seek out those who share the same interests, passions, and pursuits. At work, take the advice of someone younger. *A mystic is playing a major part in your life. Beware of the sensual undercurrents in this relationship, but go with the mood of the moment. Take your inspiration from rising vapors. If you are looking for a sign, turn down the lights and gaze at your reflection in the mirror. Steam clears your head.*

BONUS ANSWERS FOR CHANGING LINES

■   **BOTTOM LINE CHANGING:** Turn to a miracle worker or someone else who can walk on water. *A smooth character is coming into your life. Watch out for undercurrents.*

■   **MIDDLE LINE CHANGING:** Turn to a visionary or someone else who knows how to predict things. *A stormy character is coming into your life. Watch out for conflicts of interest.*

■   **TOP LINE CHANGING:** Turn to a professional counselor or someone else who is a reader and advisor of people. *A lofty character is coming into your life. Watch out for pitfalls.*

EXTRA CREDIT

To find out if you need to be cautious of a stranger, ask, **Who should I watch out for?** Cast your coins three times, noting whether each toss has produced a solid, a broken, or a changing line. Write down your three lines one above the other, and read the *italic* portion of the answers.

EXTRA, EXTRA CREDIT!

In Reading #5 you learned a very basic method of counting sticks to construct your I Ching diagrams. If you would like to use a more sophisticated—yet still relatively simple—approach, try the method described below.

First you'll need to round up 25 sticks of some kind (twigs, chopsticks, whatever)—something between 8 and 12 inches long. Once you have your sticks, you are ready to proceed. Ask one of the questions from this Reading, and then:

Remove one stick and set it aside <u>completely</u>.

1.   Divide the remaining 24 sticks into three bundles at random.
2.   Count off the sticks in the first bundle to your left **by fours.** Set aside the last group of one to four sticks in a discard pile. Keep the rest.
3.   Count off the sticks in the middle bundle **by threes.** Discard the last group of one to three sticks. Keep the rest.
4.   Count off the last bundle **by fours.** Discard the final group of one to four sticks and keep the rest.
5.   Count how many sticks you have discarded.
6.   Look up your line in the following table, based on the number of sticks you have discarded. (But don't count the first one you removed before Step 1.)

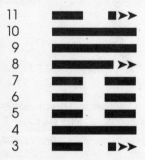

Repeat Steps 1 through 6 twice more to complete your trigram. Look up your answers in this Reading's Answer section.

This method vastly simplifies the traditional way that mystics have consulted the I Ching for hundreds and hundreds of years. While retaining much of the feeling of counting sticks in the traditional way, this method takes much less time to reach results that are statistically very close to the original.[1]

Go on to the next Reading whenever you are ready to continue.

[1] Many thanks to Michael McCormick for helping me develop and verify this simplified stick-counting method.

Reading #10

In this Reading you will "add up" the letters in your name to determine which I Ching path you are following. The trigrams provide
eight ways. You can use the Reading to see how the name you go by
influences your destiny. Or by using coins or sticks to cast a three-line
trigram, this Reading will describe the nature of any situation you
specify. Soul-searchers also can identify their spiritual path in life.

I CHING TOOLS

It just so happens that each of the three-line I Ching trigrams has a
number as well as a name:

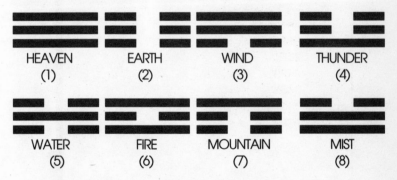

| HEAVEN | EARTH | WIND | THUNDER |
| (1) | (2) | (3) | (4) |

| WATER | FIRE | MOUNTAIN | MIST |
| (5) | (6) | (7) | (8) |

. . . but these are not just any kind of numbers. These are mystical numbers that clearly were revered by the ancient Chinese. However, the
technique used in this Reading is borrowed from Middle Eastern sages
who believed such numbers can be used to unlock the secrets of your
destiny. The key is in the letters of your name.

HOW TO

All you need to know to do this Reading is your own name! But
instead of using the full, legal name you were given at birth, use the
name you go by.

❶ Just jot down your name on the Scratch Pad. Then convert the letters in your name to numbers using this table:

1	2	3	4	5	6	7	8
A	B	C	D	E	F	G	H
I/J	K	L	M	N	O	P	Q
R/S	T	U	V	W	X	Y	Z

For example, Victoria Cox goes by the name Tory. So Tory's numbers are: (T = 2), (O = 6), (R = 1), and (Y = 7).

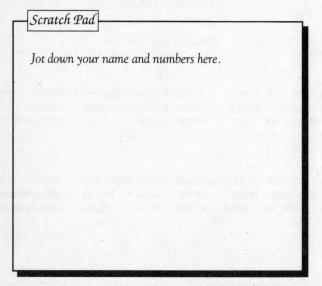

Scratch Pad

Jot down your name and numbers here.

❷ Next, add up the numbers in your name. For Tory: 2+6+1+7 = 16.

❸ Finally, reduce this number by adding its component numerals together. For Tory, 1+6=7. The object is to get a number between 1 and 8. If you still have a two-digit number at this point, combine these numerals and add again.

Note: *If you get a 9 at any point, you are very lucky indeed, for 9 is a perfect number. The number 9 is so perfect, in fact, that it would be presumptuous for us to discuss your destiny here. For the purposes of this Reading, however, convert your number 9 to a 1, and follow your inner voices in realizing your own splendiferous future.*

❹ Look up your answer by the number you wind up with. For this part of the Reading, ignore the descriptions for changing lines. (You might want to try this Reading with various nicknames or forms of your name to see which variation gives you the destiny you would prefer.)

THE ANSWERS

HEAVEN

(1). The path you are on is endless and eternal. It is the path of sky . . . the heavens . . . the Universe itself. All these things go upward and outward forever and ever. And so your path takes you to the heights. You are truly, surely headed for success. Nothing holds you down. There is no rope around your feet. There is no weight upon your back. Put body, mind, and soul into this thing you are pursuing. And do not limit your dreams. For these are the heavens you are shooting for, my friend. These are the highest heights. And there is nowhere to go but up. Be ready, willing, and able to answer when the Universe knocks. *The meaning that you seek is written in the sky. Take your cues from sun, moon, and stars. This situation empowers and enables you. This situation gives you free reign. This situation sets you free. C'mon now, take the next big step.*

BONUS ANSWERS FOR CHANGING LINES

■ BOTTOM LINE CHANGING: [Heaven ⟶ Wind] The path you are on kicks up a bit of dust at the approaching storm. Things rustle. You hustle. *Either this situation is like a breath of fresh air or else somebody is breathing down your neck! Either way, it's time to get your feelings out in the open and your tail in gear. The Universe asks nothing of you, but requires your participation.*

■ **MIDDLE LINE CHANGING:** [Heaven ⟶ Fire] The path you are on is a fiery one. The red clay bakes in the sun, and the pavement smolders under your feet. *This situation is so hot, it will burn your behind if you get caught! The Universe only points you in the general direction, but you have to steer your own wheels.*

■ **TOP LINE CHANGING:** [Heaven ⟶ Mist] The path you are on grows suddenly cloudy, and the way indiscernible, as a thick fog rolls into your life. *This situation envelopes you, clouds your senses, and interferes with your perspective. Handle the emotions of others with ever-loving care. Work on your own depth perception. And when in doubt, ask.*

EARTH

(2). It is the way of the Earth to provide a path—complete with twists, turns, forks, obstacles, and diversions—through even the wilderness. So, too, your path takes you continually forward, continuously onward down the road . . . beyond the last fork . . . beyond the next bend. The path that you are on is endless and eternal—marked by turning points, and fraught with choices. Yet nothing stands in your way for long. There is nothing you cannot get over. There is nothing you cannot get around. There is nothing you cannot get through. And so, in the matters that concern you most, your progress is assured. Keep doing what you're doing. Keep headed in the same direction. But be ready, willing, and able to make a major choice when this path splits. *The meaning that you seek will be found in Mother Nature. Take your cues from the rocks, hills, streams, and woods. This situation comforts, urges, and encourages you. This situation takes you by the hand. Come now, return the favor.*

BONUS ANSWERS FOR CHANGING LINES

■ **BOTTOM LINE CHANGING:** [Earth ⟶ Thunder] The path you are on suddenly rumbles beneath your feet like a sleeping monster. It lurches. It yawns. And then it smoothes out again. *This situation sets off the rockets inside your tummy—and I'm not talking butterflies, my friend. Just as quickly, calm prevails. And that's when you know the heartfelt truth.*

■ **MIDDLE LINE CHANGING:** [Earth ⟶ Water] The path you are on turns slick and mushy . . . soft with standing rain. Your trail of heavy footsteps sinks deeper and deeper into the red clay. *This situation is damp, dark, and slippery when wet. It smells sweet on the surface, but reeks of musk underneath. Slow down a bit and take it easy on the curves.*

■ **TOP LINE CHANGING:** [Earth ⟶ Mountain] The path you are on develops a steep uphill grade. And you will either have to huff and puff your way along or else switch to a lower gear. *This situation will surely bring you to the heights, even if the getting there is slow right now. Enjoy the scenic views along the way. And take your time arriving.*

WIND

(3). The way of the Wind is downward and inward, outward and upward. The way of the wind is circular . . . like spiral stairs . . . like whirlwinds in the fall leaves . . . like tornadoes, like hurricanes. You go round and round. You are tossed to and fro. This path that you travel is endless and eternal . . . it is the motion of the planets in their orbits . . . it is the motion of the galaxies around their cores. Like them all, your own forward progress takes you in a circular motion. The things that concern you often resolve themselves after a complete turning of the seasons or following the completion of some other natural cycle. Until then, remain flexible. Be ready, willing, and able to bend in the breeze. *The meaning that you seek will be found in the blue sky. Take your cues from the clouds. This situation shapes and molds you. This situation influences you in subtle yet persistent ways. Come on now. Why fight it?*

BONUS ANSWERS FOR CHANGING LINES

■ **BOTTOM LINE CHANGING:** [Wind ⟶ Heaven] The path you are on grows dim now, as the wind rushes by on its way back upward and the storm crackles in the distance, closing in before it moves away again. *This situation reminds you that relationships are fragile. This is a night for kissing and making up.*

■ **MIDDLE LINE CHANGING:** [Wind ⟶ Mountain] The path you are on leads to a fallen tree that blocks the way, or else comes abruptly to a windswept cliff where you must decide your next move. *This situation requires you to backtrack or take a detour from your preferred route. Which way will it be? Down over the side? Or by the back way? The choice is yours.*

■ **TOP LINE CHANGING:** [Wind ⟶ Water] The path you are on is swept by a driving rain, and you are likely to get soaked to the bone if you don't shake a leg and get a move on. *This situation requires you to let your hair down or get your hair wet. But it never hurts to be careful. If it gets to be too much for you, head for shelter.*

THUNDER

(4). The path you are on is the way of the Thunder, the way of expansion. This path is endless and eternal. The Universe itself expands ever onward and forever outward in all directions. So, too, your path takes you in many different ways at once . . . even to the far corners of the Earth. But take care on this adventuresome route. And be careful. Remember, Thunder is born of violence. And so, the path you are on is not without its dangers and repercussions. The things that concern you usually are resolved in a blinding flash of light. Be ready, willing, and able to see the truth when the inspiration strikes. *The meaning that you seek will come from things that are heard rather than seen. Take your cues from the birds returning to their nests. This situation rattles the windows and rocks the roost. This situation makes your hair stand on end. Come any closer and you may get a jolt.*

BONUS ANSWERS FOR CHANGING LINES

■ **BOTTOM LINE CHANGING:** [Thunder ⟶ Earth] The path you are on is still and quiet, now that the storm has passed through, and everything smells fresh and clean again. Any further rumbling you hear will only come from a safe distance. *This situation is well grounded. Though an occasional spark will still travel the path of least resistance, everything becomes neutral. And in the end, all things even out.*

■ **MIDDLE LINE CHANGING:** [Thunder ⟶ Mist] The path you are on is a bit hazy these days, and the air is thick. Sometimes you feel hemmed in by it. And sometimes you feel free to escape. *This situation needs a little breathing space. Let the smoke clear before you recommit. Let it have the time it takes to sort itself out. The past has a way of resolving itself.*

■ **TOP LINE CHANGING:** [Thunder ⟶ Fire] The path you are on brings you within inches of the point where lightning could very well strike . . . twice. *This situation will more than likely take you along for the ride . . . or bring you down with it. You're in for a hair-raising experience, to say the very least. It is better to speak of the past than to repeat it.*

WATER

(5). The path you are on is the way of the Water . . . constantly moving . . . constantly changing, like the rivers running down to the sea, like the tides going out . . . and coming in. Deep feelings are involved. Passions. Emotions. The way of the Water is endless and eternal. It swirls down the drain in the same motion as the galaxies spiraling down into their cores. So, too, the path you are on is one of natural progression. A birth or rebirth of some kind may be involved. The things that concern you most usually are resolved in their own good time. So go with the flow. There is no way to hurry these things along. Be ready, willing, and able to be cleansed when the healing rains come. *The meaning that you are seeking will be found along the shores. Take your cues from the things that wash up at your feet. This situation draws you in like a current. This situation carries your heart away. Come on in. The water's fine.*

BONUS ANSWERS FOR CHANGING LINES

■ **BOTTOM LINE CHANGING:** [Water ⟶ Mist] The path you are on is one of alteration. The river steams in the first light of a new day, as the water changes shape and form. You, too, are subject to transformation. *This situation promises to alter you in subtle, yet dramatic and permanent, ways. It touches you. Holds you. And then sets you free to be yourself. Everything is connected to everything else. And so be it.*

■ **MIDDLE LINE CHANGING:** [Water ⟶ Earth] The path you are on is frozen and unforgiving. Scattered patches of ice shatter under even careful footsteps. The rug has a way of being pulled out from under you. *This situation has grown cold and frigid, and there is secret longing for relief. It does no good to rue the day or curse the night. Give things a chance to sink in before you respond. The heart that hardens also melts.*

■ **TOP LINE CHANGING:** [Water ⟶ Wind] The path you are on goes down to the water's edge . . . where the breeze blows fresh, and full of spray—and where you can be alone with your thoughts. *This situation is sure to take your breath away, if you go at it head-on. It would be better to approach these things from an angle . . . and after taking a deep breath. Some things come on the breeze and some things are carried away.*

FIRE

(6). The way of the Fire is to make its own path . . . through the woods . . . across the prairies . . . up the mountains . . . the flames licking the sky, and the smoke rising. Fire changes the things it comes in contact with. It moves along by altering the things in its way—by consuming and reducing. It changes forever the things it ignites. The path you are on is one and the same. And it is endless and eternal. It is as old as the sun. You make your way along by shedding light on things and changing the things that get in your way. Matters that concern you usually are resolved through an alteration of your environment. Take stock of the things that matter to you, so you do not inadvertently toss them aside in your haste to forge ahead. But be ready, willing, and able to go when the spark ignites your soul. *The meaning that you are seeking comes to you in*

flickering candlelight. Take your cues from woodsmoke and glowing embers. This situation excites and thrills you. Something smolders deep within you. Come, warm the secret cockles of your heart.

BONUS ANSWERS FOR CHANGING LINES

■ **BOTTOM LINE CHANGING:** [Fire ⟶ Mountain] The path you are on is strewn with the cinders, stones, and ashes of your own past. Now you must make your way among these remnants with certain care, but urgent haste. *This situation has its own past to get around, crawl over, or rise out from under. It's high time to reclaim what is left and put the pieces of your own life back together. But the past has a way of coming back to haunt you, so before you move forward, set the record straight.*

■ **MIDDLE LINE CHANGING:** [Fire ⟶ Heaven] The path you are on flames with the colors of nature realizing its full potential. The leaves fall around you, and your nostrils flare to the warm scent of woodsmoke trailing upward. Relax. *This situation reaches its natural climax . . . but only when the time is right, and everything that matters is in place. You must have done something really good in a former life.*

■ **TOP LINE CHANGING:** [Fire ⟶ Thunder] The path you are on opens up into a clearing. It is here that you gather your circle of stones and heap your personal effects into a thundering bonfire of dead wood . . . blazing in the dark night . . . erasing the past for good. *This situation offers you a clean break, a fresh start, and a new beginning. But first you must abandon something else. The past would hold you hostage forever. Take only its lessons with you.*

MOUNTAIN

(7). Yours is the path of most resistance. For the way of the Mountain is obstruction . . . it is sheer . . . steep . . . treacherous. And you must feel your way along, going where the Mountain lets you go . . . going where the Mountain leads you. The path you are on demands your undivided attention—physical, mental, and spiritual—and your complete endurance. For this way is as old as the hills themselves, but you will

have to figure it out for yourself. Good luck in your quest to reach the top. The things that concern you most usually are resolved once you have proven yourself. Be ready, willing, and able to accept challenges as they come. *The meaning that you are seeking resides in the hills. Take your cues from rocks, stones, and crystals. This situation endures. This situation brings you stability. Come quickly to the point.*

BONUS ANSWERS FOR CHANGING LINES

■ **BOTTOM LINE CHANGING:** [Mountain ⟶ Fire] The path you are on is dry from drought and brittle as the tinder in a kindling box. One spark . . . and it would all go poof, except for the land itself, which will not budge no matter what. *This situation is permanent and stable to the core, but on the surface it has grown volatile . . . maybe even hostile. This is not a time to play with matches or to fight fire with fire. Rather, you must return to the basics. Trace these things back to their sources. Tend to the roots.*

■ **MIDDLE LINE CHANGING:** [Mountain ⟶ Wind] The path you are on takes you to the jagged summit of a windswept crag. There would seem to be nowhere to go from here but back down the way you came. But only you can decide what happens next. *This situation is at its peak . . . and what you see right now is just about as good as it will ever get. But are you satisfied? Or do you yearn yet for something more? Something else? The price of arrival is departure. The cost of remaining is more of the same.*

■ **TOP LINE CHANGING:** [Mountain ⟶ Earth] The path you are on follows the flat mountain ridges that the rain has worn smooth. And having come the curving distance of the steep ascent, you are now in the straightaway and can enjoy the view. *This situation has been a long time in the making. You've all been through a lot together, and you're all stronger for it. Everything eventually evens out, it seems, or at least comes to terms in the end.*

MIST

(8). The Mist moves in mysterious ways. It rises from the rivers at dawn . . . it drops into the valleys at dusk . . . it blows in from the sea. Shapeless,

dense, wispy, thin . . . the Mist encroaches, conceals, permeates, lifts—all without substance. You feel spiritual about things. You feel mystical. You dream dreams. The way of the Mist is ageless and eternal. It is like stardust. It is like the great cloudy nebula of the Universe. And the path you are on is likewise nebulous and uncertain. But new things are always in the making. New things are always taking shape. Anything could change at any moment. The matters that concern you usually are clarified in due time. Be ready, willing, and able to act on your instincts when the fog periodically parts. *The meaning that you are seeking comes from out of the blue. Take your cues from rainbows and halos around the moon. This situation is subtle and gentle. This situation is fluid. Come when Mother Nature calls.*

BONUS ANSWERS FOR CHANGING LINES

■ **BOTTOM LINE CHANGING:** [Mist ——➤ Water] The path you are on is fresh with dew and slippery with moss. Your own breath turns to vapor in the dawn's low light. *This situation invigorates you, restores you, clears your head, refreshes you, and hugs you close against its breast. Keep doing what you're doing. The silence you feel inside tells you everything. Hold these things in your heart.*

■ **MIDDLE LINE CHANGING:** [Mist ——➤ Thunder] The path you are on takes you to below the falls, where the mist rises from the thundering waters and all words are drowned out. *This situation may have a hard time finding human expression. It fails for words. But the message comes through loud and clear just the same . . . like the telltale beating of two hearts.*

■ **TOP LINE CHANGING:** [Mist ——➤ Heaven] The path you are on is flat, open . . . and nothing stands between you and the drifting clouds but the sky itself. *This situation is what you have always hoped for, longed for, wished for, and desired. The past is behind you now.*

EXTRA CREDIT

Use your coins to learn how any given situation in your life stacks up. Just ask, **What's my situation?** At work? In love? Financially? Politically? **How is my situation concerning _____ going? Where is this thing headed?** You can also try this Reading with a question like **What kind of opportunity is this?** Toss your coins three times, each time noting whether you have cast a broken (2 tails), a solid (2 heads), or a changing line (3 of a kind). Write down your three lines one above the other, and look up your answers. Read the complete answer for your trigram, but focus on any and all changing lines and anything in *italics*.

```
┌─Scratch Pad─────────────────────────────┐
│                                          │
│   Jot down your lines here.              │
│                                          │
│   line 3:                                │
│                                          │
│   line 2:                                │
│                                          │
│   line 1:                                │
│                                          │
│                                          │
│                                          │
└──────────────────────────────────────────┘
```

EXTRA, EXTRA CREDIT!

You can also use your coins or sticks to follow a developing situation. Simply ask: **How is this situation progressing?** Cast three I Ching trigrams—one for the past, one for the present, and one for the future. Read them in order and focus on the *italic* portion of the answers.

Go on to the next Reading whenever you are ready to continue.

Reading #11

How will the two of you hit it off as buddies? Lovers? Colleagues? Co-workers? Partners? Best friends? or Whatever? In this Reading, you'll find out how compatible the two of you are in I Ching terms. The Reading also works for relationships that already exist or have gone on for a long while. Give it a try for questions about your employer, banker, and stockbroker as well. For soul-searchers, this is the perfect opportunity to find out about your soul mate.

I CHING TOOLS

Everything we have seen and done in all the Readings up until now used the one-, two-, and three-line diagrams at the center of the I Ching. All of that was the heart. But now . . . now comes the soul.

By stacking two three-line trigrams on top of one another, we come in this Reading to the six-line diagrams—better known as the I Ching "hexagrams." There are 64 of these hexagrams in all, representing every double combination of trigrams possible . . . and reflecting—some say—everything in the Universe.

HOW TO

If you have not already done Reading #10, go back now and convert your name into an I Ching trigram. Keep your finger in the book! For you will be using Reading #10's How To section to convert the names of your friends and associates, too.

❶ To find out how compatible you are, start by listing the first names of the people you want to ask about. They can be anyone you are thinking of entering into any kind of relationship with, or anyone you have known for a long time. Use the name or nickname you know each person by . . . the name you would call them to their face.

81

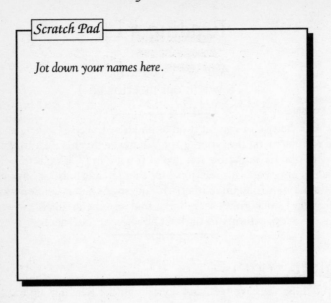

Scratch Pad

Jot down your names here.

❷ Translate each name you have listed above into an I Ching trigram by using the alphabet table in Reading #10's How To section and the trigram table from Reading #10's I Ching Tools section.

❸ Now jot down your own three-line trigram from Reading #10—and you're all set.

❹ In consulting the Answer section, look up your own trigram first, and read the answer under it for the trigram of your friend, lover, partner, or associate. To see things from the other person's point of view, look up that person's diagram first, then find yours underneath.

Note: Some of your answers may sound as if they don't match the gender of the people you are asking about. Read these answers as figurative descriptions of different kinds of relationships, not as literal physical descriptions of the parties involved. But if the shoe fits, wear it.

For more information on any hexagram consult the Quick Reference Guide.

THE ANSWERS

HEAVEN PLUS

HEAVEN

Heaven + Heaven . . . You are like blood brothers, bonded for life . . . as close as two pals can get without raising questions . . . so compatible that nothing can pry the two of you apart. *Your meeting will go best if conducted in a private place.*

EARTH

Heaven + Earth . . . You are as compatible as a grown man and his mother, bound to each other by an invisible thread . . . and a silent understanding. *Your meeting will go best if you meet each other halfway.*

WIND

Heaven + Wind . . . You are like a father and his little girl . . . two hearts poured from the same mold . . . and about as compatible as any sweet talker and a soft touch. *Your meeting will go best if you come quickly to the point.*

THUNDER

Heaven + Thunder . . . You are like a dad and his teenage son . . . about as compatible as a speed cop and a red convertible. *Your meeting—if any—will be on the fly. Go easy.*

WATER

Heaven + Water . . . You are like two good ol' fishing buddies, about as compatible as line and reel . . . with the uncanny ability to say it all without moving your lips. *Your meeting will be slow, laid-back, and easy.*

FIRE

Heaven + Fire . . . You are as compatible as two lovers on a spring night. First there are the lights up in the sky and then there are the sparks. *Your meeting will run late and long. It will go better if you take your time.*

MOUNTAIN

Heaven + Mountain . . . You are as compatible as a man and his brother. Like the hills and sky, you stand up for—and just as likely oppose—each other. *Your meeting will go better if you learn to give as well as take.*

HEAVEN PLUS

MIST

Heaven + Mist . . . You are as compatible as a grown man and his baby sister. One of you still shields, and one of you still clings. *Your meeting will go better if you simply play the part.*

EARTH PLUS

HEAVEN

Earth + Heaven . . . You are as compatible as any grown woman and her father. You can get each other's full attention, but only for 10 minutes at a time. *Your meeting will go better if you think of it as quality time.*

EARTH

Earth + Earth . . . You are as compatible as two women in the same network . . . bound by your mutual experience and your collective self-interest. *Your meeting will be best if it is spontaneous.*

WIND

Earth + Wind . . . You are as compatible as any mother/daughter team. One of you does the talking while the other listens. *Your meeting will go better if you give a little more than you take.*

THUNDER

Earth + Thunder . . . You are as compatible as any mother/son pair. One holds on for dear life, while the other cuts loose. *Your meeting will go better if you don't push the hot buttons.*

WATER

Earth + Water . . . You are as compatible as two girlfriends. You share the same wavelength, dial tone, and dress-up clothes. *Your meeting will flow along smoothly, if you just hang loose.*

FIRE

Earth + Fire . . . You are as compatible as any couple who share the same bed. One has cold feet, and the other, warm legs. *Your meeting will go better if conducted in a dimly lit place.*

EARTH PLUS

MOUNTAIN

Earth + Mountain . . . You are as compatible as any sister and her brother. One baits the hook, while the other rises to the sinker. *Your meeting will go best if you come quickly to the point.*

MIST

Earth + Mist . . . You are as compatible as two sisters. One hovers around the other like a good example, and the other humors her. *Your meeting will go like a well-choreographed dance.*

WIND PLUS

HEAVEN

Wind + Heaven . . . You are as compatible as two of the same kind. Like the wind in the sky, one is hard to tell from the other. *Your meeting will go better if it's kept on the up and up.*

EARTH

Wind + Earth . . . You are as compatible as any two things that meet in the middle. Where one leaves off, the other starts, just like the point where sky meets earth. *Your meeting will go better if you compromise.*

WIND

Wind + Wind . . . You are as compatible as two cyclones. There's bound to be some fallout when these two opposing forces collide. *Your meeting will go much better if you speak less and listen more.*

THUNDER

Wind + Thunder . . . You are as compatible as any two things that fluctuate. Both are capable of fury. Each can just as suddenly turn calm. *Your meeting will go better if you anticipate the other's mood.*

WATER

Wind + Water . . . You are as compatible as any two things that stir each other up. One quickly sets the other in motion, like whitecaps on water. *Your meeting will go better if you remain flexible and fluid.*

WIND PLUS

FIRE

Wind + Fire . . . You are as compatible as any two things that encourage each other. Where would one be without the other? *Your meeting will go better if you each defend the other.*

MOUNTAIN

Wind + Mountain . . . You are as compatible as any two things that push and resist. Each invades the other's space, but neither gives and neither takes. *Your meeting will go better if you join forces.*

MIST

Wind + Mist . . . You are as compatible as any two things that arise at the same time. One flows along with the other, like mist dancing on breeze. *Your meeting will go better if you go along for the ride.*

THUNDER PLUS

HEAVEN

Thunder + Heaven . . . You are as compatible as any two who come from the same place . . . and like the sky and the thunder, you have plenty of things to talk about. *Your meeting will go better if you discuss common interests.*

EARTH

Thunder + Earth . . . You are as compatible as two who equal each other out . . . for like the lightning striking earth, one flies off the handle and one stays firm and grounded. *Your meeting will go better if you keep it all down-to-earth.*

WIND

Thunder + Wind . . . You are as compatible as any two fellow travelers . . . and like the wind and the thunder, there is no way to predict how these two will get along. *Your meeting will go best if you keep your opinions to a whisper.*

THUNDER PLUS

THUNDER

Thunder + Thunder . . . You are as compatible as two sons of a gun. Like an all-out thunderstorm, you both have the same basic idea of how to raise some cain. *Your meeting will go best if there are no holds barred.*

WATER

Thunder + Water . . . You are like any two things that come in pairs. Like the rain and the thunder, one tends to accompany the other. *Your meeting will go better if it's just between the two of you.*

FIRE

Thunder + Fire . . . You are as compatible as any parent and offspring . . . about as similar as lightning and thunder . . . and just as likely to spark flame. *Your meeting will go better if you take each other's hand.*

MOUNTAIN

Thunder + Mountain . . . You are as compatible as two things that think alike. Just like the thunder echoing from the hills, one signals and the other mimicks. *Your meeting will go better if you cry neither uncle nor wolf.*

MIST

Thunder + Mist . . . You are as compatible as two variations on the same theme. Just like a bang and a whimper, both have the same impact. *Your meeting will go better if you express things your own way.*

WATER PLUS

HEAVEN

Water + Heaven . . . You are as compatible as an image in a looking glass. Like clouds reflecting in a lake, one mirrors the other. *Your meeting will go better if you stick to what you see in common.*

WATER PLUS

EARTH

Water + Earth . . . You are as compatible as any two things that mix with each other. Like water soaking into the earth, one gets under the other's skin. *Your meeting will go better if you try not to get on each other's nerves.*

WIND

Water + Wind . . . You are as compatible as any two that are driven. Like wind and rain in a downpour, one tends to stimulate the other. *Your meeting will go better if you try to stay calm on the inside.*

THUNDER

Water + Thunder . . . You are as compatible as the rain and the storm . . . quite similar in nature, but varied in intensity. *Your meeting will go better if you play off each other.*

WATER

Water + Water . . . You are as compatible as two of a kind can ever be. Like two streams that meet at the branch to form a river, you join forces for the better. *Your meeting will go best if you each contribute ideas.*

FIRE

Water + Fire . . . You are as compatible as two former lovers. Just as water douses fire, one throws a wet blanket on the other. *Your meeting will go better if you keep a civil tongue.*

MOUNTAIN

Water + Mountain . . . You are as compatible as any two things that shape each other . . . like the rain wearing down the hill, and the hill directing the water's flow. *Your meeting will go better if you take the path of least resistance.*

MIST

Water + Mist . . . You are as compatible as two mysteries. Like a fog blowing over the sea, one conceals, while the other hides. *Your meeting will go better if you swear to keep a secret.*

FIRE PLUS

HEAVEN

Fire + Heaven . . . You are as compatible as any two things that form a contrast. Like a shooting star in a jet-black sky, one lights up the other's life. *Your meeting will go better if you know a good thing when you see it.*

EARTH

Fire + Earth . . . You are as compatible as the mother and child in her arms. As the earth forms a nest for the fire, one cradles and comforts the other in the dead of night. *Your meeting will go better if you feel for each other.*

WIND

Fire + Wind . . . You are as compatible as any two who nurture each other. Like the wind and the fire, one only encourages the other. *Your meeting will go better if you keep things out in the open.*

THUNDER

Fire + Thunder . . . You are as compatible as any two things that are highly charged. Like the fire and the thunder, one complements the other. *Your meeting will go better if you play off of each other's energy.*

WATER

Fire + Water . . . You are as compatible as two friends on a picnic. One brings the charcoal and one the ice, and together they share a time that is good. *Your meeting will go better if you divide things fair and square.*

FIRE

Fire + Fire . . . You are as compatible as two flames melding into a single light. Each of you kindles the other. And oh, what a night! *Your meeting will go better if you combine forces.*

MOUNTAIN

Fire + Mountain . . . You are as compatible as any two forces with different intentions . . . for like a fire on the hill, one consumes, while the other endures. *Your meeting will go better if you come to a meeting of the minds.*

FIRE PLUS

MIST

Fire + Mist . . . You are as compatible as a leader and a follower. Like a headlight through the fog, one lights the way for the other. *Your meeting will go better if you accept some good advice.*

MOUNTAIN PLUS

HEAVEN

Mountain + Heaven . . . You are like a boy and his mentor. Just as the mountain attempts to meet the sky, one rides on the shoulders of the other. *Your meeting will go better if you keep things on the up-and-up.*

EARTH

Mountain + Earth . . . You are like an old married couple. Over the years the hills and the valleys have evened out and you have met each other halfway. *Your meeting will go better if you agree on basic principles.*

WIND

Mountain + Wind . . . You are as compatible as brother and sister. Like the wind in the hilltops, you whisper in each other's ears . . . and make each other giggle. *Your meeting will go better if you play it sweet and innocent.*

THUNDER

Mountain + Thunder . . . You are like native sons. You both draw your inspiration from the same place, and you share the same beliefs. *Your meeting will go better if you play by the ground rules.*

WATER

Mountain + Water . . . You are like two priests with slightly different inspirations. Just as the mountains are holy and the waters are sacred, you make your separate ways to the same end. *Your meeting will go better if you start off with a silent prayer.*

MOUNTAIN PLUS

FIRE

Mountain + Fire . . . You are like two who share the same passion. Just as the fire leaps upwards and the hills reach for the sky, you both aim for the same heights. *Your meeting will go better if you agree on a common goal.*

MOUNTAIN

Mountain + Mountain . . . You are like twin brothers . . . for just as twin peaks rival each other, you learn to establish your own identity. *Your meeting will go better if you challenge instead of test.*

MIST

Mountain + Mist . . . You are as compatible as two kids raised by the same mom. Like the mist on the hills, you are part of the same experience. *Your meeting will go better if you compare notes.*

MIST PLUS

HEAVEN

Mist + Heaven . . . You are like two things made for each other. Like the sky and the clouds, one provides the context for the other. *Your meeting will go better if you do what comes naturally.*

EARTH

Mist + Earth . . . You are like two things that gravitate toward each other. Just as the mist envelopes the land, you have a way of forming a silent bond. *Your meeting will go better if you stick together.*

WIND

Mist + Wind . . . You are like two nebulous forces. Just as the wind swirls the mist, one molds and gives the other shape. *Your meeting will go better if you remain open to the possibilities.*

91

MIST PLUS

THUNDER

Mist + Thunder . . . You are like two things that balance each other out. You are like the mist and the thunder—one is quiet, and the other loud. *Your meeting will go better if you seek a middle ground.*

WATER

Mist + Water . . . You are as compatible as two nuns. Like the mist dancing on the water, you both tap into the common source. *Your meeting will go better if you share the experience.*

FIRE

Mist + Fire . . . You are like two beautiful dreamers. Just as the fire gives off its cloud of smoke and steam, your separate visions come from the same source. *Your meeting will go better if you find a catalyst.*

MOUNTAIN

Mist + Mountain . . . You are as compatible as two kindred spirits . . . and like the mist-shrouded hills, you seem to keep bumping into each other. *Your meeting will go better if you feel your way along.*

MIST

Mist + Mist . . . You are as compatible as twin sisters. Like the mist and vapor, you seem to meld, always hearing what the other is thinking . . . always knowing what the other will say next. *Your meeting will go as planned . . . and as it should.*

EXTRA CREDIT

How will our meeting go? To find out, toss your coins three times for yourself and three times for the person you are getting together with. Read the results as solid (2 heads), broken (2 tails), or changing (3 of a kind) lines. First look up your answer, according to the trigram you threw for yourself, ignoring any changing lines. Find your associate's trigram under yours, and read the *italic* part of the answer. If any changing lines are involved, translate each into its opposite (solid into broken; broken into solid), then look up the new trigrams that result.

This Reading also works for questions like: **How will our date go?**

How will this partnership work? How will the get-together be? But you may have to interpret the answers a bit.

EXTRA, EXTRA CREDIT!

If you would rather use sticks to determine your compatibility with others, first ask, **How compatible am I with so-and-so?** and cast a trigram. Then ask, **Is so-and-so compatible with me?** and cast a second trigram. Look up your answers as before.

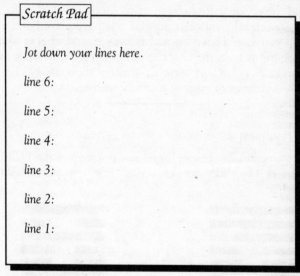

Scratch Pad

Jot down your lines here.

line 6:

line 5:

line 4:

line 3:

line 2:

line 1:

Go on to the next Reading whenever you are ready to continue.

Reading #12

Who Was I in a Former Life?
(What do I have coming to me?)

According to Eastern thought, we each have lived many lives and have had the opportunity to learn many lessons. This Reading will help you consider the various roles you may have played in the past, the lessons you should have learned as a result, and what it all means for the coming year. In the East they call the past's influence on the future karma. But—in keeping with Western thought—it's simply a matter of turning your fate into destiny.

I CHING TOOLS

As you learned in Reading #11, one way to interpret the I Ching six-line hexagrams is to read them as two three-line trigrams stacked on top of one another:

HEAVEN/EARTH

FIRE/THUNDER

That's exactly what we'll continue to do in this Reading.

HOW TO

❶ Clasp your three coins in your hand and ask your question: **Who was I in a former life? What have I learned? How can I overcome my past? What's my karma?**

❷ Toss your coins six times, noting each time whether you have cast a solid (2 heads), a broken (2 tails), or a changing line (3 of a kind).

| Scratch Pad |

Jot down your lines here.

line 6:

line 5:

line 4:

line 3:

line 2:

line 1:

---

❸ In consulting the answers, look things up according to the top three lines you have cast. Then consult the entry for the bottom three lines. Also, don't forget to look up the diagram that results if you translate changing solid lines into broken lines, and changing broken lines into solid lines.

For more information on any hexagram consult the Quick Reference Guide.

THE ANSWERS

HEAVEN OVER

HEAVEN

Heaven/Heaven: In a former life, you must have lived on the Great Plains—where the sky is everything, and the people feel small beneath it. For now you have no further need of humility. In coming to the end of your journey this year, you have already embarked on a new start. May your next wish come as easy.

HEAVEN OVER

EARTH

Heaven/Earth: In a former life, you must have lived under the stars—and seen the passing of many a moon. For now, you understand that there is a purpose to waiting for things to cycle up. In this year, opposites come together. And the rest is history. Quick! Make your next wish.

WIND

Heaven/Wind: In a former life, you must have been a sailor on the high seas—in the days of clipper ships when stars and breeze meant the difference between returning safely or wallowing adrift—for now you know the importance of direction in your life. And, at last, you can steer your way clear this year. Starlight . . . Star bright . . . Make your next-best wish tonight.

THUNDER

Heaven/Thunder: In a former life, you must have done the Thunder Dance—in the days when the sky gods needed no reason to deny us rain. For now that you know that some prayers are never answered, you are ready for whatever befalls you this time around. But wish you may and wish you might just the same—for when in doubt, it cannot hurt to ask.

WATER

Heaven/Water: In a former life, you must have lived on the East Coast—where the clouds and the Full Moon rise from the depths of the sea. For now that you know all things come and go in sequence, you can ride the waves of change this year. Make a wish over your shoulder, and watch for the signs of great things to come.

FIRE

Heaven/Fire: In a former life, you must have been a cowboy—cooking over an open fire somewhere out under the stars. For now that you have learned to gather wood and keep the matches dry, you are prepared to cope with the cold, damp weather in store this year. Oh well . . . if things get too dark and scary, you can always light a fire. Wish, if you've got 'em.

HEAVEN OVER

MOUNTAIN

Heaven/Mountain: In a former life, you must have been some kind of mountain man—living up in them thar hills. For now that you have learned to recognize the other animals by their footprints and the droppings they have left, you are free to leave your own tracks this year. Where shall it be this time, my friend? Your wish is thy command.

MIST

Heaven/Mist: In a former life you must have lived on Chincoteague—where the ponies roam in the mist and mire. For now that you have learned to tread carefully while you wait for the veil of fog to lift, you are no longer a victim of the night. Keep your fingers crossed this year. Close your eyes. And make your wish.

EARTH OVER

HEAVEN

Earth/Heaven: In a former life, you must have lived on the Big Prairie—where nothing but flat, open stretches of grass lay in every direction. For now that you have learned how to put up fences, you are free to define your own limits this year. How will you have it? For what will you wish?

EARTH

Earth/Earth: In a former life, you must have lived on a different planet—far, far away. For now that you have overcome this time and distance, you find yourself in a strange new place where everything is topsy-turvy. In this case, opposites trade places and step into each other's shoes this year. Make a wish upon a stone you toss into the woods.

EARTH OVER

WIND

Earth/Wind: In a former life, you must have lived in the Great Southwest—where the dry winds blow dust instead of rain. For now that you have learned about the center of things, you are free to kick up a little dust yourself this year and make your own sidewinding way along. Make your wish on a wishbone.

THUNDER

Earth/Thunder: In a former life, you must have lived on the San Andreas Fault—where the earth is inclined to rumble and tremble from time to time. For now that you have learned that nothing is firm and stable—not even the earth—you are free to negotiate your own deal with the Powers that Be. Wish for what you will.

WATER

Earth/Water: In a former life, you must have lived on the Great Mississippi—where the muddy water snakes through the earth. For now that you have learned to recognize the signs of rising water, you are free to control a flood of emotions this year. Toss a coin into the fountain. Make your earnest wish.

FIRE

Earth/Fire: In a former life, you must have lived near Mount St. Helens—where hot ash sometimes blows from the center of the earth. For now that you have come to know the anger of the gods, you are free to make your peace with the Powers that Be this year. But quiet the rage within you first. Make a wish and not a curse.

MOUNTAIN

Earth/Mountain: In a former life, you must have been a pioneer who crossed the Gap at Cumberland and headed for the lands out West. For now that you have learned your way around these hills, you are free to stay put this year. Make a wish on a handful of Mother Earth.

EARTH OVER

MIST

Earth/Mist: In a former life, you must have lived on the West Coast—where the fog rolls in at dawn and the sun sinks into the sea at dusk. For now that you have witnessed these mysterious things in real life, you are free to look for them in yourself this year. Wish well. May you find what you are seeking.

WIND OVER

HEAVEN

Wind/Heaven: In a former life, you must have been an eagle—soaring on an updraft above the canyon floor. For now that you have encircled your territory, you are free to defend it in the coming year. Blow a wish to the winds and make your New Year's resolution.

EARTH

Wind/Earth: In a former life, you must have lived in the woodlands—where the winds rustle the autumn leaves free of their branches, to drift down. For now that you have learned to tell time by the changing seasons, you are free to keep yourself occupied in all four of them. Make a wish on an acorn, and it will grow into a tree.

WIND

Wind/Wind: In a former life, you must have lived in Hurricane Andy's path—and the only calm to be found was in the eye of the storm. For now that the Powers that Be have shown you their stuff, you are free to rebuild, redefine, reconstruct—and take your chances if you like. Take a deep breath. And hold out hope for relief. Make a big wish on a piece of debris.

THUNDER

Wind/Thunder: In a former life, you must have lived where it stormed a lot—and the wind was always knocking to get in, and the thunder was always rattling the windowpanes. For now that you know all storms blow over in the end, you are free to ride them out this year,

WIND OVER

if you so choose. When you see lightning streak—but quick!—make your biggest wish.

WATER

Wind/Water: In a former life, you must have lived on the Outer Banks of Carolina—where wind and sea is all there is and all you can expect there will ever be. For now that you know how the sands drift and the currents pull, you are free to alter your own course just as easily. Which way will you go this year? What will you wish for next?

FIRE

Wind/Fire: In a former life, you must have lived in Atlanta—when the winds fanned the flames and the whole city burned. For now that you have learned to bury the past and its dead, you are free to imagine again. Give your new wishes their chance in the sun.

MOUNTAIN

Wind/Mountain: In a former life, you must have lived in the Appalachians—where the earth is more or less divided east to west. For now that you have come to know the nature of the obstacles in your path, you are free to climb over them or go around some other way. Wish on a fallen rock by the edge of the turnpike.

MIST

Wind/Mist: In a former life, you must have lived in New Orleans—where everything is always damp, especially the breeze. For now that you have come to expect the unexpected storm, you are well on your way to understanding everything there is to know. Make a wish on a lucky token found on the street . . . or thrown from a float.

THUNDER OVER

HEAVEN

Thunder/Heaven: In a former life, you must have lived in timberlands—where the wolf still answers when the thunder calls. But now that you know to look for reasons when the noises start, you are sure to make it through the coming nights. Make a wish on a buckeye and settle in for the duration.

EARTH

Thunder/Earth: In a former life, you must have made moonshine in the hills of Tennessee—where they used to brew white lightning in the days of Prohibition. For now that you have learned the laws of human nature, you are free to use your own devices to get around the rules this year. Swear by the Good Book, but make a wish with this one.

WIND

Thunder/Wind: In a former life, you must have lived on the Graveyard of the Atlantic—where the winter gales smash ships to shore. For now that you have learned to salvage what you can of the past's wreckage, you are free to patch things up again this year. Make a wish on a winging gull.

THUNDER

Thunder/Thunder: In a former life, you must have lived in D.C.—in fact, your own footsteps must have thundered through the Halls of Justice. For now that you have learned the ins and outs of campaign promises, you are free to do as you damn well please. Write your wish upon a dollar bill—but quick!—before it turns into a quarter.

WATER

Thunder/Water: In a former life, you must have gone down the white waters—holding on for dear life in the thundering torrent. For now that you have learned how to avoid the hidden rocks, you are free to navigate the coming obstacle course. Hold your breath. And make a wish.

THUNDER OVER

FIRE

Thunder/Fire: In a former life, you must have been a blacksmith in the colonies—hammering out the hot steel at your forge. For now that you have learned how to gain strength from raw energy, you can direct your own powers to the job at hand. Make a wish on a horseshoe.

MOUNTAIN

Thunder/Mountain: In a former life, you must have lived in the Catskills—where legend says the Elves go bowling in the thundering hills at night—for now that you have learned to pick up spares and count these complex scores, you are free to join the big leagues. Make your wish, take your aim, and follow through.

MIST

Thunder/Mist: In a former life, you must have lived on the Great Divide—where the thundering waters throw spume as they separate, some flowing east and some flowing west. For now that you appreciate the need to choose between two separate paths, you have the power to decide the future for yourself. Make a wish before you split.

WATER OVER

HEAVEN

Water/Heaven: In a former life, you must have lived in the Pacific Northwest—where the seasons are varied but all rainy. For now that you know about subtle distinctions, you are free to read the signs of the coming changes for yourself. Make a wish on a passing cloud.

EARTH

Water/Earth: In a former life, you must have lived on a floodplain—where the rising waters brought both disaster and the fresh soil of renewal. For now that you know what it takes to be prolific, you are free to increase your output this year. Throw a coin onto the water lily. And make your wish.

WATER OVER

WIND

Water/Wind: In a former life, you must have lived on the Jersey shore—where the winds of change and the waters of chance attract the gamblers. For now that you know the odds are against you, you are free to try your luck anyway this year. Put your money where your mouth is. Make a wish on your lucky number.

THUNDER

Water/Thunder: In a former life, you must have lived on the Niagara—at the brink of those thundering waters that constantly spill over the edge of the Horseshoe Falls. For now that you have learned not to look down or lean too far over the rail, you are free to use your high position as a competitive advantage this year. Make a wish on a rainbow.

WATER

Water/Water: In a former life you must have lived on the Great Lakes—where the icy northern waters empty into each other. For now that you have battled the cold gales of November, you are free to settle in for the duration of the long winter ahead. Make a wish on a freshwater pearl.

FIRE

Water/Fire: In a former life, you must have lived on the Frontier—across the jagged Ohio River, which separates north from south and east from west. For now that you have spent some time in the wilderness, you are free to claim it for yourself and burn the bridges to your past. Make a wish on a match.

MOUNTAIN

Water/Mountain: In a former life, you must have been from Nantucket—where the rocky land rises from the bottom of the sea (and the limerick is king). For now that you have learned the benefits of isolation—and how to pass the hours alone—you are free to go back to the mainland, if you can find the time. Cast out a wish on the high tide.

WATER OVER

MIST

Water/Mist: In a former life, you must have lived where the mist rose from the lake at dawn and where the clouds rolled in at dusk. For now that you have come to know the uses for windshield wipers and fog lamps, you are free to step into the thick of things this year . . . and find your way back out. Make a wish on the fly.

FIRE OVER

HEAVEN

Fire/Heaven: In a former life, you must have lived where the chaparral grows dry in the sun before bursting into spontaneous flames. For now that you know what a dry spell means, you are ready to thank your lucky stars for the first sign of relief. When it rains, it pours this year. Burn a candle. Make a wish.

EARTH

Fire/Earth: In a former life, you must have lived in New Mexico—where everything is barren moonscape burnt by the sun into adobe. For now that you know what it is like to thirst for something, you are free to quench your desire . . . and to follow your hunger. Make a wish on turquoise.

WIND

Fire/Wind: In a former life, you must have lived in Florida—where the Caribbean air blows hot from the tropics. For now that you know how to spot the Portuguese man-of-war and other jellyfishes, you are safe to make your way barefoot. Make a wish on a sand dollar—but quick!—before it shatters into pieces of eight.

THUNDER

Fire/Thunder: In a former life, you must have lived in the Bible Belt—where hellfire and brimstone are taught. For now that you have seen the light and felt the burning waters on your forehead, you are free to witness the Gospel truth this year. Make a wish at Sunday sunrise.

FIRE OVER

WATER

Fire/Water: In a former life, you must have drunk the firewater—that the white man brought. For now that you know how to get some kicks, you still must walk the fine line this year between remedy and excuse. Place your wishes in an empty bottle and set them all adrift.

FIRE

Fire/Fire: In a former life, you must have lived south of the border—where the warmth collects and never ends. For now that you know the taste of red-hot chili peppers, how will you ever be cool again? Next year is more of the same. Cross your heart, make a wish, and don't drink the water.

MOUNTAIN

Fire/Mountain: In a former life you must have lived in the Smokey Mountains—where the fall colors light up the hills. For now that you have come to appreciate the bigger picture, you are free to return to the city, if you must. At any rate, the coming year brings you home again. Make a wish on a wooden nickel.

MIST

Fire/Mist: In a former life, you must have sent up smoke signals—and just in the nick of time! For now that you appreciate the need to cry out for help sometimes, you are free this year to get the helping hand you need. Make a wish on a trail of burning incense.

MOUNTAIN OVER

HEAVEN

Mountain/Heaven: In a former life, you must have lived in the Rockies—where the jagged crags brush the jet streaks. For now that you have trained in these high altitudes—and gotten over the nosebleeds—you can compete anywhere . . . anytime. Go for the gold this year. Make your wish, and give me five.

MOUNTAIN OVER

EARTH

Mountain/Earth: In a former life, you must have lived in the Great Valley—with mountains on either side. For now that you have lived in the shadow of others for a good long while, it is your turn to step out front and center. Make your next wish standing up. This is your year of years.

WIND

Mountain/Wind: In a former life, you must have lived in the Blue Ridge Mountains—where the way is steep and the crosswinds rock the trucks. For now that you have learned to take a few S-curves for yourself, you are better off. Ease up a bit and make a wish going into the tunnel. Next year is a straight stretch.

THUNDER

Mountain/Thunder: In a former life, you must have lived in the White Mountains—where the first light of day touches on the good old U.S. of A. For now that you know how to live on the edge, you are free to come back to the center. Keep the best. And do some wishful thinking this year.

WATER

Mountain/Water: In a former life, you must have lived near the Finger Lakes—where the hills reflect in the many waters. For now that you have looked at things from right side up and upside down, you are entitled to your own opinion. Wish well and often . . . especially this year. A reward could come your way.

FIRE

Mountain/Fire: In a former life, you must have lived near a hilltop tree—where lightning once struck. For now that you have seen the damage firsthand, you know to keep your distance in the future. You learn from your past failures this year. Make a wish under an old oak tree, and tie a ribbon in it if you please.

MOUNTAIN OVER

MOUNTAIN

Mountain/Mountain: In a former life, you surely lived in the high hills—where the waters start. For now that you know the source of the things happening in your life, you can reach your own conclusions and make your own choices. Shout your wish to the distant hills . . . and listen for the hills' reply.

MIST

Mountain/Mist: In a former life, you must have lived on the shores of a mountain lake—where the rising mists obscure the dawn. For now that you know about the things that happen quietly, you are free to keep these secrets to yourself another year. Make a wish on the New Moon.

MIST OVER

HEAVEN

Mist/Heaven: In a former life, you must have lived where the clouds painted moving pictures in the sky—and you watched them for the signs and seasons. For now that you know how everything follows a grand pattern, you are free to see the hand of God in your own life this year. Make a wish and say your silent prayers at the Crescent Moon.

EARTH

Mist/Earth: In a former life, you must have lived in a mystical land—where spirits roamed the woods and gave us things to talk about. For now that you have learned to acknowledge the Powers that Be, you must learn also to appease and petition this year. Give them tokens. Make your wish on the rising moon.

WIND

Mist/Wind: In a former life, you must have lived in the time when the spirits intervened in human affairs. For now that you appreciate how the winds of change work at altering things, you can turn change to your own

107

advantage this year. Make a wish whenever you see a halo 'round the moon.

Mist/Thunder: In a former life, you must have lived in a place where the thunder gods had names and duties. For now that you know the purpose of ceremony, you can get down to the business of working with the Powers that Be. Make a wish on the eclipsing moon, but only as the light is returning.

Mist/Water: In a former life, you must have paid homage to the spirit of a great river. For now that you have been cleansed by the sacred waters, you are free to go in peace to either sin again or sin no more. You make a big choice this year. Make a wish on a Quarter Moon.

Mist/Fire: In a former life, you must have lived in a place where fire was regarded as God's gift. For now that you have felt the warm glow upon your face and hands, you are free to feel the glow within yourself. Act on impulse this year. Go where the spirit leads you. Make a wish at the Full Moon.

Mist/Mountain: In a former life, you must have lived in a land where the spirit of the mountains called the people. For now that you have heard the call for yourself, you have no choice but to follow it this year. Make a wish on a third Quarter Moon and count your many blessings.

Mist/Mist: In a former life, you must have lived in a land where the spirits controlled everything. For now that the spirit has awakened in you again, you are free to come to terms with the past and move on to the present. Make a wish. Good luck. And Happy New Year.

EXTRA CREDIT

What do you have coming this year? Cast six lines to find out. Just ask your question: **What do I have coming to me this year?** Then, using either coins or sticks, cast an I Ching hexagram. Look up your answer.

EXTRA, EXTRA CREDIT!

You can also use I Ching numerology to conduct this Reading. To find out what any specific year holds for you, jot down the trigram you constructed for yourself in Reading #9. Next, construct a two-line diagram based on your age in the year you are asking about (see Reading #6). Stack this two-line diagram on top of your trigram. Then toss your coins once to complete the sixth line of your I Ching hexagram. In consulting the answers, look things up according to the top three lines of your hexagram. Then consult the entry for the bottom three lines.

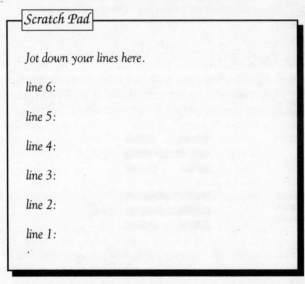

Scratch Pad

Jot down your lines here.

line 6:

line 5:

line 4:

line 3:

line 2:

line 1:

Go on to the next Reading whenever you are ready to continue.

Reading #13

WHAT CHANGES WILL THERE BE?
(What will heal my spirit?)

The I Ching is especially famous for its ability to forecast change. In this Reading, you will cast a six-line hexagram in order to see how a current relationship, arrangement, or situation is likely to change if it stays on its current course. Since the answers also suggest actions you can take to make this outcome happen (or not happen), it's a good place to turn for advice on deciding current moves. Soul-searchers will also find this Reading a useful tool in gauging and directing their spiritual progress over this or many lifetimes.

I CHING TOOLS

To conduct this Reading, you will toss your coins six times to get a hexagram . . . but you will continue to think of it as two trigrams, one over the other, as in the trigram for Water over Wind, below:

In order to consider the changes you can expect—for this Reading anyway—the bottom trigram will represent the present state of things. It is changing into the top trigram, which shows you what things will be like in the future.

HOW TO

❶ Clasp your three coins in the palm of your hand, while you concentrate on your question: **What changes can I expect?** At work? At home? With my money? **How is my relationship with _____ changing?**

Will we get together? Come closer? Drift farther apart? **How will my career unfold?** My campaign progress? My soul evolve?

❷ With your question firmly in mind, cast your coins six times, noting each time how they land. (2 or more heads = a solid line; 2 or more tails = a broken line; and 3 of a kind = a changing line.)

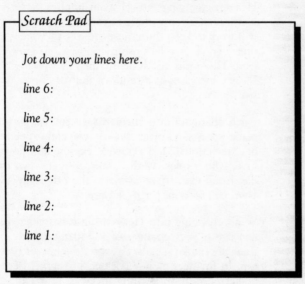

Scratch Pad

Jot down your lines here.

line 6:

line 5:

line 4:

line 3:

line 2:

line 1:

❸ Look up your answer. Just as in past Readings, the answers are organized according to the TOP three lines you have cast. If you have any changing lines in your hexagram, don't forget to convert them to their opposites, and read also for the resulting diagram.

For more information on any diagram, consult the Quick Reference Guide.

THE ANSWERS

HEAVEN

HEAVEN/
HEAVEN

Heaven changing into Heaven implies perfection and continuity. So any changes that come along right now will work to keep things just the way they are—which is pretty good. A relationship continues to grow through care. The status quo is maintained by working together. Money increases as a result of mutual effort. *Your spirit soars.*

HEAVEN/
EARTH

Earth changing into Heaven suggests the horizon, the place where land meets sky. So you can expect changes of a transitional kind. At work, explore new horizons. In love, switch roles. With money, split it down the middle. In all else, strive to meet "the other guy" halfway. *Your spirit seeks the perfect balance.*

HEAVEN/
WIND

Wind changing into Heaven suggests smoke rising. So you can expect changes of a shifting nature. In love, there are smoke signals. At work, the hot air rises to the top. In finance, money goes up in smoke. Best send a prayer upward on burning incense. *Your spirit takes its cues from a higher source—which is in no hurry. (But it never hurts to ask.)*

HEAVEN/
THUNDER

Thunder changing into Heaven suggests heat lightning, flashing in the distance. So you can expect changes of the enlightening kind. In love, you are informed in a flash. At work, you must quickly batten down the hatches. With money, it is always best to play it safe. *Your spirit longs to cut loose from its restraints.*

HEAVEN/
WATER

Water changing into Heaven suggests the clouds reflecting on the surface of a lake. So you can expect changes of a backwards nature. In love, ponder your situation in front of a mirror. At work, press onward but glance over your shoulder from time to time. With money, consider how to reverse the picture. *Your spirit wants to experience things both ways.*

HEAVEN

HEAVEN/FIRE

Fire changing into Heaven suggests a shooting star. So you can expect changes of the quickly burning-out variety. In love, there is spark without flame. At work, whatever is up in the air will soon come down. And with your money, burn a few bucks on something ephemeral (perhaps computers or electronics equipment). *Your spirit wants to hit the ground running.*

HEAVEN/
MOUNTAIN

Mountain changing into Heaven suggests the hills fading into the sky at dusk. So you can expect changes of the blending kind. In love, you grow to resemble each other. At work, you find your fit in the overall scheme of things. And with money, you *are* what you buy. Try to accept these things. *Your spirit wants to belong.*

HEAVEN/MIST

Mist changing into Heaven suggests fog rising and dispersing. So you can expect changes of a nebulous kind. In love, you drift. At work, you grasp after the answer. With money, it flies to and fro. Let your dreams lead you down your proper trail. *Your free spirit wants to shoot for the stars.*

EARTH

EARTH/
HEAVEN

Heaven changing into Earth implies perfect harmony. So you can expect changes that will restore things to their proper balance. In love, a physical attraction develops emotional depth through commitment. Balance work with family cares, and the money evens out. *Your spirit sings.*

EARTH

EARTH/EARTH

Earth changing into Earth implies endurance and stability. So you can expect mild changes of a weathered nature. A love tempers itself. Friends become family. A job is no longer regarded as work. There is a regular rhythm and a reason for everything. Lie back and kick up your feet. The moment is now. Enjoy it. *Your spirit is content.*

EARTH/WIND

Wind changing into Earth suggests dust settling. So you can expect changes of a filtering-out nature. In love, a whirlwind romance comes back to earth. At work, things quiet down and shake themselves out. In general, things get resolved by being sorted. Old accounts are settled up in good time. *Your spirit needs to shed a little excess baggage.*

EARTH/
THUNDER

Thunder changing into Earth suggests hail the size of golf balls. So you can expect changes of the high-impact variety. In love, keep your hat on. At work, keep your head down. With money, keep your wallet in your pocket. This storm brings a welcome change of pace. *Your spirit stands at the rain-streaked window watching the sky fall . . . without regret.*

EARTH/WATER

Water changing into Earth suggests muddy floodwaters running off. So you can expect changes of the rising and receding kind in your life. In love, be soft as putty and change to suit the other if you must—or else reassess and regroup. At work, expand beyond the limits of your job. And with your money, insure everything. *Your spirit needs a healthy dose of fertilizer.*

EARTH

EARTH/FIRE

Fire changing into Earth suggests a campfire going out. So you can expect changes of an expunging nature. In love, set the record straight even if the flame goes out in the process. In the workplace, empty the ashtrays and spend more time outdoors. With money, sift through the dark recesses of the drawers. An era ends. You'll have to adjust. *Your spirit longs for the good old times.*

EARTH/
MOUNTAIN

Mountain changing into Earth suggests a valley lying in the shadow of a hill. So you can expect changes of the downhill, shady kind. In love, come up for air. At work, go on break for 15 minutes, and let it work itself out. With money, give it a holiday. Emerge into the light, or else retreat into the shadows. *Your spirit can hardly wait for Friday.*

EARTH/MIST

Mist changing into Earth implies the arrival of freezing rain. So you can expect changes of a crystallizing nature. In love, let it sparkle like blue-white diamonds. At work, make it gleam like glass and chrome. And with money, let it dazzle like a Gold Card hologram. This is your moment to solidify your position and announce your arrival. *Your free spirit could get used to this.*

WIND

WIND/HEAVEN

Heaven changing into Wind indicates turbulence. So the ride ahead may be a tad bumpy. Meetings are subject to interruption. Friends are delayed. Plans are disrupted. Funds take a temporary nosedive. A slight misunderstanding occurs. But these minor trials and tribulations pass in the breeze. Roll with the punches. *Your spirit holds its breath.*

WIND

WIND/EARTH

Earth changing into wind suggests rustling grasses. So you can expect changes of a murmuring kind. Lovers whisper sweet nothings into each other's ears. Workers hear it on the grapevine. Money talks—and people will listen to anything. At night, the message comes in a memorable dream. Pay attention. *Your spirit wants to ride the wind.*

WIND/WIND

Wind changing into Wind suggests a cyclone. So you can expect changes of a blustery nature. In love, a relationship spirals downhill fast. At work, things pick up quickly. A financial strategy goes like clockwork but may prove counterproductive in the end. Better make contingency plans. *Your spirit longs to go the distance, but things outside your control interfere.*

WIND/
THUNDER

Thunder changing into Wind suggests the arrival of a scattered shower. So you can expect changes of the passing variety. For lovers, there are quarrels (but kisses in the aftermath). At work, there is reorganization (again!). And with money there is constant fluctuation. Just weather it through. In the end, it all comes back to normal. *Your spirit wants to vent some steam.*

WIND/WATER

Water changing into Wind suggests waves breaking on the beach. So you can expect changes of the fanning-out variety. In love, keep sending and receiving signals. At work, extend feelers. With money, determine the pattern of income and outflow. The seventh wave's a sailer. *Your spirit wants to be in sync with Father Time and Mother Nature.*

WIND

WIND/FIRE

Fire changing into Wind suggests flames licking up the sides of the chimney. So you can expect changes of the roaring kind. In love, it's "Me Tarzan, You Jane." At work, your candle burns at both ends. And with money, you might as well set fire to a hundred-dollar bill. *Your spirit seems to be in a rip-roaring mood.*

WIND/
MOUNTAIN

Mountain changing into Wind suggests a belching volcano. So you can expect changes of a dark and unexpected kind. In love, there is a pregnant moment of silence and suspense. At work, the Powers that Be express sudden anger. With money, the vultures circle overhead. There's nothing to do to prepare. Be careful. *Your spirit longs for a breath of fresh air.*

WIND/MIST

Mist changing into Wind suggests a fog bank blowing in. So you can expect changes of a drifting nature. In love, two boats rock in the same wake. At work, your view is blinded by a smoke screen. With money, a passing fancy lures you into impulse buying. Think twice. And wait another second before you decide. *Your free spirit wants to see the big picture.*

THUNDER

THUNDER/
HEAVEN

Heaven changing into Thunder indicates a sudden disturbance in the atmosphere. So you can expect changes of a flashing kind. There are sudden revelations (but you can't believe everything you hear). Lovers spat (but love endures). The market crashes (but recovers fast). *Your spirit comes to its senses in a blinding flash.*

THUNDER

**THUNDER/
EARTH**

Earth changing into Thunder implies tremors. So you can expect changes of an earthshaking nature. A good relationship rocks. A business arrangement shifts. The stock market quakes. You'd best hold on to your hat. And get ready . . . for soon the #$% hits the fan. *Your spirit seeks temporary shelter.*

THUNDER/WIND

Wind changing into Thunder suggests a fast-approaching storm. So you can expect changes of a threatening kind. In love, all hell breaks loose. At work, the chips fall where they may. And with money—as usual—it goes down the drain. Witness the telltale signs for yourself. And prepare. *Your spirit wants to run for cover.*

**THUNDER/
THUNDER**

Thunder changing into Thunder suggests a violent storm right overhead. So you can expect changes of the most unsettling, disturbing, or window-rattling kind. In love, World War III kicks off. (Be careful of an outburst.) In the workplace, heads roll without warning or excuse. Wall Street rumbles, the Dow tumbles. *Your spirit could use a couple of aspirin.*

**THUNDER/
WATER**

Water changing into Thunder suggests a storm growing in intensity. So you can expect changes of the rapidly escalating kind. In love, the little things wind up getting to you. At work, pent-up hostilities are about to let fly. And with money, it's all just a matter of time now. Cool off. Calm down. *Your spirit wants to spout off.*

THUNDER/FIRE

Fire changing into Thunder suggests (goodness, gracious!) great balls of fire.[1] So you can expect changes of an explosive nature. In love, flaring passions end in a moment of rapture. At work, hotheads overreact and tempers prevail. With money, it is an Act of God. Be careful not to retaliate. *Your spirit wants to spill its guts.*

---

[1] Thanks to Jerry Lee Lewis.

THUNDER

THUNDER/
MOUNTAIN

Mountain changing into Thunder suggests an avalanche. So you can expect changes of a snowballing nature. In love, don't look back! At work, get out the shovel. With money, hold on to your skis. And don't look up! The sky is falling! *Your spirit wants you to make it down this hill in one piece.*

THUNDER/MIST

Mist changing into Thunder suggests an unexplained and unexpected noise. So you can expect changes of the startling kind. In love, someone wants to play hide-and-seek. At work, someone comes up behind you. With money, the statement doesn't jibe. Enjoy the rush! It's only adrenaline. *Your free spirit wants to see you get out of here alive.*

WATER

WATER/
HEAVEN

Heaven changing into Water implies rain. So you can expect rapid changes in barometric pressure, accompanied by sudden mood swings. There is something unnerving in love—yet at the same time, refreshing. Go with the silent, pensive mood at work. Money pours in (but easy come, easy go). *Your spirit thirsts for renewal and gains revival.*

WATER/EARTH

Earth changing into Water suggests clay. So you can expect changes of the soft, mushy kind. Things are like putty in your hand. A lover or contact molds you. Investments are soft, at best. And there is much going back and forth at work. Be flexible and open to suggestion, but assume your own shape. *Your spirit is evolving not as it wills, but as you direct.*

WATER

WATER/WIND

Wind changing into Water suggests mineral springs. So you can expect changes of a sparkling, healing, therapeutic nature. In love, exchange favors. At work, pat each other on the back. With money, blow it on bottled water. And in general, take it easy. *Your spirit is refreshed.*

WATER/
THUNDER

Thunder changing into Water suggests a storm moving off. So you can expect changes of the reassuring kind. In love, you agree to new terms. At work, the damage is assessed and written off. And with your money, you see yourself through. Return to your senses. Count your lucky stars. *Your spirit wants to wipe the slate clean and start all over again.*

WATER/WATER

Water changing into Water suggests the juncture of two rivers. So you can expect changes of an ongoing, ever-flowing, mother-loving kind. In love, it's a never-ending story . . . but with a new ending each time. At work, a team effort pays off big down the line. And with money, the cash flow just keeps on streaming by. *Your spirit wants to go where this current leads.*

WATER/FIRE

Fire changing into Water suggests steaming ashes. So you can expect changes of a rapidly evaporating nature. In love, the memory lingers after the flame has gone. At work, it's time for making new plans. And with money, you wind up with the short stick. Clean up and be done with it. *Your spirit longs to put the past behind.*

WATER/
MOUNTAIN

Mountain changing into Water suggests the spring waters running off. So you can expect changes of the exhilarating kind. In love, take the plunge. At work, get in the swim of things. And with money—what the heck!—dive off the deep end. *Your spirit needs to get a little wet behind the ears.*

WATER

WATER/MIST

Mist changing into Water suggests steam forming on the windowpanes. So you can expect changes of the steamy kind. In love, the rear windows fog up. At work, the ventilation system drips. With money, your pocket change turns green (with envy?). The feeling in your bones is right. *Your free spirit is tempted to leave a special message on the mirror.*

FIRE

FIRE/HEAVEN

Heaven changing into fire implies the arrival of a comet or a shooting star. So you can expect changes of an erratic, unpredictable nature. In love, a friendship heats up (so don't be taken by surprise!). At work, tempers flare. A deal turns to ashes, yet there is money left to burn. *Your spirit is awakened from its peaceful slumber by a sudden craving.*

FIRE/EARTH

Earth changing into fire suggests flint on steel. So you can expect the kind of changes that spark. An old flame is rekindled. Something is touched off at work. Money burns a hole through your pocket. And in general, tongues lash. Try to separate your urges from your desires. *Your spirit lights a fire under you.*

FIRE/WIND

Wind changing into Fire suggests flames being fanned. So you can expect changes of a rapidly escalating kind. For lovers there is candlelight and whispers. For workers, there are power surges. Money turns to ashes. You need to cool things off, or else take the heat. *Your spirit spreads itself a little thin.*

FIRE

FIRE/THUNDER

Thunder changing into Fire suggests lightning striking in a burst of flame. You can expect changes of the remote, unlikely kind. In love, you are stricken at first sight. At work, you are singled out. With money you are showered from out of the blue . . . perhaps twice. *Your spirit stirs suddenly, sending shivers all the way down to your socks.*

FIRE/WATER

Water changing into fire suggests a piece of wood that won't light. So you can expect changes of a sputtering, smoking kind. In love, you'll iron things out eventually in a series of fits and bursts. At work, you'll put things on the back burner. (Let it simmer.) And with money, you'll hang it up (to dry?). *Your spirit wants to ignite, but it hasn't aged enough . . . yet.*

FIRE/FIRE

Fire changing into Fire suggests an eternal flame. So you can expect changes of a permanent nature. In love, the mercury shoots to the highest degree—and stays there. At work, there is always a fire to put out (for this is just a different day). And with money—it lights up the night. (What's it good for, anyway?) *Your spirit longs to do the town.*

FIRE/
MOUNTAIN

Mountain changing into Fire suggests a thin trail of smoke rising from the hills. So you can expect changes of a signaling nature. In love, look deeply into each other's eyes. At work, read between the lines. With money, rake it in—and heap it on the fire of your needs. *Your spirit longs to feast its eyes on the signs of welcome changes.*

FIRE

FIRE/MIST

Mist changing into Fire suggests swamp gas, rising and glowing. So you can expect changes of the close-encounter variety. In love—just when you thought you'd seen it all . . . a pleasant surprise. At work, be prepared for the extraordinary. With money—it's all done with mirrors. Pinch yourself if you don't believe it's really happening. *Your free spirit longs to see the candle waiting in the window.*

MOUNTAIN

MOUNTAIN/
HEAVEN

Heaven changing into Mountain suggests clouds clinging to the hilltops. So you can expect changes of a gathering, lingering nature. Lovers rendezvous! Workers touch base. A business soon expands its grasp, but payments and earnings are both extended over time. Stick it out a little longer. *Your spirit aspires to the heights, but these things take time.*

MOUNTAIN/
EARTH

Earth changing into Mountain suggests foothills. So you can expect changes of a gently rolling kind. A love builds gradually. The employment situation slowly, surely improves. Money becomes increasingly sufficient. Watch for the patterns, and time your moves. *Your spirit seeks the downhill course, but first you must press upward.*

MOUNTAIN/
WIND

Wind changing into Mountain suggests towering fluffy clouds altering shape. So you can expect changes of a superficial nature. In love, change your appearance. At work, change your look. With money, arrange the numbers differently. *Your spirit wants to gain perspective.*

MOUNTAIN

MOUNTAIN/
THUNDER

Thunder changing into Mountain suggests a storm echoing in the distance. So you can expect changes of the reverberating kind. In love, avoid setting off a chain reaction. At work, be neither gun-shy nor trigger-happy. And with money, save it for a rainy day. *Your spirit longs for stability in an environment of change.*

MOUNTAIN/
WATER

Water changing into Mountain suggests a river gorge cut into the hills. So you can expect changes of the coursing, cliff-hanging variety. In love, things come to a thrilling climax! At work, everyone waits with bated breath. And with money, things turn over fast. Watch out for the white water ahead. *Your spirit longs for the thrill of going down the rapids.*

MOUNTAIN/
FIRE

Fire changing into Mountain suggests a brush fire on the hill. So you can expect changes of a leveling nature. In love, you're back to home plate again (and trying to get to first base). At work, you have returned to ground zero (and you get to start all over again). With money, it's back to the drawing board. *Your spirit rallies to the challenge and rises to the opportunity.*

MOUNTAIN/
MOUNTAIN

Mountain changing into Mountain suggests still peaks stacking off into the distance. So you can expect changes of a perpetual nature. In love, hang on to each other for dear life. At work, hang in there to the bitter end. And with money, hang loose. Focus on that which endures. *Your spirit—in its heart of hearts—knows what counts.*

MOUNTAIN

MOUNTAIN/
MIST

Mist changing into Mountain suggests mist-shrouded hills. So you can expect changes of a lofty nature. In love, keep your promise. At work, keep your word. With money, keep it in the proper perspective. And in general, pay homage to your God. *Your free spirit longs for a definite sign. This is it. Your wish is granted.*

MIST

MIST/HEAVEN

Heaven changing into Mist suggests high-flying clouds. So you can expect changes of the wispy, mutable kind. In general, things are still firming up and taking shape. A relationship is evolving. A deal has not yet solidified. Financial conditions are still up in the air. But the first inklings are there. Keep a lookout. Feel your way. *Your free spirit is open to the possibilities.*

MIST/EARTH

Earth changing into Mist suggests dew on the grass. So you can expect changes of a refreshing nature. Things are just getting started here. Love is fresh. The workday is bright and new. And all monetary possibilities exist. Take care—and all the necessary precautions. *Your free spirit has never felt so unrestricted, or the flesh more alive.*

MIST/WIND

Wind changing into Mist suggests steaming breath on cold air. So you can expect changes of the spine-tingling kind. In love, take a walk in the moonlight. At work, get up and going before the fog burns off. With money, watch it evaporate. Observe closely. *Your free spirit follows its inspiration . . . wherever it leads.*

MIST

MIST/THUNDER

Thunder changing into Mist suggests the aftermath of a storm. So you can expect changes of the back-to-normal kind. In love, it is the morning after. At work, it is the next day. With money—and all else near and dear to you—hold on to what you've got. *Your free spirit heaves a sigh of relief.*

MIST/WATER

Water changing into Mist suggests a steaming river at dawn. So you can expect changes of an eerie kind. In love, there is a secret admirer, or a funny coincidence. At work there is an unseen eye. And with money there is a secret source. Try to get outside yourself. Rise to the situation. *Your free spirit wants to get away from it all.*

MIST/FIRE

Fire changing into Mist suggests the smell of woodsmoke clinging. So you can expect changes of the lingering, pervasive kind. In love, let your feelings move you (and pick up on the scents). At work, let the spirit call you (and go where you must). And with money, give some of it up. *Your free spirit longs to linger longer.*

MIST/
MOUNTAIN

Mountain changing into Mist suggests fog on the Pennsylvania Turnpike. So you can expect changes of a hair-raising kind. In love, you enter the tunnel. At work, there seems to be a light at the end. And with money, it's a downhill run from here. Better slow down and get there a minute later. *Your free spirit does its best to steer you clear.*

MIST/MIST

Mist changing into Mist suggests something endless and eternal. So you can expect changes of the cosmic kind. In love, it is simply meant to be. At work, it is in the cards. And with money, it is up to the stars. Good luck with the draw. Good luck on your feet. *Your free spirit wants to go along for the ride.*

EXTRA CREDIT

How are you coping with your lot in life? To find out, use your coins or sticks to cast an I Ching hexagram. Just ask, **What will heal my spirit? What does my soul require?** or **How is my spirit progressing?** Look up your hexagram and focus on the *italic* portion of the answer. To trace your soul's progress over time, construct three hexagrams and read them as past, present, and future.

EXTRA, EXTRA CREDIT!

For a more complete Reading, just look up your I Ching hexagram in the Quick Reference Guide's Master Answer section. You will find your hexagram listed in the same order as it was here—look up the top three lines first, then the bottom three. 1) Read the full description for your primary diagram. 2) Then consult the Bonus Answers for any changing lines. 3) Finally, convert changing lines into their opposites and look up the resulting hexagram you receive.

Go on to the next Reading whenever you are ready to continue.

Reading #14

How will a current business deal progress? A career path? A love affair? An investment? In this Reading you will toss your coins six times to find out what you need to do to succeed in anything . . . and everything. This Reading also works great for choosing lucky numbers. And soul-searchers are sure to find the answer here.

I CHING TOOLS

As we have seen throughout this book, I Ching diagrams can be read in many ways. In this Reading, you will find a number encoded in your hexagram. Here is the code:

6th line solid =	1
5th line solid =	2
4th line solid =	4
3rd line solid =	8
2nd line solid =	16
bottom line solid =	32
Broken lines in any position =	0

This formula is the same method that modern computers use to count and organize data.[1] In this code, only solid lines have a "value." Depending on where a solid line falls in the hexagram, it is worth 1, 2, 4, 8, 16, or 32 "points." Broken lines are worth zero. To get your hexagram's number, you would just total the values for its solid lines.

If these "binary" numbers are just not your thing, don't worry about it. You don't have to do the math to complete this Reading. You'll find your answer by looking up the hexagram in the usual way. The answer will tell you what your diagram adds up to and give you additional things to think about as well.

[1] In fact the I Ching was instrumental in the development of the mathematical theory behind computers.

HOW TO

❶ Clasp your three coins in the palm of your hand, while you concentrate on your question: **What is my key to success?** In this relationship? With this job? In financial affairs? With this project? **What success will come of this?** Joint venture? Idea? Plan? Project? Affair? **How should I proceed?** Or—for soul-searchers—**What's the answer for me?**

❷ With your question firmly in mind, cast your coins six times, noting each time how they land (2 heads = a solid line; 2 tails = a broken line; 3 of a kind = a changing line).

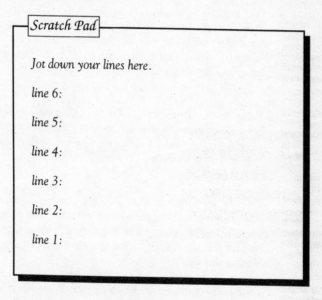

Scratch Pad

Jot down your lines here.

line 6:

line 5:

line 4:

line 3:

line 2:

line 1:

❸ Look up your answer. The answers are organized according to the trigram represented by the TOP three lines you have cast. If you have any changing lines, don't forget to convert them to their opposites and read also for the resulting hexagram.

❹ The Answer section for this Reading performs a special trick. After you look up your answer, follow the "See Also" reference, which will refer you to a related hexagram. That hexagram, in turn, will refer you to another . . . and so on and so forth. You can stay on this "thread" for as long as you like, but generally three to five hexagrams are enough to give a complete course of action.

For more information on any diagram, consult the Quick Reference Guide.

THE ANSWERS

HEAVEN

HEAVEN/
HEAVEN

Your lucky number is 63 . . . which in I Ching terms represents completion. All else builds up to this lucky moment, this sudden ending . . . and this new beginning. *See also: Water/Fire.*

HEAVEN/
EARTH

Your lucky number is 7 . . . the number of days between phases of the moon. So give these things a week to heal, build, or repair themselves. Allow stability to rule for the moment. *See also: Earth/Water.*

HEAVEN/
WIND

Your lucky number is 31 . . . the turning point, when you cannot possibly go back and yet you resist going forward. Still the temptation is great to consummate this bargain. Be careful in crossing over this line. *See also: Mist/Mountain.*

HEAVEN/
THUNDER

Your lucky number is 39 . . . a perfect number, which indicates the meeting of like minds. Things that are done simply and in concert with others will impress the most—like thunder and lightning. *See also: Water/Mountain.*

HEAVEN/
WATER

Your lucky number is 23 . . . which indicates that things are happening through pull and push, like the moon and the tides. You find yourself acted upon or stuck in the middle. It does no good to resist. *See also: Mountain/ Earth.*

HEAVEN

HEAVEN/FIRE

Your lucky number is 47 . . . which indicates you are experiencing the stress of belonging to a group. But suddenly you will see the light—like stars in the sky. Commitment will bring contentment. *See also: Mist/Water.*

HEAVEN/
MOUNTAIN

Your lucky number is 15 . . . which indicates you will make progress by retreating. The conditions are set by the Powers that Be. Like clouds caught on mountains, you must hasten to escape. *See also: Earth/Mountain.*

HEAVEN/MIST

Your lucky number is 55 . . . which indicates success coming from subtle moves. Like the mist gently treading on the heels of sky, you must risk offending the Powers that Be if you ever wish to rise. *See also: Thunder/Fire.*

EARTH

EARTH/
HEAVEN

Your lucky number is 56 . . . which indicates a change of scenery is in order. Be like a traveler in friendly skies. Sit elbow to elbow with total strangers. And retreat into yourself. Take in the bird's-eye view. *See also: Fire/Mountain.*

EARTH/EARTH

Your lucky number is 0 . . . for this is a pregnant moment. The past is buried—like last year's rubble under newly turned earth—and the slate is wiped clean. All things are possible. And all things are uncertain. What will you do tomorrow? *See also: Fire/Water.*

EARTH

EARTH/WIND

Your lucky number is 24 . . . which indicates that further progress comes now from settling down. Like the seed carried on the breeze to its planting place, your period of drifting will end by returning to your home. *See also: Earth/Thunder.*

EARTH/
THUNDER

Your lucky number is 32 . . . which indicates that progress will come on schedule. Just as the yellow shoots break through the soil in their own good time, you, too, will succeed by being persistent. *See also: Thunder/Wind.*

EARTH/WATER

Your lucky number is 16 . . . which is an encouraging sign. Just as many waters flow inside the riverbanks as one collective force, you will gather strength in numbers. The cause that benefits the most generates its own enthusiasm. *See also: Thunder/Earth.*

Your lucky number is 40 . . . which indicates that your solution lies in letting go of the past. Like the campfire stamped out with earth, the flame that carried you through the night has served its purpose. A new path opens to you. *See also: Thunder/Water.*

EARTH/FIRE

EARTH/
MOUNTAIN

Your lucky number is 8 . . . which indicates that success emerges from following a set routine. Just as the mountains remain only if the valleys stay put, they also serve who only run in place.[2] Remain loyal. Stay true. *See also: Water/Earth.*

EARTH/MIST

Your lucky number is 48 . . . which is a good sign. Just as the mist gathers on the earth, you, too, are rising to the fore. Gather your inner strength and outer courage now . . . and go to the meeting place. *See also: Water/Wind.*

[2]Thank you, John Milton.

WIND

WIND/HEAVEN

Your lucky number is 59 . . . which indicates slow, sure progress. Just as the winds aloft blow scant clouds slowly apart, success comes from tending to things a little at a time. You spread yourself in many directions. *See also: Wind/Water.*

WIND/EARTH

Your lucky number is 3 . . . which indicates progress through the powers of observation. Like the wind lifting up the dust and dropping in the seeds—you must tear up the old before you plant the new. Learn from trials and errors. *See also: Water/Thunder.*

WIND/WIND

Your lucky number is 27 . . . which indicates success through deep thought and penetration. Just as the winds come at things from many different directions at once, you must consider all the angles—if you wish to get to the heart of things. *See also: Mountain/Thunder.*

WIND/
THUNDER

Your lucky number is 35 . . . which indicates success from being aggressive. Just as wind and thunder make their rumbling way across the sky, so, too, must you rev your own engines or toot your own horn. Look sharp. Be quick. Act fast. *See also: Fire/Earth.*

WIND/WATER

Your lucky number is 19 . . . which indicates success that comes from picking up and moving. Just as the wind lifts and separates the waters, your progress depends on sorting things out. Disperse what you can and dispense with the rest. *See also: Earth/Mist.*

WIND/FIRE

Your lucky number is 43 . . . which indicates success through breakthrough. Just as the air fans the flame until the wood finally breaks under its own weight, you arrive at the point where past efforts amount to the destruction of roadblocks. Your family is rooting for you. *See also: Mist/Heaven.*

WIND

WIND/
MOUNTAIN

Your lucky number is 11 . . . which indicates progress through inner peace. Just as the wind descends upon the mountain, let the calm descend upon you. Everything is sure and certain. And you will know the truth at last. *See also: Earth/Heaven.*

Your lucky number is 51 . . . which indicates success through sudden inspiration. Just as the wind stirs the mist and moves it, your own ideas make their fleeting way. In a moment of unsuspecting silence, a big idea takes hold of you. *See also: Thunder/Thunder.*

WIND/MIST

THUNDER

THUNDER/
HEAVEN

Your lucky number is 60 . . . which is a very strong and powerful sign. Just as the thunder rattles the sky, you gain now through the shaking of cages. You are your own boss[3]—at last! Now's the time to set some rules and limitations for yourself. *See also: Water/Mist.*

THUNDER/
EARTH

Your lucky number is 4 . . . which indicates success resulting from naïveté. Just as the first April showers come as a breath of fresh air, you will achieve much through honest integrity. Give up youth, but never innocence. *See also: Mountain/Water.*

THUNDER/WIND

Your lucky number is 28 . . . which indicates progress from exerting pressure. Just as the thunder rolls in on the thrust of the winds—you find success by pushing from behind and under. Persistence pays off here. *See also: Mist/Wind.*

[3] Thanks to The Sailor.

THUNDER

THUNDER/
THUNDER

Your lucky number is 36 . . . which is a perfect number for those who love plenty of excitement. Just as the lightning lights up the sky, the fireworks go off inside you. Enjoy the thrill of this spectacular moment. *See also: Earth/Fire.*

THUNDER/
WATER

Your lucky number is 20 . . . which indicates success through thought-out actions. For just as peaceful waters are as quickly dark with rage, so you must stir into immediate action once your thoughts have idled long enough. *See also: Wind/Earth.*

THUNDER/FIRE

Your lucky number is 44 . . . which indicates success that comes as the result of being in the right place at the right time. Just as lightning strikes a tree at random, you must seize the opportunity when it presents itself. *See also: Heaven/Wind.*

THUNDER/
MOUNTAIN

Your lucky number is 12 . . . which indicates a number of small successes. Just as the thunder echoes from the hills, your progress comes from repetition. Little by little, you get there in the end. *See also: Heaven/Earth.*

THUNDER/MIST

Your lucky number is 52 . . . which indicates progress through mysterious ways. Just as voices echo through the mist, you hear the ancient call. The time has come to remain still . . . in the arms of someone. *See also: Mountain/Mountain.*

WATER

WATER/
HEAVEN

Your lucky number is 58 . . . which indicates success coming after a long wait. Just as the rivers and the stars are in no hurry to get where they are going, take your pleasure in the journey to get there. *See also: Mist/Mist.*

WATER/EARTH

Your lucky number is 2 . . . which indicates success through union. Just as the water and the earth join forces to make things grow, your success will come from cementing a relationship . . . perhaps with a kiss. *See also: Earth/Earth.*

WATER/WIND

Your lucky number is 26 . . . which indicates success through word of mouth. Just as the rain is driven by the wind, you are made stronger by others pushing from behind. *See also: Mountain/Heaven.*

WATER/
THUNDER

Your lucky number is 34 . . . which indicates success through struggle. Just as the pouring rain uproots the plants it is attempting to water, you may feel uprooted by outside forces attempting to help you. Sink your roots in a better place. *See also: Thunder/Heaven.*

WATER/WATER

Your lucky number is 18 . . . which indicates that progress comes from making a difficult passage. Just as the crossing of water is often tricky, you journey now among life's pitfalls. Success awaits you on the other side. *See also: Mountain/Wind.*

WATER/FIRE

Your lucky number is 42 . . . which indicates success in the past. Just as the fire is reduced to smoldering ash by water, you have accomplished all you can . . . for now. *See also: Wind/Thunder.*

WATER

WATER/
MOUNTAIN

Your lucky number is 10 . . . which indicates progress that comes from standing still. The drizzling rain slickens the mountain trail and slows the ascent. Take a break until the weather clears. Slow down the pace. *See also: Heaven/Mist.*

WATER/MIST

Your lucky number is 50 . . . which is a very good sign. Just as the water transforms itself into mist—and the mist into water—you will surely realize your dual purpose. Pay attention to the inklings in your bones. *See also: Fire/Wind.*

FIRE

FIRE/HEAVEN

Your lucky number is 61 . . . which indicates success through insight. Just as the shooting star streaks a glowing path across the night, your progress comes in a flash of genius. *See also: Wind/Mist.*

FIRE/EARTH

Your lucky number is 5 . . . which indicates success through inaction. Just as the earth contains the fire, you succeed by holding back. It is by waiting that you assure progress. *See also: Water/Heaven.*

FIRE/WIND

Your lucky number is 29 . . . which indicates progress through deep concentration. Just as the flickering flame eventually brings the watched pot to boil, you arrive at your destination after some time and much effort. *See also: Water/Water.*

FIRE

FIRE/THUNDER

FIRE/WATER

FIRE/FIRE

FIRE/
MOUNTAIN

FIRE/MIST

Your lucky number is 37 . . . which indicates progress through reform. Just as the fire thunders its way through the wood, your success comes from biting off as much as you can chew and changing things in the process. *See also: Wind/Fire.*

Your lucky number is 21 . . . which indicates success from finishing what you've started. Just as the green wood sputters before it lights, your success depends upon turning a spark into a flame. Keep trying. You're almost there. *See also: Fire/Thunder.*

Your lucky number is 45 . . . which indicates success through experience. Just as the fire gathers its strength from the things in its path, you will gain from each new obstacle you face. *See also: Mist/Earth.*

Your lucky number is 13 . . . which indicates success from traveling in good company. Just as the signal fire in the wilderness seeks human compassion, your journey depends upon the kindness of strangers.[4] *See also: Heaven/Fire.*

Your lucky number is 53 . . . which indicates success through separation. Just as the heat of the sun eventually lifts the fog, you will find what you are seeking by taking the time. Get off by yourself. *See also: Wind/Mountain.*

[4] Thanks to Tennessee Williams's *A Streetcar Named Desire.*

MOUNTAIN

MOUNTAIN/
HEAVEN

Your lucky number is 57 . . . which indicates progress from getting to the center of things. Just as the mountains penetrate the clouds, you need to pierce the veil of secrecy. Discover what the heart knows. Find the truth. *See also: Wind/Wind.*

MOUNTAIN/
EARTH

Your lucky number is 1 . . . which indicates progress through wearing away at the outsides. Just as every mountain eventually flattens out again, success comes now from whittling away at something old and outworn. Make way for the new. *See also: Heaven/Heaven.*

MOUNTAIN/
WIND

Your lucky number is 25 . . . which indicates progress arising from endurance. Just as the wind wears down the mountain through persistence, your success comes from continuing to do what you do . . . and be who you are. *See also: Heaven/Thunder.*

MOUNTAIN/
THUNDER

Your lucky number is 33 . . . which indicates success from soul-searching. Just as the thunder rumbles in the volcano, the call stirs within you. Retreat to the wilds . . . and think things over. *See also: Heaven/Mountain.*

MOUNTAIN/
WATER

Your lucky number is 17 . . . which indicates progress from going with the flow. Just as the water follows the path of least resistance through the hills, you will find success by steering around the obstacles in your way. *See also: Mist/Thunder.*

MOUNTAIN/
FIRE

Your lucky number is 41 . . . which indicates progress on the surface. Just as the autumn hills are a blaze of color, reveal your true colors. This is the ultimate key to your success. Let shine what shows. *See also: Mountain/Mist.*

MOUNTAIN

MOUNTAIN/
MOUNTAIN

Your lucky number is 9 . . . which indicates progress arising from matters of principle. Though the mountains are steep and difficult to cross, your success is counted all the greater once you reach the top. Live up to your own ideals. *See also: Wind/Heaven.*

MOUNTAIN/
MIST

Your lucky number is 49 . . . which indicates progress through radical change. Just as the mist alters the state of things—even to obstruct the mountain—so success comes to you now through chance and change. Free spirits of the world unite! You have nothing to fear but fear itself.[5] *See also: Mist/Fire.*

MIST

MIST/HEAVEN

Your lucky number is 62 . . . which indicates progress up the ladder. Just as the mist ascends to the sky, so now you will rise. What shall you become this time? *See also: Thunder/Mountain.*

MIST/EARTH

Your lucky number is 6 . . . which indicates progress from getting your act together. Just as the earth comes face-to-face with mist, success stares you straight in the mirror. Consult the one who looks back at you. *See also: Heaven/Water.*

MIST/WIND

Your lucky number is 30 . . . which indicates progress through constant change. Just as the wind swirls the mist as it passes, you succeed by learning how to stir things up. Be creative. *See also: Fire/Fire.*

[5] Thanks to both Karl Marx and Winston Churchill.

MIST

MIST/THUNDER

Your lucky number is 38 . . . which indicates success that comes from seeking. Just as the faint voices come crying through the fog, you succeed by heeding when your secret name is called. *See also: Fire/Mist.*

MIST/WATER

Your lucky number is 22 . . . which indicates progress through a natural process. Just as the mist rises up from the still river, you succeed by drawing from the endless stream within you. Go to the source. *See also: Mountain/Fire.*

MIST/FIRE

Your lucky number is 46 . . . which indicates progress through transformation. Just as the smoking fire signals the changing of one thing into another, your success comes from making yourself over. Let your inner light shine through. *See also: Earth/Wind.*

MIST/
MOUNTAIN

Your lucky number is 14 . . . which indicates progress by making connections. Just as the mist connects with the mountain, your success comes from networking. Get in touch with the Powers that Be. *See also: Fire/Heaven.*

MIST/MIST

Your lucky number is 54 . . . which in I Ching terms represents contentment. All else builds up to this perfect moment of completion, when all that is left to do is ride off into the sunrise. *See also: Thunder/Mist.*

EXTRA CREDIT

Pick 4! To get your three, four, six, or eight lucky numbers for Saturday night's lottery drawing, concentrate really hard on your question: **What are my lucky numbers?** Toss your coins six times, look up your hexagram, and note its number. Then follow the "See Also" references until you have all the numbers you need. Along the way, skip any hexagrams that represent numbers larger than the numbers in your lottery or raffle. (Another way of using hexagrams to select winning numbers is described in the Appendix.)

EXTRA, EXTRA CREDIT!

Of course, the best way to find your lucky numbers is to construct your hexagram by counting sticks. Try the method described in Reading #9—which uses 25 sticks—or consult the Appendix for instructions on using the traditional method of 50 sticks.

Go on to the next Reading whenever you are ready to continue.

Reading #15

How Will it All Turn Out?
(What's the magic word?)

How will this relationship wind up? Your situation resolve itself? A
problem get fixed? The way get chosen? In this final formal Reading
you will toss your coins six times to find out where anything you
want to know about is ultimately leading. For here we come at last to
the "bottom line," the "end of the story," and the start of a new chapter. From here on out, all the rest is up to you.

I CHING TOOLS

In this Reading, you will be using your coins or sticks to cast a six-line
I Ching hexagram. You have been playing with the hexagrams for several Readings now, but in this Reading, you will learn their names.

The 64 I Ching hexagrams have had many names assigned to them
over the years. Perhaps it's because their Chinese names are difficult to
translate. Or perhaps it's simply because the I Ching has such a hard
time holding still!

Different people see different things in these diagrams—and what they
see changes from time to time. In this Reading you will learn the names
that *I Ching in Ten Minutes* uses for the six-liners. But by this point,
these names will come as no surprise to you. In fact, if you have done the
last several Readings, you already have a feeling for what the names
should be.

There is a long tradition for reading each hexagram as two trigrams,
one above—and one below—the other. In *I Ching in Ten Minutes*, the
natural images of the trigrams have been taken quite literally. Each
hexagram name simply reflects the combined natural effect of two trigrams coming together.

HOW TO

❶ Clasp your coins in your hands (or use sticks if you've got 'em) and
ask your question: **How will it all turn out?** This courtship? This marriage? This separation? **What will the final outcome be?** With this

investment? This pending deal? This contract? **What's the bottom line?**
On this job? This assignment? This new opportunity? **Where will my
soul-search lead?**

❷ With your question in mind, toss your coins six times, noting each
time how they have landed—or use your sticks—to construct a hexagram. (From here on out, consult Reading #16 if you need help in using
sticks or coins.)

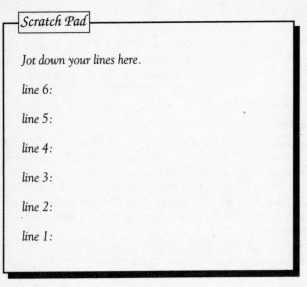

Scratch Pad

Jot down your lines here.

line 6:

line 5:

line 4:

line 3:

line 2:

line 1:

❸ Look up your answers. (As always, look up the top three lines of your
hexagram first, then the bottom three.)

**For more information on any diagram, consult the Quick Reference
Guide.**

THE ANSWERS

HEAVEN

HEAVEN/
HEAVEN

THE UNIVERSE. Heaven over Heaven . . . sky beyond sky . . . stars upon stars . . . Whatever else it is, it will be big . . . huge . . . enormous . . . and everlasting. This is something that will change you forever . . . and for the good. A relationship achieves its full potential. The time for the Big Event comes soon. *In a word, the outcome is Cosmic.*

HEAVEN/
EARTH

THE NORTH STAR. Heaven over Earth . . . the Big Dipper twirling round the North Star, forever constant and abiding. Though your view of the Big Picture may not always be clear, you are on the direct path of destiny. If you're honest with yourself, a recurring problem will be resolved. All things considered, everything balances out in the end. *The magic word is Truth.*

HEAVEN/
WIND

CLOUDS IN MOTION. Heaven over Wind . . . Wind under Heaven . . . the clouds blowing in the sky . . . meeting up with one another . . . blending for the moment . . . going their separate ways. In your life, a passing interest leads to a brief encounter, rendezvous, liaison, or private meeting. Even these fleeting moments have their meaning in the overall scheme of things. *The magic word is Silence.*

HEAVEN/
THUNDER

THE DISTANT THUNDER. Heaven over Thunder . . . Thunder under Heaven . . . the distant rumble that catches you off guard . . . and puts you on notice. And oh, but it's the same old story—it's just another storm. Still, there are many means to the same end—many ways in, and many ways out, of the same situation. Stay true to your nature, and feel free to express your feelings. *The magic word is Self-determination.*

HEAVEN

HEAVEN/
WATER

THE MOON & THE TIDES. Heaven over Water . . . Water under Heaven . . . the tides rising under the pull of the Full Moon. This situation involves forces outside yourself . . . things tugging at you relentlessly—deep, ever-conflicting emotions. Still, the situation is fluid. Once you make the choice for yourself, the outcome will be obvious. *The magic word is Give-and-take.*

HEAVEN/FIRE

THE CONSTELLATIONS. Heaven over Fire . . . Fire under Heaven . . . the stars burning brightly in a sky blacker than ink and darker than night. Never were two things less alike or more compatible. In your own life, two unlikely things combine to make something rather spectacular happen. Equals and opposites have a way of attracting. This is a match made in heaven. *The magic word is Union.*

HEAVEN/
MOUNTAIN

THE SUNSET HILLS. Heaven over Mountain . . . Mountain under Heaven . . . the hills silhouetted by the setting sun . . . the Crescent Moon above . . . and the Evening Star on the horizon. This much is certain: At the end of the day, the day is done—and not a moment too soon . . . or a second too late. Keep all things in perspective. You gain the most by taking a step back. *The magic word is Distance.*

HEAVEN/MIST

THE MIST RISING. Heaven over Mist . . . Mist under Heaven . . . the mist rising from the river at dawn . . . the mist rising from the trees at dusk. Either way you choose to go, the path goes ever onward and the way is ever up. Tread softly, my friend. Examine your beliefs. Listen for your inner voices. And follow when your soul calls. *The magic word is Vision.*

EARTH

EARTH/
HEAVEN

THE DUSK & THE DAWN. Earth over Heaven . . . the sun rising in the east as if arriving . . . the Crescent Moon sinking in the west, as if returning. Your current situation involves walking the fine line that separates equals from opposites. The outcome depends on how you look at things. Is it dusk? Or is it dawn? The past and the future meet on this line. This is a time of transition. *The secret word is Decision.*

EARTH/EARTH

THE GREAT WIDE OPEN. Earth over Earth . . . Earth beneath Earth . . . Earth within Earth . . . Earth changing into Earth . . . land stretching as far as the eye can see. What is, is. What endures, endures . . . and what does not, does not. The outcome of your situation depends on your ability to expand your horizons. There are many things on this earth to be had, once you decide what it is you want. *The secret word is Openness.*

EARTH/WIND

THE WHIRLWIND. Earth over Wind . . . a cyclone swirling . . . the autumn breeze stirring up the fallen leaves . . . the spring wind kicking up dust. The direction of these things is onward, outward, and upward. Surely you will rise in the process. A relocation or resettling is in store as a result of an uplifting experience. *The secret word is Returning.*

EARTH/
THUNDER

THE REPEATING THUNDER. Earth over Thunder . . . the thunder reporting . . . the echo repeating itself again and again and again in a steady rumble. Your situation is like an old record. You already know how it ends. As it did in the past, the same old urge compels you forward again. Listen, they're playing your song. *The secret word is Instant-replay.*

EARTH

EARTH/WATER

THE FOUNTAINHEAD. Earth over Water . . . Water below Earth . . . the dark subterranean sea . . . the underground river . . . the hidden spring that bubbles up to the surface. The outcome depends on tapping into unseen sources. In order to succeed, you must gather strength from within. A trip or mission is in store. Fight the good fight. *The secret word is Self-reliance.*

EARTH/FIRE

THE FLICKERING FLAME. Earth over Fire . . . Fire under Earth . . . the campfire kicked out with dirt . . . the light wavering . . . the flame darkening. The outcome of your situation involves a fading light. The sun sets on an era. The passion goes out of a heart. Or something wounds the ego. Pump up, restore, and reinvigorate yourself first. Empty out the ashes later. *The secret word is Rekindle.*

EARTH/
MOUNTAIN

THE BIG VALLEY. Earth over Mountain . . . Mountain below Earth . . . the Grand Canyon sinking into the depths . . . the Great Valley lying in the shadow of the Alleghenies. Your situation rests in the depths as much as it depends on the heights. Be still and patient. In the presence of powers greater than yourself, keep silence. *The secret word is Hush.*

EARTH/MIST

THE CREEPING MIST. Earth over Mist . . . Mist under Earth . . . the musty soil below the surface . . . the dark, rich, fertile earth making ready to renew itself. Your own situation is no less promising . . . and no more demanding. Great things are in the process of happening (even as we speak). Extend feelers. *The secret word is Inspiration.*

WIND

WIND/HEAVEN

THE COMET'S TAIL. Wind over Heaven . . . the wispy clouds sculpted out of ice . . . the trailing light behind the spark of a comet. The outcome of your journey—whether slow or fast—is to the quick. And nothing gets in the way now, except for progress itself. Extend yourself beyond the past. Conditions have a way of favoring the underdog. *The key word is Small-but-Mighty.*

WIND/EARTH

THE DRIFTING CLOUDS. Wind over Earth . . . the clouds passing slowly overhead . . . the clouds changing shape . . . the changing air breathing down upon you. The outcome of this situation depends upon your own reaction to the rising signs. You are about to observe something. Something is about to reveal itself to you. Watch. Listen. *The key word is Witness.*

WIND/WIND

THE COLD FRONT. Wind over Wind . . . Wind below Wind . . . winds coming from all four directions at once . . . winds going up . . . winds crashing down. The outcome of this rapidly changing situation depends on how well you can bend with the breeze. An influential source is numb to the touch. You must get under the skin. *The key word is Flexibility.*

WIND/
THUNDER

THE STORM BREWING. Wind over Thunder . . . the first signs of the storm thickening in the distance . . . the brisk breeze . . . the swaying trees . . . and the faraway sound of thunder. The tempo picks up suddenly in your life again. Be ready—some tense moments lie ahead. But in the end, the outcome is beneficial . . . for all concerned. *The key word is Get-set.*

WIND

WIND/WATER

THE DRIVING RAIN. Wind over Water . . . Water below Wind . . . the driving rain falling once again, like silent tears streaking the windowpane. In the end, things that come together tend to have a falling out. Distill the fact from fiction. Dispel the fiction from the facts. Discover the truth in between. *The key word is Separation.*

WIND/FIRE

THE WARM FRONT. Wind over Fire . . . Fire under Wind . . . a tropical breeze blowing in from the Islands . . . a warm front coming up from the South . . . a strong draft stoking the last fire of winter in the hearth. As you turn your sights outward now, a bright day greets you. All these days are yours. *The key word is Summer.*

WIND/
MOUNTAIN

THE CLOUDS GATHERING. Wind over Mountains . . . the clouds rolling up over the hills . . . the clouds catching and sticking to the peaks . . . the clouds gathering their strength. So, too, your slow but steady progress builds into crescendo. Once the power gathers within you, there can be no stopping your release. *The key word is Expansion.*

WIND/MIST

THE SWIRLING MIST. Wind over Mist . . . Mist below Wind . . . the salt spray in the air . . . the damp mist blowing in from the sea . . . the fog drifting in the headlights. What exists on the outside is now hidden from view. But—as always—truth lies at the center. There is no need now to look outside your own heart. *The key word is Self-realization.*

THUNDER

THUNDER/
HEAVEN

THE GREAT THUNDER. Thunder over Heaven . . . the greatest thunder of them all . . . the one that set the whole shebang in motion . . . the Big BANG . . . the Big Beginning. The outcome of your current situation carries an equal wallop—at least it feels that way to you. This is the moment you have been waiting for. *The key word is Climax.*

THUNDER/
EARTH

THE HOLLOW THUNDER. Thunder over Earth . . . the low rattle at the front of a storm . . . the hum of the coming thunderheads . . . the sputtering of the first rain letting loose. The final outcome of this endeavor is icing on the cake. Contentment comes in the aftermath of great excitement. (Anticipation can be fun.) *The key word is Buildup.*

THUNDER/WIND

THE TRAILING THUNDER. Thunder over Wind . . . Wind under Thunder . . . the thunder cracking straight above you . . . sending aftershocks in all different directions. The outcome of this experience is not yet known, but the possibilities are good. It is only by riding out the storm that we survive it. Stand up to the challenge. Remain persistent. *The key word is Self-preservation.*

THUNDER/
THUNDER

THE THUNDERBOLT. Thunder over Thunder . . . Thunder below Thunder . . . thunder to the left of you . . . thunder to the right of you . . . thunder all around you. In a word, the outcome of your deliberations is shocking. In a sudden, flashing light, you see the truth. Take a deep breath—you are going to need it! *The key word is Jump-start.*

THUNDER

THUNDER/
WATER

THE YOUNG THUNDER. Thunder over Water . . . the thunder of the water crashing over Niagara Falls . . . the thunder of water pulsing down the gorge. The outcome of this situation depends upon your getting over something. To be youthful is itself an act of daring. And at the moment, you are double-dog dared. *The key word is Forge-straight-ahead.*

THUNDER/FIRE

THE THUNDER BALL. Thunder over Fire . . . the ball of fire dropping from the sky . . . the lightning-struck tree! . . . the sudden fire . . . as if a gift from the gods. The outcome of your current situation will likewise come from out of the blue. This is a blessing in disguise. Your candle drippeth over. *The key word is Think-quick.*

THUNDER/
MOUNTAIN

THE RECEDING THUNDER. Thunder over Mountain . . . the jolt that rattles the hills and yet does not faze or change them. The outcome of your current situation is determined by the forces at play. But surely these Powers that Be will not steer you wrong. Take things as they come . . . one by one . . . one at a time—and your progress is certain. *The key word is Step-by-step.*

THUNDER/MIST

THE OLD THUNDER. Thunder over Mist . . . the ageless sound of the waves crashing on the beach on the nights when the fog blows in from sea. The outcome of this relationship involves the union of opposite things—a marriage perhaps, at least of the minds. Work on things together . . . and they will only get better. *The key word is Diligence.*

WATER

WATER/
HEAVEN

THE MILKY WAY. Water over Heaven . . . the great river of the Milky Way . . . stretching across space, time, and endless distance. The outcome of your current situation is a decision to keep to your present course. A calculated move is considered . . . but calculated inaction is advised. *The key word is Self-sustaining.*

WATER/EARTH

THE ANCIENT RIVER. Water over Earth . . . the old river meandering on its slow course down to the delta . . . taking the runoff and the deadwood of the ages with it. Your current situation involves an ongoing and continuous process. The old is constantly recycled and renewed. The several and separate are made whole and one again. *The key word is Long-term.*

WATER/WIND

THE DRINKING WATER. Water over Wind . . . the spring gushing from the rock face (and into green bottles) . . . the cool air rising from the city reservoir on its way to the tap and the coffee maker. Your current situation involves a matter of personal taste and the utmost discretion. Where people come together to drink, there is idle talk. *The key word is Think-before-you-speak.*

WATER/
THUNDER

THE WHITE WATER. Water over Thunder . . . the roar of the river churning up rapids . . . the spume and the spray of the waves crashing on the beachhead. Your current situation takes you for one heck of a ride or throws you for one incredible loop. It's time to ride the waves and shoot the rapids. Hang on. Things are always the most difficult at the start. *The key word is Take-a-deep-breath.*

WATER

WATER/WATER

THE DEEP. Water over Water . . . Water beneath Water . . . waters to the depths of the deep. The current situation involves deep feelings and emotional tides of the risky kind. There are many blind alleys here—ditches and deadends. Be careful, my friend. And take care. *The key word is Watch-out-for-the-unknown.*

WATER/FIRE

THE BOILING WATER. Water over Fire . . . the hiss of the teakettle about to whistle . . . but not quite yet. A watched pot won't boil until you turn your head. Big things are about to happen in your life . . . but since you're not paying attention, you are in for a big surprise. *The key word is Blink-of-an-eye.*

WATER/
MOUNTAIN

THE RAINWATER. Water over Mountain . . . the drizzling rain that blends in with the haze . . . the rain you can hardly see, and that hardly touches you. Your current situation is both dark and mysterious. The thing you are going after may prove to be elusive . . . or slippery when wet. *The key word is Keep-plugging.*

WATER/MIST

THE MORNING DEW. Water over Mist . . . the mist rising from the lake . . . the kind of day that steams the car windows in the morning . . . and creeps into your bones at night. Your current situation is like a dampness settling into your joints. You've got to go with your inklings on this one . . . and come what may. *The key word is Tap-in.*

FIRE

FIRE/HEAVEN

THE SHOOTING STARS. Fire over Heaven . . . the sparkling streaks of a meteor shower . . . as if, one by one, the stars were winking out. Yet—all in all—it's a great sign. A period of material well-being is certainly in store. (If I were you, I'd make a BIG wish.) *The key word is Thank-your-lucky-stars.*

FIRE/EARTH

THE BRUSH FIRE. Fire over Earth . . . the grass fire raging out of control . . . clearing away everything that gets in its path. The outcome of your current situation involves an Act of God. In the days ahead, you trade the past for a new and promising future. And everything old is new again. *The key word is Self-renewal.*

FIRE/WIND

THE LICKING FLAMES. Fire over Wind . . . the fanning of the flame in the kindling . . . the paper catching. . . the snapping of the bark . . . and at last the roaring blaze. The outcome of your current situation will soon be known—and it would be a shame to spoil the surprise. A fire under you is suddenly lit. *The key word is Go-for-it.*

FIRE/THUNDER

THE FIRE BREAKING UP. Fire over Thunder . . . the rip-roaring blaze that soon folds in upon itself . . . sputtering and breaking into pieces as it goes. This is a situation that involves proving something about and for yourself. Take on as much as you can chew—but spit out the rest. Make reforms. *The key word is Bite-the-bullet.*

FIRE/WATER

THE GREEN-WOOD FIRE. Fire over Water . . . Water under Fire . . . the fire that can't catch because the wood is too wet . . . the fire that sputters because it's not ready to burn yet. Your situation is like green wood. If not now . . . later. When another season is behind you—then. *The key word is Keep-up-the-good-work.*

FIRE

FIRE/FIRE

THE ETERNAL FLAME. Fire over Fire . . . Fire beneath Fire . . . fire behind you . . . fire before you . . . fire! . . . fire! . . . fire! Well, don't just sit there. Get out and wet down the roof! (Or at least take a cold shower!) You've really got your hands full this time. And once started, a fire like this is tough to put out. *The key word is Hot-potato.*

FIRE/
MOUNTAIN

THE SIGNAL FIRE. Fire over Mountain . . . the smoke of a lone campfire trailing up from among the trees . . . a sure sign of fellow travelers out roughing it in the wilderness. This situation involves a cry for help or a signal to return. Strangers are involved. Come to the rescue. But keep your distance. *The key word is Check-it-out.*

FIRE/MIST

THE GUIDING LIGHT. Fire over Mist . . . like the torch that lights the dim and murky way in front of you . . . like the beam of headlights . . . flashlights . . . searchlights. The situation you are in involves two things. First you must find the Guiding Light. And then you must be willing to follow it. Choose with care, my friend, both what you accept and what you reject. *The key word is Choice.*

MOUNTAIN

MOUNTAIN/
HEAVEN

MOUNTAIN OF THE GODS. Mountain over Heaven . . . the Himalayas . . . the Rockies . . . craggy peaks jutting like church spires to the stars. Your current situation involves a series of events in the past that have built up on one another. If you want to get what you have coming to you next, look back. Start with a prayer for guidance. *The secret word is In-retrospect.*

MOUNTAIN

MOUNTAIN/
EARTH

VALLEY OF THE SHADOW. Mountain towering over Earth . . . the dark valley stretching away beneath . . . little by little the rock face chipping off and rolling away. Your situation changes daily, yet in small ways that are not always clear to the naked eye. The gist of a matter lies below its surface. Be brave. And face the facts. Get to the heart of things. *The secret word is Dig-into-it.*

MOUNTAIN/
WIND

THE SMOKING VOLCANO. Mountain over Wind . . . the black smoke smelling of sulfur from the center of the earth . . . the volcano huffing and puffing. The current situation leaves you short of breath, and musses up your hair. Though you may feel unsettled right now, it is only a temporary disruption. These things, too, will run their course and pass in no time. Recovery is certain. *The secret word is Let-go-of-it.*

MOUNTAIN/
THUNDER

THE MOUTH OF THE VOLCANO. Mountain over Thunder . . . the slow build-up of the lava rising from the center . . . pushing boulders out of its maw. The outcome of this situation is dependent on simply one thing: How much can you take? It's time to be awed! You're in for a big surprise. *The secret word is Open-wide.*

MOUNTAIN/
WATER

THE RIVER GORGE. Mountain over Water . . . the crystal-clear mountain spring waters cascading down over the boulders. This situation gives you a thrill a minute. And there is never a dull moment. This situation is an experience in itself. There is no need to look further. This is IT. *The secret word is Enjoy.*

MOUNTAIN

MOUNTAIN/
FIRE

THE AUTUMN HILLS. Mountain over fire . . . like the hills ablaze in autumn colors along the Skyline Drive. Whatever happens between now and then, you'll receive quite a send-off in the end. Focus on the things that remain ever-green. But adorn yourself from time to time. And tend to the length and color of your hair. *The secret word is Self-improvement.*

MOUNTAIN/
MOUNTAIN

THE MOUNTAIN PASS. Mountain over Mountain . . . the ridges running off to the horizon, until they blend in with the sky. Your situation involves a matter of many high principles. It's a difficult route you have chosen. And there are many gaps to fill . . . but also gaps to pass through. Look out . . . for shortcuts. *The secret word is Go forth.*

MOUNTAIN/
MIST

THE SHRINKING HILLS. Mountain over Mist . . . Mist under Mountain . . . the mist gathering in the valley, cutting down visibility and obscuring the panoramic view. Your situation involves losing sight of something . . . but only for the moment. To see your way clear, you must hunt down and overcome the elusive. Retreat now to your mist-covered hills. *The secret word is Hide-and-seek.*

MIST

MIST/HEAVEN

THE NORTHERN LIGHTS. Mist over Heaven . . . the slow fingers of the Northern Lights spreading over the sky like tendrils. The outcome of this matter involves your taking flight and soaring to the heights. All things that were, now must make room for the new things that are coming into being. By looking ever up and out, you will soon make the breakthrough. *The watchword is Change.*

MIST

MIST/EARTH

SCATTERED PATCHES OF FOG. Mist over Earth . . . the intermittent wisps passing by, streaming off to their distant gathering place. The situation you are in involves a random series of events. Put your money where your mouth is—but before you place your bets, compute the odds of your success. Timing is everything. *The watchword is Chance.*

MIST/WIND

THE FOG BANK. Mist over Wind . . . a bank of fog drifting by the outlying areas and socking in the airport. Both planes and plans are subject to unexpected delay these days. If you want to see your way clear of these blinding roadblocks, better turn on your radar and switch off the fog lamps. This is a time to feel your way. *The watchword is Autopilot.*

MIST/THUNDER

THE FOGHORN. Mist over Thunder . . . Thunder below Mist . . . the ringing of the bell warning of shallows . . . the blast of the coast guard siren cutting through the pea soup. The situation you are in has you pitted against the Powers that Be . . . and the Forces of Nature. There is a voice in the wilderness. And it is quietly calling your name. Follow it to a sure, safe passage. *The watchword is Sighs-and-whispers.*

MIST/WATER

THE VAPOR. Mist over Water . . . the mist hovering above the lake . . . the mist trailing from the river . . . the mist clinging to far banks. The road you are on is clouded with false barriers and figments of the imagination. To find the essence, you must first strip off the layers of illusion. Take on adversity. *The watchword is Cut-through-it.*

MIST

MIST/FIRE

WOODSMOKE. Mist over Fire . . . the steam rising from the campfire or the hearth . . . the toasty smoke blowing back into the house. Your situation involves a feeling that lingers long after the fire has gone out. There are many ways and many purposes. But you will make the most lasting mark by doing as the spirit moves you. *The watchword is Imprint.*

MIST/
MOUNTAIN

THE LINGERING FEELING. Mist over Mountain . . . the low, fleecy cloud, wrapped like gossamer to the mountain . . . the 747 streaking over. Your situation involves a trade-off between inertia and quantum leap. Though similar things like to hang out together, and opposites also attract, as always, truth lies in the middle. *The watchword is Self-balance.*

MIST/MIST

THE GREAT NEBULA. Mist over Mist . . . Mist under Mist . . . Mist upon Mist . . . Mist inside Mist . . . like the giant clouds of swirling gas glowing in Virgo as the new stars shine their first. The outcome of this whole ball of wax and stardust will be whatever it shall be . . . and in its own time. Without rhythm there is only the blues. Joy comes first to those who tap their feet and kick their heels. *The watchword is Dance.*

EXTRA CREDIT

To receive a thought for the day, ask: **What's the magic word?** Cast six lines and look up your hexagram in the answers, focusing on the *italic* portion. Then look up your diagram in the Master Answer section to see what else you can expect today. (And don't forget to read for changing lines.)

EXTRA, EXTRA CREDIT!

What will the new year bring? Cast a six-line hexagram for each month to get your "horoscope" for the year. Consult the answers in this Reading or use the Master Answer section on page 176.

Go on to the next Reading whenever you are ready to continue.

Reading #16

WHERE DO I GO FROM HERE?
(How do I ask my own questions!)

In this Reading, you get to fly solo. From here on out, in fact, everything is up to you! You can ask whatever you want, whenever you feel like it. And not to fear . . . the answers in the back of the book will help you interpret the results for yourself. Here are just a few tips and reminders . . . .

I CHING TOOLS

All you need to consult *I Ching in Ten Minutes* are three coins. Many people use plain, old Lincoln pennies. But if you feel luckier with dimes, quarters, or commemoratives, why not? Or how about pennies from the year you were born? These tools are just a means to an end—for the object is to toss an I Ching line.

Depending on how your three coins land, you will wind up with one of four different I Ching lines:

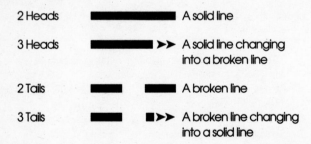

2 Heads	▬▬▬▬	A solid line
3 Heads	▬▬▬ ➤➤	A solid line changing into a broken line
2 Tails	▬ ▬	A broken line
3 Tails	▬ ■➤➤	A broken line changing into a solid line

But again, each line is just a tool—for the object is to cast an I Ching diagram. If you have worked your way up through the book, you know that there are many kinds of I Ching diagrams—one-liners, two-liners, three-liners, and six-liners—each of which can be used as tools for various purposes.

From here on out, we will be using the six-liners—the I Ching hexagrams—as our primary tools.

HOW TO

To construct your I Ching hexagram, you first need to get your question clearly in mind.

How to Ask. No question is off limits, but the I Ching method works best with questions that are fairly pointed and specific. You will often get a very literal answer to your question. So you might want to write it out in advance so you remember exactly what you asked.

Though most authorities frown on asking the very same question more than once on the same day, you are free to ask for details and approach the same question from various angles. In fact, a very effective technique is to ask a series of questions along the same lines.

For example, if you want to know about your job, you could construct a series of questions like this:

YES/NO	Is this a good time to ask for a raise?
WHAT IF	What if I apply for that new opening?
WHAT	What will happen if I stay where I am for another year?
WHO	Who should I get in touch with?
WHEN	When will things improve?
WHERE	Where should I focus my attention now?
HOW	How can I make myself more valuable to the boss?
WHY	Why am I feeling distracted at work?

To zero in on things, it helps to include a time frame in your questions.

What will happen in my love life (this week)?
How will my money go (this year)?
What will be the outcome if I end this relationship (tomorrow)?
How will I do on my project (this month)?
Where will I be with regard to money (in five years)?
Will I (ever) get ahead?

In fact, to zero in even more, you can ask the very same question again and again, as long as you change the time frame each time.

If in doubt, err on the side of being overly specific: "How should I prepare for the job interview I have next Friday at 3:15 with Big Company, Inc., in NYC?" . . . You get the idea. You can't go wrong by providing complete details, even if the question gets long.

There are certain standard question formats that will consistently produce excellent results. They are (and you get to fill in the blanks):

What's going on with _____?
How's the current situation at _____?
What action should I take to_____?
How should I react to _____?
What are the chances that _____?
What will the outcome be with regard to _____?
How will things change at _____?
What should I do to create a change in _____?

Having said all that . . . my primary advice to you is, sit back, relax, and ask about whatever your heart desires. . . .

WORK	When will I find a better job?
LOVE	How does so-and-so really feel about me?
MONEY	Where should I invest my money?
STRATEGY	What will make the best impression?
GENERAL	What's going on in my life?

. . . or your soul craves:

SPIRITUAL	What is my mission?
	What is my purpose?
	What do I need to learn?
	How can I be a better person?
	How can I make my contribution?
	How should I pursue my destiny?

Once you have formulated your question, you are ready to cast your I Ching hexagram . . . almost.

How to Psyche Up. At this time, you might want to ring a bell, light a stick of incense, or burn a candle. Some people like to face in a certain direction when they consult the I Ching—some say north, some say west, some say south. Some like to take a few deep breaths or say a prayer before they begin. Others would rather go for a walk or take a hot bath. Do whatever seems right and natural for you, even if it's nothing at all.

How to Toss Coins. There's no right or wrong way to do this . . . honestly! Whatever way you toss your coins, they will eventually come up heads or tails. Clasp the coins in your palm like dice . . . shake until done . . . throw. Or clasp the coins between the palms of both hands as if you are saying a prayer . . . rattle them together until done . . . open your hands, and let 'em fall.

You'll know when it's time to release them, because at that moment you'll let go. You simply cannot let go at the wrong time. So quit worrying about it, okay? The real trick to tossing coins is not how to hold them or when to release them but to keep your mind focused on the question. If you keep your question in mind, the coins will fall just as they should at this time.

If a coin rolls away, let it go. But go after it and find out how it landed. After all, it had to work pretty hard to come up that way, didn't it? Or throw that coin again—whatever feels right at the time.

Write down each line immediately after you throw it. Is it solid (mostly heads) or broken (mostly tails)? Is it changing (3 of a kind) or static (2 of a kind)? Construct your lines freehand, using dashes, rules, and arrows. Use the chart in the I Ching Tools section of this Reading or develop your own shorthand.

In writing your hexagram, the only rule you need to follow is: *Start at the bottom and work your way up.* Each time you toss your coins you will be adding a line above the line you cast before. Stop after you've cast six of them.

Put your coins and pencil aside and consult the Answers.

THE ANSWERS

Once you have cast your six lines, just turn to the Master Answer section of the Quick Reference Guide and find your hexagram.

Look up your Answer. The 64 I Ching hexagrams are arranged there in blocks of eight, based on the top three lines of the hexagram you have cast. These "upper trigrams" are arranged in the following order:

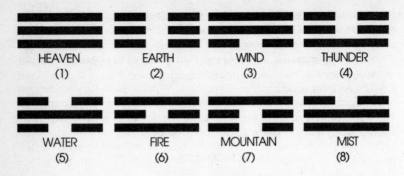

| HEAVEN (1) | EARTH (2) | WIND (3) | THUNDER (4) |

| WATER (5) | FIRE (6) | MOUNTAIN (7) | MIST (8) |

Once you find the section that deals with your hexagram's upper tri-gram—Heaven Signs, Earth Signs, Wind Signs, etc.—look up the bot-tom three lines of your hexagram.

The lower trigrams are presented in the exact same sequence as the upper trigrams. So if you have cast:

WATER/WIND

. . . you look up Water Signs (the fifth section), then find Wind (the third trigram in Water Signs).

Using the Answer Section. If your diagram has no changing lines, it represents your complete answer. This primary hexagram tells the whole story of your current situation. All you have to do is look it up in the back of the book. The Master Answer section includes a general descrip-tion of each hexagram, plus separate interpretations for questions about work, love, money, or strategy. You'll want to focus on the section that most closely relates to the question you asked. If no category exactly matches, try the strategy section and the opening description for your hexagram.

If there are no changing lines, just look up your hexagram. Once you read this answer, you're done. Ask another question for more details, clarification, or further instructions.

If there are changing lines in your diagram, ignore them at first and look up your primary hexagram in the Master Answer section. This primary hexagram gives you an idea of how things are going. In the bonus section, also read the answers for any and ALL lines that are changing in your hexagram. These answers will give you tips, suggest actions you should consider taking, or sometimes add detail to the outcome you can expect. Then . . .

Convert your changing lines into their opposites—solid into broken and broken into solid—to create a new hexagram. Let's say your primary hexagram was Fire over Mountain, with the second and sixth lines changing (remember to count from the bottom up):

FIRE/
MOUNTAIN

You'd read for Fire over Mountain, including the BONUS ANSWERS for lines 2 and 6 changing. Then you'd convert these changing lines into their opposites to derive the resulting hexagram, Thunder over Wind:

THUNDER/
WIND

This resulting hexagram shows you what the current situation is changing into. Consult the answers for this new hexagram just like you did for the first one. (But BONUS ANSWERS no longer apply.) You're done now. Ask another question.

A Note on Changing Lines. It is the changing lines that make the I Ching method so dynamic. Any I Ching hexagram can change into any other hexagram, depending on which (and how many) lines alter in the process. If no lines change, you are in a rather solid situation. If all lines are changing, you are in a situation that is totally reversing itself—your hexagram is changing into its opposite. Most situations fall in between these two extremes. Usually you can expect to cast hexagrams with one, two, or three changing lines. In reading the answers, we focus on the lines that are changing, because it is these changes that create the new hexagram . . . the new situation. Think carefully about the tips that are provided for changing lines in the BONUS ANSWERS, since these are the means by which you will influence your own destiny.

Interpreting your Answers. The answers in the Quick Reference Guide will give you a general feeling for what your hexagram represents. But a solo Reading also involves reading between the lines and thinking about things for yourself. Feel free to take key words or individual phrases from the answers or to ask for more detail on any question. Also don't be afraid to draw your own conclusions or make your own observations. Much is in the eye of the beholder, and the future, as always, is in your own hands.

All power to you.

EXTRA CREDIT

To Construct Your Hexagram by Drawing Sticks. First make your sticks, using 16 sticklike objects (twigs, dowel sticks, pick-up sticks, chopsticks—even toothpicks will do). With a black marker draw lines around the middle of eight of them. With a red marker, add dots to one of these lined sticks and to three of the sticks with no lines. It's that easy. Now put your sticks into a bowl or bag, ask your question, reach into the container, and draw one stick out at random. Look at your stick and read it as:

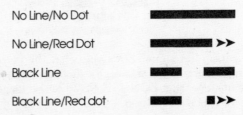

No Line/No Dot

No Line/Red Dot

Black Line

Black Line/Red dot

Write down your line, then *return the stick to its container*. Repeat the process five more times to construct your six-line hexagram. Stack each new line on top of the one you drew before. Look up your diagram in the Master Answer section. (This simple method approximates the odds that are involved in a very ancient and traditional, but complex, procedure for counting through 50 sticks several times to get the same answer.)

EXTRA, EXTRA CREDIT!

To Count Sticks. Another way to use sticks to get your hexagrams is to count sticks. First you'll need to round up 25 sticks of some kind (twigs, chopsticks, whatever)—something between 8 and 12 inches long. Pass your sticks through the smoke of burning incense three times if you like, ask your question, and then . . .

Remove one stick and set it aside <u>completely.</u>

1. Divide the remaining 24 sticks into three bundles at random.
2. Count off the sticks in the first bundle to your left **by fours.** Set aside the last group of one to four sticks in a discard pile. Keep the rest.
3. Count off the sticks in the middle bundle by **threes.** Discard the last group of one to three sticks. Keep the rest.
4. Count off the last bundle **by fours.** Discard the final group of one to four sticks and keep the rest.
5. Count how many sticks you have discarded (but don't count the stick you took away at the very start).
6. Look up your line in the following table, based on the number of discarded sticks:

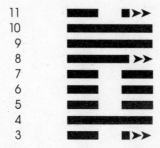

Repeat Steps 1-6 five more times to complete your hexagram. Look up your answers in the Master Answer section. (This method will give you the feeling of traditional stick counting and set a meditative mood. It also comes very close to producing the same statistical results as the traditional method of counting 50 yarrow stalks.[1] Have fun with it.)

---

[1] I Ching enthusiast and mathematical wizard Michael McCormick consulted the classical *Book of Changes* after he and I had finished working out the details of this method. To paraphrase, the counsel was that it was a fine way for people to become familiar with the oracle. The author invites your comments.

Quick Reference Guide
to the
I Ching Hexagrams
AND
Their Meanings

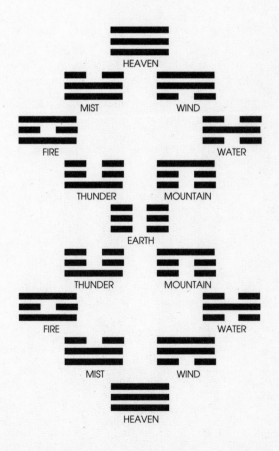

HEAVEN

MIST   WIND

FIRE   WATER

THUNDER   MOUNTAIN

EARTH

THUNDER   MOUNTAIN

FIRE   WATER

MIST   WIND

HEAVEN

READINGS FOR THE SMALLER DIAGRAMS

I Ching in Ten Minutes makes use of *all* of the I Ching diagrams, including one-liners, two-liners, and three-liners (trigrams). These "smaller" diagrams are all put to work in the Readings section of this book. Starting with one-line diagrams, the Readings quickly build up to six-line hexagrams, which are also treated in greater detail in the Master Answer section.

If you would rather jump ahead and start reading hexagrams in the Master Answer section that follows, just go ahead. But first you will want to read the instructions in Reading #16. For those who would like to know more about using the smaller I Ching diagrams, this overview summarizes the things you can do in the Readings section of the book.

ONE-LINE READINGS

Sometimes casting a single I Ching line is enough to give you the answer you are looking for, especially if what you had in mind was a quick sign. One-liners will work fine for any question you would consider deciding on the "flip of a coin." But the odds are actually quite different! And you will receive some interesting surprises when you use this method.

I Ching in Ten Minutes uses one-line Readings to do the sort of things that the I Ching was probably first used for. In fact, Reading #1 asks one of the most common questions addressed by ancient Chinese fortune-tellers, simply: Are conditions favorable? One-liners are also demonstrated in Reading #2—where they are used to help you think about the basic Forces of Nature operating in your life—and in Reading #3, to get an I Ching horoscope.

Tips. Casting a few one-liners is a good way to warm up and an excellent way to begin every session with your coins or sticks. A good question to start out with is, Is this a good time to consult the I Ching? See Reading #1 for the answer.

TWO-LINE READINGS

Two-line Readings are very good at quickly sizing up the current situation and making short-term plans. They produce straightforward forecasts based on the current state of things. As such, they are highly recommended for *what if* lines of questioning, where you want to consider the outcome of various options open to you.

Two-line diagrams are a very ancient and early application of the I

Ching method. Thousands of years ago such oracles were consulted routinely on simple matters like weather forecasting, route planning, and scheduling. *I Ching in Ten Minutes* puts these ancient applications to modern use. See Readings #4, #5, and #6.

Tips. Since two-liners are good at giving you a quick barometric Reading, they serve as a fine jumping-off point for any line of questioning. After warming up with one-liners, you can start delving into an issue by casting two lines. Use Reading #4 to compute the odds of a particular thing happening. Use Reading #5 to get your bearings and set your sights. Use Reading #6 to help you plan your calendar or pinpoint events in time.

THREE-LINE READINGS

Three-Line Readings are highly suited to the task of assessing relationships. Use them to think about people, places, and things and to ask *who*, *what*, *when*, and *where* questions about anything.

Three-line diagrams are the cornerstone of I Ching and—even after thousands of years—provide us with a very useful way to think about things. The ancient oracle was often used to forecast whether a particular marriage would be auspicious or to deal with other family matters. *I Ching in Ten Minutes* demonstrates three-liners in Readings #7, #8, #9, #10, and #11, where they are used to assess relationships and determine human compatibilities.

Tips. For people on the go—and for people who don't want to carry their book around with them!—three-line diagrams are a very practical device. Once you get a feeling for the eight trigrams—Heaven, Earth, Wind, Thunder, Water, Fire, Mountain, and Mist—you will find yourself in a good position to cast the I Ching on the fly. (If you have not completed the first part of the book, I suggest you give these three-liners a try.)

READINGS FOR THE HEXAGRAMS

Six-line Readings are good for anything and everything! . . . but especially for deep or complex questions, like *why* and *how*. By long-standing tradition, six-liners are well suited for tackling the most complex problems and issues and for making strategic or political decisions. But they also work swell for everyday decision making too.

Over the centuries six-line hexagrams have served as the blueprints for military campaigns and for forming political strategy, as well as serving as a basis for describing deep philosophies and religious ideas. You will find the six-line diagrams demonstrated in Readings #11, #12, #13, #14, and #15, as well as being treated in the Master Answer section immediately following this overview. For complete instructions see Reading #16.

Tips. Six-liners have come to be regarded as the traditional way of using the I Ching method. There are many theories about them and numerous finely honed techniques for interpreting them. If you are interested in knowing more about I Ching's fascinating history and theory, see the source list at the back of the book.

To find your hexagram in the Master Answer section, look it up in terms of the trigram formed by the top three lines. Your top trigram will place you in one of eight sections:

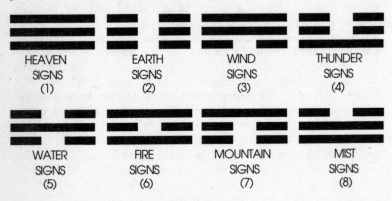

HEAVEN	EARTH	WIND	THUNDER
SIGNS	SIGNS	SIGNS	SIGNS
(1)	(2)	(3)	(4)

WATER	FIRE	MOUNTAIN	MIST
SIGNS	SIGNS	SIGNS	SIGNS
(5)	(6)	(7)	(8)

Once you find your "sign" in the Master Answer section, flip forward to your lower trigram. Read your answer. . . .

Reading Your Primary Hexagram. First look at your hexagram. Each hexagram is defined in terms of the two trigrams that form it. Taken together, these trigrams imply a certain relationship existing in the natural world. Look at the name that has been assigned to the hexagram and read its general description to get an idea of what this combination of trigrams implies.

Then zero in on the portion of the answer that relates most closely to your question. Is it work? love? money? or strategy? When in doubt, consult the strategy section—though you will also find clues in other portions of the answer. The point is, since these are general answers, everything in every answer may not directly apply to your situation. Look for the things that leap out at you . . . and read with the idea of getting a general impression.

If no lines are changing in your hexagram, the I Ching is not necessarily saying that your situation is permanent or unchanging—for nothing remains without change. But the implication certainly is that your situation can be sized up by looking at a single hexagram.

Reading Your Changing Lines. More than likely at least one line will be changing. By consulting the BONUS ANSWERS for each changing line in your hexagram, you will be given additional information about your unique situation. These answers will provide extra details, give you ideas about how best to proceed, or indicate additional things you should think about. You might think of these hints as action items.

Reading Your Resulting Hexagram. How many—or which—lines change in your primary hexagram are not as important as the result of the changes they create. By transforming solid changing lines into broken lines—and broken changing lines into solid lines—you will derive a new hexagram. This resulting hexagram is read just like your primary hexagram. It serves to add additional depth and detail to your understanding of your current situation and informs you of how things can be expected to turn out, given their current course.

Since this outcome is highly dependent on what actions you choose to take in the interim, it is not necessarily a done deal. If the resulting hexagram is not what you hoped for, you can always ask the I Ching how you might alter this outcome or what you might do to achieve the end result that you desire.

Occasionally you will find that one hexagram—along with its BONUS ANSWERS—results in a new hexagram that seems entirely contrary or unrelated. This can be due to a variety of factors, but the implication is usually that everything is not within your total control. In these cases, you will want to flesh out anything you don't understand by asking additional questions.

For help in forming questions—and for complete instructions—see Reading #16. For additional ways to use the Quick Reference Guide, also see "How to Get Your Money's Worth"—at the back of the book.

HEAVEN

Heaven Signs

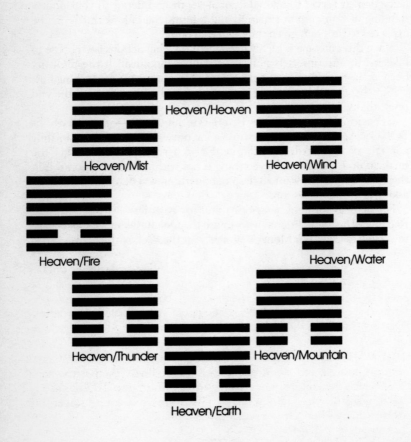

Heaven/Heaven

Heaven/Mist

Heaven/Wind

Heaven/Fire

Heaven/Water

Heaven/Thunder

Heaven/Mountain

Heaven/Earth

THE UNIVERSE

HEAVEN/HEAVEN

Heaven over Heaven. *Think about it.* This is a diagram about creative energy . . . the cosmos spreading out from here to eternity in a constant act of creation, self-realization, self-fulfillment, and personal renewal. Since you have drawn the sign of The Universe, it is clear you are "at one" with it. So you have no choice in this matter. Each star, planet, and moon is designed to be a little different—it seems. And so you, my friend, are destined To Become . . . yourself.

For WORK questions. Creativity! A call goes out for new ideas in the workplace. New skills are sought. New voices are heard. The good news is, it's your chance to influence the way things turn out. This is your once-in-a-lifetime. <u>Outcome</u>: You get to do things your way for a change.

For LOVE questions. Diversity! An ad gets posted on the electronic boards (well, it never hurts to advertise), but only the Universe is perfect! The good news is, you are about to trade in your criteria and prejudices for a stroll in the moonlight. Remain open to the possibilities. Live, love, and let live. <u>Outcome</u>: True love is in the stars for you.

For MONEY questions. Idiosyncrasy! An ATM transaction shuffles money in and out of accounts with the speed of light. Fortunes can be made here overnight. What you need is less bookkeeping and more creative risk taking. Pursue that wacky idea of yours. Believe in yourself. <u>Outcome</u>: Your big break comes at your own hand.

For STRATEGY questions. Chance! You're in a situation where anything is possible and everything follows a time line. Whether you are a star, comet, meteor, moon, or planet, it's your turn now To Become . . . what and who you are. <u>Outcome</u>: The ordinary becomes something extraordinary when left to its own devices.

BONUS ANSWERS FOR CHANGING LINES

Line 6: This is the right place. Situations and circumstances are on your side to make a big move. Good luck!

Line 5: If not now, when already? Quit procrastinating. Take the big leap.

Line 4: C'mon! Take a chance. Step out on a limb. Risk, and you stand to gain plenty. Risk not, and fate takes over.

Line 3: Let your love find you. Things will happen for you once you get in touch with your true self. The person must love you for who you are.

Line 2: Dare to raise your head. The old is out. Stand out by being different.

Line 1: This is the right time. Styles come and go, but right now, you are in. It all comes naturally to you.

THE NORTH STAR

HEAVEN/EARTH

Heaven over Earth. *Think about it.* This diagram is about things that are constant . . . the firm earth beneath your feet . . . Polaris, fixed, true, dependable, and trustworthy in its relationship to earth. Since you have drawn the sign of The North Star, it is clear that you are involved in an ongoing relationship. Equals and opposites attract, they say. But what holds them together is a mystery. In this case, the bond that is formed is permanent . . . even if the glue has not quite set, or the cement completely dried.

For WORK questions. Inertia! It's business as usual. Nothing but the world is expected of you—and yet management changes its mind with the phases of the moon. Still the books balance out by the end of the day. And the pay's okay. <u>Outcome</u>: It's a deal you can live with.

For LOVE questions. Equilibrium! The fireworks went off in the sky. The earth moved beneath your feet. Sparks flew from your locked lips. And then you woke one day to find yourself committed. Give each other enough time, enough space, and enough distance. <u>Outcome:</u> This one will last.

For MONEY questions. Balance! Debits and credits mount up to the sky (but interest payments stretch on forever). Not to worry . . . Your income meets your obligations, and you make it pay to pay. Keep at it. In the end, you wind up better off than you expected. <u>Outcome:</u> You struggle . . . and survive.

For STRATEGY questions. Standstill! This situation involves some give and take . . . some check and balance. You'll want to aim for an arrangement that meets the other party halfway, while not compromising your own position. <u>Outcome:</u> Great minds share the same vision.

BONUS ANSWERS FOR CHANGING LINES

Line 6: Listen to your gut. Despite all facts and reason, go with your hunches.

Line 5: Tend to the feelings of others. But from your own depths discern the truth.

Line 4: Stand by the woman. Nurture the woman in your life, or cultivate what is female in yourself.

Line 3: Stand by the man. Defend the man in your life, or express your own male side.

Line 2: Tend to the senses. See. Touch. Taste. Hear. Smell. The writing is on the wall.

Line 1: Listen to your heart. Believe completely. Care genuinely. Open up to yourself entirely.

CLOUDS IN MOTION

HEAVEN/WIND

Heaven over Wind. *Think about it*. This is a diagram about random events . . . the clouds constantly reshaping themselves, grouping and regrouping—until one transitory moment blends into the next. Having drawn the sign of Clouds in Motion, it is clear that something is passing through your life. Chance meetings and spur-of-the-moment departures play a part. Try to remain flexible as these winds of change sweep you along.

For WORK questions. Touching Bases! Impromptu meetings are in store . . . in the elevator, rest room, hall, or passing through an opened door. Though fleeting, these brief encounters can be personally rewarding . . . if you act fast. <u>Outcome</u>: You make the most of a little something.

For LOVE questions. Chance Meetings! You brush into each other. Eyes lock. A few words are exchanged. It is a brief—if not dangerous—liaison . . . a small event really—and yet it leaves a lasting imprint. <u>Outcome</u>: This is one for the scrapbook.

For MONEY questions. Temptations! It's one of those chances "to get in on the ground floor" of something potentially sky-high. Add up the odds for yourself—but go with your hunches. This window of opportunity is brief . . . and the impulse is fickle. <u>Outcome</u>: Ante up, my friend—or kiss it good-bye.

For STRATEGY questions. Idle Thoughts! Clouds swirl in the bottomless cups of sugar-free decaffeinated. Doodles appear on the agenda margins. For preoccupation and distraction there is only the one cure. <u>Outcome</u>: You benefit from a little change of pace.

BONUS ANSWERS FOR CHANGING LINES

Line 6: Keep your ears peeled. There is something you must hear for yourself. Go to the source.

Line 5: Keep your sights high. There are both ends and means to be considered. Justify both.

Line 4: Keep your assets in mind. There are some things of yours that need to be protected. Consider insurance.

Line 3: Keep your butt covered. There are some personal risks involved, not necessarily of your own making. Beware. Be wary.

Line 2: Keep your priorities in line. There are a few things you must do before you are finished. What are they?

Line 1: Keep your eyes peeled. There is something you must see for yourself. Look for it.

THE DISTANT THUNDER

HEAVEN/THUNDER

Heaven over Thunder. *Think about it.* This is a diagram about things that creep up on you . . . the thunder rumbling like a murmur in the distance—giving fair notice. Since you have drawn the sign of The Distant Thunder you should keep your ears, eyes, and nostrils open for the early signs. What is about to happen is only the natural culmination of a series of unseen events. By getting in sync with things going on at a distance, you will be ready for the opportunity when it strikes.

For WORK questions. Stand By! On the upper floors the Powers that Be are flexing their muscles. Meetings take place behind closed doors. And rumors float the halls. An announcement is forthcoming. <u>Outcome</u>: A change in attitude comes down the line.

For LOVE questions. Tune In! You've got a feeling in your bones, that's all—or is it? Some tension is building up in the background. You simply pick up on it . . . and jump to conclusions. Better confront this one head-on. And let the chips fall. <u>Outcome</u>: It all blows over. Whew! False alarm!

For MONEY questions. Turn Off! You are operating in the dark on this one, for no one knows for sure which way the winds will blow. There are mixed signals . . . but enough signs of looming trouble to concern you. Prepare for the worst, but hope for the best. <u>Outcome</u>: Plan B is put into effect.

For STRATEGY questions. Drop Over! This is a situation in which an element of surprise is involved. There is nothing certain about the weather, news, or sports . . . it's all in the shock value. <u>Outcome</u>: You are in for a surprise visit.

BONUS ANSWERS FOR CHANGING LINES

Line 6: Hear no evil. Ignore a gibe written between the lines, a slur spoken under the breath, or a backhanded comment.

Line 5: Act surprised. Something tips you off in advance or otherwise spoils the surprise. With tact and grace, compose your reply.

Line 4: Hedge your bets. Though you may be certain or feel sure, it never hurts to have contingency plans. Make some just in case.

Line 3: Plead innocence. Just because you feel guilty doesn't mean you are. Consider all the extenuating circumstances.

Line 2: Remain faithful. Stay true to your pledges, honor your commitments. But most of all be honest with yourself.

Line 1: Speak no evil. Keep your negative thoughts to yourself. The whole truth is unknown. And who are you to judge?

THE MOON & THE TIDES

HEAVEN/WATER

Heaven over Water. *Think about it*. This is a diagram about things that cycle continuously . . . like the moon moving through its phases and the tides rising and ebbing. Since you have drawn the sign of The Moon and the Tides, you should look for recurring patterns in your own life. Things that cycled up in the past will cycle up—and down—again. Once you learn to recognize these patterns in your life, you will be better able to anticipate, use, and take advantage of them.

For WORK questions. That Time of Week! Mondays and Fridays come especially to mind . . . and paydays, whatever day they fall on. The best work is done when conditions favor it and the mood of the moment is right. An artificial deadline comes in due time. <u>Outcome</u>: Things cycle up according to their own schedule.

For LOVE questions. That Time of Month! There's a time for everything . . . and everything in due time. New Moon. Full Moon. Crescent Moon. Quarter Moon. High tide . . . low tide—and all the currents in between. Keep track on your calendar of the things that happen in cycles, especially your sex life. <u>Outcome</u>: He's got the feeling, and she's in the mood.

For MONEY questions. That Time of Season! The time is fast approaching for the end of an accounting period. The day of reckoning comes. It all gets added up and netted out. Another closing of the books occurs. And you see it all in black and white (and red all over?). <u>Outcome</u>: It's time to rephase the budget.

For STRATEGY questions. That Time of Year! The situation you are in involves the use of a clock, calendar, and calculator. At least two factors are at play . . . and many variables. For best results, schedule things out ahead of time and base your plans on past experience. <u>Outcome</u>: It goes like clockwork.

BONUS ANSWERS FOR CHANGING LINES

Line 6: The tide is coming in. Things are starting to build up again. A high point is approaching. You are on a roll. Go for it.

Line 5: Harvest at Full Moon. Take in now the results of your labors and see what you have accomplished.

Line 4: Plant at Quarter Moon. Give ideas a chance to sprout and take root. Try out some new things. Give it your best shot.

Line 3: Wish at Crescent Moon. Make plans early. Set sights. Chart a course. Dream on . . .

Line 2: Wait at New Moon. Before a new thing can start, an old thing must finish up. Be done with it. Be satisfied.

Line 1: The tide is going out. Things are winding down again. A low point is coming . . . and a fresh start.

THE CONSTELLATIONS

HEAVEN/FIRE

Heaven over Fire. *Think about it.* This is a diagram about fitting into the scheme of things . . . the stars in the sky shining continuously, each in its place, each with its own identity. Having drawn the sign of The Constellations, it is clear you feel a sense of belonging. But it is only by being yourself—and burning with your own light—that you wind up connecting all the dots . . . and achieving your own destiny. There is a story for every life and a moral for every story.

For WORK questions. The Great Hunter! It's clear as the stars in Orion's belt that it's time to find what you are seeking. The hounds are sent to fetch the wild geese. The fox is still on the run. Be like the Great Hunter. Follow the signs. Pick up the scent. Pursue the things you regard as important. <u>Outcome</u>: It's time to set your sights. Take aim.

For LOVE questions. The Seven Sisters! Like Orion forever chasing the Pleiades, there is an eternal passion here . . . and an eternal quest. There may be safety in sticking together. However, one is inclined to split off and go a separate route. Is it you? Or is it your friend who is after something new? <u>Outcome</u>: Go your separate ways, but keep in touch.

For MONEY questions. The Big Bear! It's clear as the dippers in the night sky, two accounts are involved here. And one is substantially bigger than the other. But as long as you don't dip into savings too much, you'll be okay. <u>Outcome</u>: Invest in your dream. But hold a little in reserve.

For STRATEGY questions. The Zodiac! Your situation involves a dozen different things happening at once. An Aries, Leo, or Sagittarius may play a leading role, but regardless of the astrological signs, multiple personalities are involved . . . and more than one hidden agenda. You must look between the lines. And read the story for yourself. <u>Outcome</u>: By setting yourself apart, you wind up fitting in.

BONUS ANSWERS FOR CHANGING LINES

Line 6: The scorpion hustles. So must you, if you want to get where you are going . . . fast.

Line 5: The lion springs. When the opportunity presents itself, you must be ready to leap into action. Jump on this chance.

Line 4: The fish swim in groups. Take your cues from those you hang out with. Join a popular school of thought.

Line 3: The ram lowers its head. Looks like you'll be butting heads on this one in order to hold your current position.

Line 2: The bull bucks. You must be a little bullheaded yourself if you hope to get someone off your back. Charge!

Line 1: The crab crawls sideways. You, too, must take a few sidesteps in order to move forward.

THE SUNSET HILLS

HEAVEN/MOUNTAIN

Heaven over Mountain. *Think about it.* This is a diagram about with-drawing . . . the sun setting behind the hills, lighting up the clouds, and calling it a day. Since you have drawn the sign of The Sunset Hills, it's time for you to wind down, too. Withdraw now to the place you call home. Retreat to the shadows of your private life, your intimate relationships, and your own rules.

For WORK questions. End of the Day! The time clocks are punched out. The lights are turned off and the computers powered down. Traffic winds its way up and down the rolling hills, following the taillights home. It's time to eat a little something and play Wheel of Fortune. <u>Outcome</u>: Another day, another sawbuck.

For LOVE questions. On Into the Night! It's time to hit the hay . . . but who said anything about turning in? The day may well be shot, but the night's a-wasting. It's time to draw the blinds, don't you think? Let your hair down. Live a little. <u>Outcome</u>: It's nobody's business but your own.

For MONEY questions. The Midnight Hour! This is the time to give your money—and all the other cares of the day—a well-deserved rest. Count off bills by hundreds—if you must—to put yourself to sleep. But don't let your money keep you awake. <u>Outcome</u>: The answer comes in a symbolic dream.

For STRATEGY questions. The Livelong Night! This situation involves things done in the privacy (safety and sanctity) of your own four walls. How the day goes may be more or less out of your control. But when the dusk comes, you get to post your own signs and make your own rules. <u>Outcome</u>: Wait till the midnight hour.

BONUS ANSWERS FOR CHANGING LINES

Line 6: The cost of freedom. To free yourself, first extend the benefit of the doubt to the actions, habits, and customs of others.

Line 5: Feel free to run the risk. Chance takes no sides, of course, but comes at its own will. Bet carefully. Set limits.

Line 4: Feel free to change. Nothing is meant to remain the same for ever . . . not even you. Change in your own way.

Line 3: Feel free to come at your convenience. But once you commit to something, honor your word.

Line 2: Feel free to go. Movement is unrestricted now. Nothing holds you back . . . except limits you place upon yourself.

Line 1: The price of freedom. To be free, you must give way to others without giving up everything yourself.

THE MIST RISING

HEAVEN/MIST

Heaven over Mist. *Think about it.* This is a diagram about walking softly . . . like mist treading the water or stepping upward on windy stairs. It is about how things behave in nature and how behavior changes things. Having drawn the sign of The Mist Rising, it is clear you are conducting yourself in a rather soft-spoken, quiet way. But nothing else would do right now, since you are walking a thin line . . . you are treading on the tail of a tiger. Forces that outweigh you in size or numbers would like to set your boundaries for you. So you have no choice now but to creep around these artificial limitations.

For WORK questions. Walking a Thin Line! You'll have to watch your p's and q's for now. Do nothing to draw attention to your own ambitions or ideas. Whisper gently what they want to hear. And when they are not looking, make your move. <u>Outcome</u>: The tiger's eye is lulled shut. You are safe to run circles around him.

For LOVE questions. Floating on Air! There is a ritual involved here . . . and a little role-playing. One flits mysteriously around the other, who watches in silence with glazed-over eyes. A little flimsy underwear should do the trick, I'd say. <u>Outcome</u>: The tiger purrs in the aftermath, creating the perfect opportunity to ask a favor.

For MONEY questions. Treading Water! Are the bankers salivating to have your business? Or are they licking their lips before eating you alive? Miss a payment and you'll find out what's what. <u>Outcome</u>: The tiger is inclined to bite even the hand that feeds him. Throw tidbits while you plan your escape.

For STRATEGY questions. Rising Above! The situation that confronts you is not without threat. To get where you are going, you must either bend or get around the rules. This is not an easy path to take. Use camouflage to reduce the risk. <u>Outcome</u>: The tiger is easily fooled by appearances. Put up a smoke screen. Let him think he's won.

BONUS ANSWERS FOR CHANGING LINES

Line 6: Destiny is achieved. By reacting to the inevitable in your own way, you carve out your own identity.

Line 5: The prey outsmarts the predator. There is a benefit from both a bluff and a surprise. Make your move suddenly, decisively.

Line 4: The predator threatens the prey. Two options exist—stand your ground or make your getaway. Which shall it be?

Line 3: The weak resist the powerful. Consider things from the bottom up. What do they want? How can they get it?

Line 2:   The powerful oppress the weak. Consider things from the top down. What would you do? How do they think?

Line 1:   Fate is dealt. So congrats! Or, tough luck! Either way, what you do as a result is up to you . . . and all that really matters.

EARTH

Earth Signs

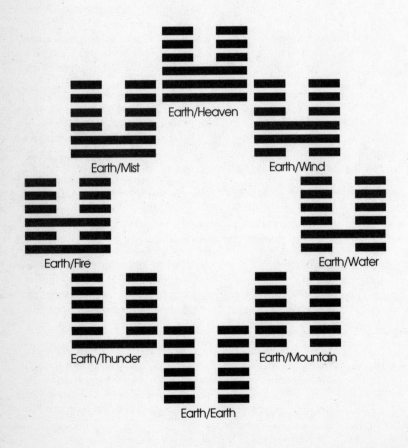

Earth/Heaven

Earth/Mist

Earth/Wind

Earth/Fire

Earth/Water

Earth/Thunder

Earth/Mountain

Earth/Earth

THE DUSK & THE DAWN

EARTH/
HEAVEN

Earth over Heaven. *Think about it.* This is a diagram about things quietly exchanging places . . . like the day gliding into the night at twilight, and like the night trailing off into the day at dawn's early light. Since you have drawn the sign of The Dusk and The Dawn, it is clear you are on the cusp. One era moves toward the horizon and runs smack dab into a new one. And at the very moment of transition, there is unqualified peace.

For WORK questions. Passing the Reins! The ship of state—or the helm of the corporation—changes hands (again). It is the twilight of a passing regime now . . . and the dawn of a new era. Things will certainly be different. But will they be better? Nothing stays the same. <u>Outcome</u>: Every Good Boy Does Fine. TGIF.

For LOVE questions. Passing the Mark! You've made it! A turning point comes in a relationship. Friendship crosses over into love. A difficult period runs its natural course. And the two of you ride off into the sunset. <u>Outcome</u>: You get a second chance.

For MONEY questions. Passing the Buck! Consumer confidence is back after a long hiatus. Bye-bye, economic downturn. Hello, happy new day. As you rebuild your collection of electronics equipment, snazzy new cars, and square footage under roof—try to do it with cash up front this time. <u>Outcome</u>: Uncle Sam sets the lead.

For STRATEGY questions. Passing the Torch! These are times of transition, all right, for once again the torch has been passed. But though the former ways are done and gone, the latter ways have yet to make their mark. The sure past is over, and the unknown is coming soon. Have faith. <u>Outcome</u>: A welcome change brings peace and prosperity to the people.

BONUS ANSWERS FOR CHANGING LINES

Line 6: When will the latter come? These things happen in their own time. Suddenly what was the future is now.

Line 5: Take a big leap of faith. Trust in your own vision of the Great Unknown . . . and walk forward with confidence.

Line 4: Take a step forward. Turn your headlights on high beam, and head into the tunnel. There's light on the other side.

Line 3: Take a brand-new look. Reassess. Reconsider. Reappraise . . . And reapprise.

Line 2: Take a long look back. Before you close the door and walk away forever and for good, look now . . . and remember.

Line 1: Where has the former gone? What's done is done. The time has come to leave the past to its shadows.

THE GREAT WIDE OPEN

EARTH/EARTH

Earth over Earth. *Think about it.* This is a diagram about things that are subject to the Forces of Nature . . . the windswept prairies, the rain-drenched mountains, the crop-covered hills and valleys, the sunbaked deserts—all things that are not only open but receptive to change. Having drawn this sign of The Great Wide Open, you, too, must be open and receptive—to the forces from without, as well as those that come from within. There are things that change you. And there are things you can change.

For WORK questions. Time & Temperature! Do you run by the clock, or does the clock run you? It seems there are not enough hours in the day or days in the week to cope with the changes that have come about so quickly. And yet nature has a way of recovering fast . . . even from disaster. <u>Outcome</u>: The work climate improves . . . and then the economy.

For LOVE questions. Tops & Bottoms! One is aggressive and the other docile. One dominates, while the other submits. Without the one, where would the other be? And so it goes to prove the point: It takes two to do the work of Mother Nature. Play your part. <u>Outcome</u>: There is a sudden role reversal.

For MONEY questions. Oil & Silicon! There's liquid gold in them thar fields—or is it computer chips? Natural resources come and go, and so do the needs for them. But though the price of real estate rises and falls, the land—regardless of its perceived worth—endures. Invest in it, and you will never be without a place to go. <u>Outcome</u>: It's time to reevaluate things.

For STRATEGY questions. Give & Take! This is a situation where fate plays a leading role. The Forces of Nature are involved . . . and The Powers that Be. But all things considered, it is you who determine what these Acts of God will mean. The answer lies in your natural response. <u>Outcome</u>: Build on the foundation that already exists.

BONUS ANSWERS FOR CHANGING LINES

Line 6: There is a reason for every reaction. Look for the rationale. But trust in your own instincts.

Line 5: The soul replies. The question is: What in your heart of hearts do you need to do with your life?

Line 4: The Great Spirit calls. How could you even consider not answering? You have no choice but to go where this voice leads.

Line 3: The laws of nature apply. In this case, it is best to do what seems right at the moment. Go with your hunches.

Line 2: The Powers that Be have spoken. It is best to go along with the rules . . . at least for now.

Line 1: There is a cause for every action. Look for the reasonable explanation below the surface. But believe what you will.

THE WHIRLWIND

EARTH/WIND

Earth over Wind. *Think about it.* This is a diagram about things pushing upward . . . like dust, leaves, and debris ascending on a whirlwind . . . like the crocuses pushing upward through the half-frozen earth . . . like people rising above their own roots. Since you have drawn the sign of The Whirlwind, it is clear you are making progress. You are advancing. It is a growth experience you are involved in. And growth is the goal.

For WORK questions. Starting on the Bottom! Though the opportunity may seem small or insubstantial at first, it will grow and grow—until it may even threaten to take your breath away. The possibilities are great. But finish the groundwork first. Do each small task to completion. <u>Outcome</u>: You make the most progress by moving with the prevailing winds, rather than against them.

For LOVE questions. Putting Down Roots! You're right. It's a big decision to move into a new place and start a new life together. And the closet space is only the first of the turf storms. Allow each person room to get unpacked. Let each get moved in. <u>Outcome</u>: Things will work out over time . . . once the dust settles.

For MONEY questions. Working Your Way Up! Some luck out. They grow up in the richest earth under the best weather conditions. But others have to struggle against poor soil, stiff winds, and lack of rain. Neither is prepared for everything. And time is the great leveler. <u>Outcome:</u> What struggles at first, catches up in the end. What thrives at first, does not always come out ahead.

For STRATEGY questions. Hit the Ground Running! This situation involves dramatic change. Whether you are just starting out for the first time or have been recently transplanted by the winds of change, you must adjust quickly to your new environment. Set about the task at hand. Map out a plan for making rapid progress. Pace yourself. <u>Outcome:</u> What's done at the start pays off down the line.

BONUS ANSWERS FOR CHANGING LINES

Line 6: Nurture the early results. Encourage the things that get off to a strong start. Help the things that struggle along at first.

Line 5: Get up to speed quickly. To hit the ground running, put in extra time at first.

Line 4: Work around shortcomings. Weaknesses are strengths when viewed from a different angle. Find what suits you.

Line 3: Give more than what you take. Any extra is sure to come back to you in the end, as all things tend to even out.

Line 2: Do more than what is required. That which is necessary is not always sufficient. Less is not more.

Line 1: Plant the seed of an idea. Things that need to get started eventually might as well get started now.

THE REPEATING THUNDER

EARTH/THUNDER

Earth over Thunder. *Think about it.* This is a diagram about things that occur over and over again . . . the thunder itself coming up over the ridge, the roll of the thunder echoing on the hills, the hills themselves rumbling with stirrings of life. Having drawn the sign of The Repeating Thunder, you are experiencing an old, familiar feeling. Whether by force of habit only or by genetic imprint, you find yourself repeating a behavior pattern. But how will the same old sequence of events turn out this time . . . in a Universe where the very same thing never happens twice?

For WORK questions. Do It Till You Get it Right! Typos, transposed numbers, and other quality-control errors creep into your life. (Better

197

double-check.) Or something more insidious rears its ugly head again in the workplace. Old habits die hard. Old problems resurface until they're laid to rest. And old patterns repeat themselves to death. <u>Outcome</u>: What have you learned this time?

For LOVE questions. Don't Stop Doing What You're Doing! This is one of those habits you don't want to break. This is an addiction you can live long and well with and die with a smile on your face. Keep up the good work. (Where did you learn how to do that, anyway?) <u>Outcome</u>: Everything's okay on this end.

For MONEY questions. Don't Repeat Past Mistakes! It may seem like it's the same old story at the end of the month. So the systems and budgets and plans went haywire again—what the hay? Nothing ever built was made to last forever. Test out new approaches to the same old problems. <u>Outcome</u>: Take a deep breath, and learn a lesson from the past.

For STRATEGY questions. Try, Try Again! You are in a situation that involves the same old traps you've fallen into before. And it probably involves the same old lessons you should already know. Still, each repetition adds to the understanding. Most experiments fail . . . but keep experimenting. <u>Outcome</u>: The third time's the charm.

BONUS ANSWERS FOR CHANGING LINES

Line 6:   The peace is reestablished. Things quiet down, settle out, and stabilize again—but in a new order. Refit yourself into the scheme.

Line 5:   Try out something entirely new. Toss out the old methods and reengineer the whole ball of wax. Look for efficiencies.

Line 4:   Fine-tune the machine. Take steps to fix a few minor but important things. But if it ain't broke . . .

Line 3:   Play out a scenario. Consider what you would do if . . . and when. Now, how can you get there from here?

Line 2:   Deal with the crisis of the day. React. Respond. Think fast. Put out today's fire. And then go home.

Line 1:   The peace is disturbed. But things need to be shaken up once in a while. Let the dust fly. It will surely settle again.

THE FOUNTAINHEAD

EARTH/WATER

Earth over Water. *Think about it.* This is a diagram about things that gather strength . . . like the underground river bursting out at the spring. Having drawn the sign of The Fountainhead, it is clear you are about to emerge from the trenches yourself, having gathered sufficient strength and nerve to let loose or pitch in. It takes only one to become a martyr to a cause. But strength can also come from joining forces with others. The many waters flow as one.

For WORK questions. Army of Ants! There's a group project in the works. A ditch needs to be dug. A barn needs to be raised. A highway needs to be constructed. A competitor needs to be withstood. Lend one another a helping hand, and whistle while you work. <u>Outcome</u>: Collective force results in bridges being built.

For LOVE questions. Gushing of Wellsprings! There are lots of factors involved in this relationship. Lots of preconditions exist . . . and plenty of feelings. A passion pursued with both the right intention and human compassion makes the most headway. <u>Outcome</u>: There is an outpouring of the emotions.

For MONEY questions. Combined Resources! Few have the financial resources to do everything they'd like to do. But by combining accounts and sharing risk, a larger effort can be pulled off. Put everything in writing up front in order to protect your own . . . assets. <u>Outcome</u>: A joint effort is pulled off.

For STRATEGY questions. Collective Force! This situation requires not only teamwork, but team spirit. How will you unite the group? Hatred rallies just as easily as—or easier than—love. But does the end justify your means? And what are you setting yourself up for? <u>Outcome</u>: A few with conviction sway and move the many . . . for better or worse.

BONUS ANSWERS FOR CHANGING LINES

Line 6: There is a secret plan. You have not been told the truth—at least not the whole truth. The means do not justify the ends.

Line 5: The troops are rallied. Marching orders are issued. Your choices are made for you now. No use crying over spilt . . . ashtrays.

Line 4: Opinion leaders are recruited. The outspoken (and obnoxious) sound off. Speak up now or forever hold your peace.

Line 3: An emotional appeal goes out. Morals come now backed up with scientific evidence. But beware the twisted stat.

Line 2: A front is put up. Don't be taken in by the politics. Below the fine rhetoric and the high ideals lie cold, cruel power facts.

Line 1: There is a secret motive. So take the reasons and excuses you hear with a certain degree of cynicism.

THE FLICKERING FLAME

EARTH/FIRE

Earth over Fire. *Think about it.* This is a diagram about faith that endures a test. The flame struggles under the dirt heaped upon it, and the light of truth wavers. Having drawn this sign of The Flickering Flame, you must be experiencing a dark, difficult moment of doubt. Whether the world has turned against you is almost beside the point. The spirit that remains in you must fight now for its very light. You must believe as hard as you can in what is good and right and true . . . especially the truth that resides in you.

For WORK questions. The New Guard! Those who would rather see things done the old way had best cover their eyes now. The passion that once raged here has had its very heart and soul cut out. And what is left of the founding father's dream can be put on a flip chart. It is not enough to know how to do things. You must also believe in what you are doing. <u>Outcome</u>: It's time to realign your thinking.

For LOVE questions. The Old Flame! You bump into each other again—after all these years and many miles. And it's hard to believe, isn't it? Somewhere deep inside, a long-lost coal of a rapid heartbeat suddenly resuscitates. But what does it mean this time? <u>Outcome</u>: A long-forgotten feeling flares up again, briefly. Burn, baby, burn.

For MONEY questions. Empty Pockets! That old gold card hasn't lost its sparkle, has it? That hologram's still flashing rainbow colors, right? Or does it just not get accepted anymore? Well, they were good times, weren't they? Better return to a cash basis. <u>Outcome</u>: Something puts a cramp in your style, at least for now.

For STRATEGY questions. Repression! This is a situation where the truth that once seemed so bright and eternal has been all but stamped out. Yet no matter how repressed by half-truths—or the restraints others would place upon your very thoughts if they could—the last remaining ember burns. Hold it close to you. <u>Outcome</u>: Wait. Watch. And bide your time. All things change.

BONUS ANSWERS FOR CHANGING LINES

Line 6: Those were the good old days. Here's to the good old tomorrows.

Line 5: You can never go home again. Don't even think about what could have been. Focus on what might yet be.

Line 4: It was fun while it lasted. But is it over yet? Only time will tell what goes and what remains.

Line 3: Things aren't what they used to be. But neither is this the be-all, end-all. Live. Learn. Grow. Change with the changes.

Line 2: Here's mud in your eye . . . cheers! . . . and all that. Make a pact to keep in touch. Write. Phone. Fax.

Line 1: These are the good old days. And when you look back on all of this tomorrow, you will at least smile . . . if not laugh.

THE BIG VALLEY

EARTH/
MOUNTAIN

Earth over Mountain. *Think about it.* This is a diagram about things that are whittled down to size or carved out . . . like the mountain worn away little by little, washed into the valley below, and carried off. Having drawn the sign of The Big Valley, you are in a situation where you walk in the shadow of someone larger than yourself or higher in station. (And don't we all?) Yet here, as in all else, one force moderates the other, and both make up the larger picture. Carry your own weight. Do your part. Hold up your end. By chipping away at things, you make an impact.

For WORK questions. Integrity! The small and the large both make a contribution. Be proud of your role, even though you stand in the background. They can't do it without you. And in the end, the spoils are divided. Just keep doing what you're doing. <u>Outcome</u>: A major contribution is made after all is said and done.

For LOVE questions. Modesty! This is a good and decent relationship — even if it does occur with the lights out. You really have nothing to hide, for you are loved for who you are. But long shadows and low whispers set the mood—and the sounds of nature operate in the background. One initiates; one responds. <u>Outcome</u>: It is a tender moment.

For MONEY questions. Humility! It is not a sure thing that the rich will only get richer. And it is not certain that the poor will remain without means. It's all on paper anyway. Keep things in perspective. And count your nonnegotiable blessings as goodwill. <u>Outcome</u>: You never know what matters in the end.

For STRATEGY questions. Take It Easy! This is a situation that looks more or less permanent to the eye. But what is firm disintegrates constantly. And what is soft, hardens over time. The process is slow, moderate, but inevitable. <u>Outcome</u>: You can forestall, but you cannot reverse the laws of nature. It is better to participate in the process than to resist.

BONUS ANSWERS FOR CHANGING LINES

Line 6: Every mountain is made low. That which is high eventually wears down. Abide now. But await the day.

Line 5: Hold on for dear life. Something happens as fast as an avalanche—and with as little warning.

Line 4: Anticipate a reversal. Things can still go either way, but be prepared—just in case you lose your edge.

Line 3: Listen for the signals. The unexpected happens, but most changes can be predicted if you watch for signs.

Line 2: Watch for subtle changes. Little by little, small things add up. Consider the seemingly minor and insignificant.

Line 1: Every valley is built up. That which is low does not remain low forever. Build on top of what you've already got.

THE CREEPING MIST

EARTH/MIST

Earth over Mist. *Think about it.* This is a diagram about things that sneak up on you . . . like the mist swirling by the windows or the fog creeping up the bank. Having drawn the sign of The Creeping Mist, you are in for a surprise of sorts, for things of a deeply moving nature are approaching—or catching up to you. Powers of a spiritual kind are involved here . . . powers that move in mysterious ways and reveal themselves in startling truths. There is nothing to do but watch and wait for the surprise ending.

For WORK questions. Vision! Listen to someone at work who not only has inside information, but also has the insight to figure out what the ambiguous rumors mean. Trust in a leader who emerges from the smoke screen of gibberish. Listen to your common sense. <u>Outcome</u>: The veil is lifted for a moment for a sneak-peek.

For LOVE questions. Character! You've suddenly hooked up with a most enchanting partner—the kind who keeps you guessing and never ceases to amaze. There is heart and body, of course, but it is the soul you adore—the mirror image of yourself. <u>Outcome</u>: Turn off the fog lights— you are done scanning for a mate.

For MONEY questions. Foresight! The visibility is no more murky from the low-lying areas than it is from the dizzying heights. In hindsight, it's always the unforeseen that makes the biggest spike in the charts. To glimpse even the foreseeable future, you'll need a crystal ball. <u>Outcome</u>: The dark glass clears suddenly . . . and suddenly you see.

For STRATEGY questions. Advancing Power! This is a situation that is due to unseen but active forces operating upon you. Then the answer emerges from powers you didn't even know you had. It is as if you were walking through a mist that suddenly lifts. <u>Outcome</u>: The answer comes so fast, it floors you. Quick! Write it down.

BONUS ANSWERS FOR CHANGING LINES

Line 6: Power recedes. A moment of grandeur passes. A door closes. Or a final decision is at last reached. A wish is used up.

Line 5: Note the passing thought. What is the nature of the things you keep coming back to? This is your answer.

Line 4: Consider . . . but wait to hear more. It is too soon to make a judgment call on this one. Gather more information.

Line 3: Clear the steam from your glasses. It is time to see things in a new light. Insist on clarity.

Line 2: Feel your way. Advancement is just this: One step at a time, you move forward. Easy does it.

Line 1: Power approaches. You will need to either take a step forward or two steps back. Things continue by reversing. Make a wish.

WIND

Wind Signs

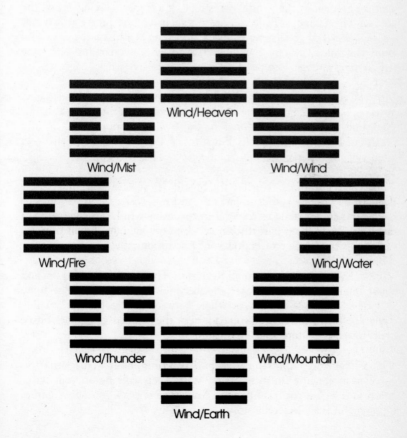

Wind/Heaven

Wind/Mist

Wind/Wind

Wind/Fire

Wind/Water

Wind/Thunder

Wind/Mountain

Wind/Earth

THE COMET'S TAIL

WIND/HEAVEN

Wind over Heaven. *Think about it.* This is a diagram about small things that make progress . . . the clouds trailing headlong into a stiff counter breeze . . . the windblown streak of a comet. Having drawn the sign of The Comet's Tail, you are up against some pretty stiff winds yourself. But the good news is, every underdog shall have its day. And yours is coming . . . fast. Smallness has a way of overcoming—or using size to its advantage. Use yours.

For WORK questions. Small Hurdles! Good news for the little guy! What appears a major hurdle to the big guy is something you can just duck under. The future belongs to those who are not only lean and mean but flexible and nimble. But most of all, you've got to believe in what you are doing. <u>Outcome</u>: Small becomes big enough.

For LOVE questions. Nurture the Small! Those who are young or new need to be prepared—but for what? And how? The future belongs to those who are prepared to respond to the unknown. Learn to cope with change yourself, then pass this knowledge on. <u>Outcome</u>: Small wonders never cease to amaze you. Follow your inspiration.

For MONEY questions. Small Restraint! The little things add up, and small amounts—taken all together—become large sums. Exercise some willpower. The answer lies somewhere between saving it all for a windy day and blowing it as fast as you can. Seek the balance. <u>Outcome</u>: Three cents tossed is a future read. Ask again.

For STRATEGY questions. Small is Triumphant! This situation involves a dramatic finish to a slow start. Keep working on your skills. Keep mastering the technique. And always play your best game. <u>Outcome</u>: It is a Cinderella story.

BONUS ANSWERS FOR CHANGING LINES

Line 6: The little guy comes out on top. Take a lesson from the dark horse. Come from behind to finish first.

Line 5: Small keeps coming. Whatever you do, don't give up now. A breakthrough is just around the corner.

Line 4: Fine-tuning improves results. A few small adjustments are all that's needed now.

Line 3: Small successes multiply. Many little things contribute to the whole. Do each task well and to completion.

Line 2: Early results encourage. Take heart. Stay at it. And keep your fingers crossed.

Line 1: The little guy starts out on the bottom. Take a lesson from the underdog. Rise above.

THE DRIFTING CLOUDS

WIND/EARTH

Wind over Earth. *Think about it.* This is a diagram about things that are seen in other things . . . just like the clouds forming into random but easily recognizable shapes—the inkblot tests of the sky. Having drawn the sign of The Drifting Clouds, it is clear you have been thinking deeply about something. You have been contemplating a change. You have been watching and waiting for your chance . . . you have been looking for a sign. Now all you have to do is recognize it. Trust it, when it comes.

For WORK questions. Scattered Effort! Everybody seems to be going in a different direction—if not 10 different directions at once! And just when you thought you'd seen it all, another change gets dealt. Center yourself. Breathe deeply. Focus. Consider things from a different angle. All of a sudden things take a whole new shape. <u>Outcome</u>: Who would have thunk it?

For LOVE questions. Passing Thoughts! You have been thinking about something you're "not supposed to"—staring out the windows again and daydreaming. Fantasies are taking shape in your mind. Perhaps it's time you explored them . . . or dismissed them completely. The question is . . . <u>Outcome</u>: Who would you rather be with?

For MONEY questions. Calm before the Storm! It hardly looks like a Black Friday, does it? Let alone Black Monday! See what you will in the rumors of war. Take what you can from the latest polls. Weigh your risks. Plot your potential gains. And—most of all—pay attention to your hunches. Decide for yourself. <u>Outcome</u>: What did you conclude?

For STRATEGY questions. Look & Listen! You are in a situation that is changing slowly but rapidly at the same time. Rather than jumping on the first thing that moves, it's best to step back, look upward, and consider. Contemplate the big picture. What do you see? What does it look like to you? <u>Outcome</u>: Where will you be tomorrow?

BONUS ANSWERS FOR CHANGING LINES

Line 6: An act is premeditated. Take this current silence as consent and make your move. The winds are with you now.

Line 5: Cross your fingers and ride the winds. Forces greater than your own resolve are involved. Flow with them.

Line 4: Weigh the evidence against the reality. Separate what is possible and probable from what is otherwise only imaginable.

Line 3: Imagine what it would really be like. Picture things the way you want them to turn out. And imagine yourself there.

Line 2: Retreat, meditate. Prepare yourself for the impending changes by retreating into your own silence. The answer lives there.

Line 1: A premonition occurs. Take the current silence as an omen of what is surely coming. Brace yourself for the good news.

THE COLD FRONT

WIND/WIND

Wind over Wind. *Think about it.* This diagram is about things that get to you . . . the storm howling outside, rattling the windows, pounding at the door, penetrating even the weather stripping—trying desperately to get in. Having drawn the sign of The Cold Front, you can feel these changes in your very bones. The raging of an actual storm stirs everything up, shakes the deadwood from its place, and informs you of who's the boss. You may also be experiencing the effects of your own inner weather, or you may feel pressured from someone in a position of authority. At any rate, it's time to take cover.

For WORK questions. Slipping through Cracks! Something gets forgotten until it's long overdue. And the Powers that Be are none too pleased—it seems—with you. Don't sweat it. It'll all blow over, like a storm that rattles off. Salvage what you can. . . . <u>Outcome</u>: *Mea Culpa!* You may kiss the ring now.

For LOVE questions. Knock Before Entering! Whatever goes on outside these closed doors had better stay out there. And whatever goes on inside had best abide by the basic rules. Hide out under the covers while the latest crusade passes by. What they don't know about you won't hurt them. <u>Outcome</u>: It is better to pretend than to give in.

For MONEY questions. Kneel in Submission! A knock comes pounding on the door in the dead of night. The phone rings "not at this hour" again. It may well be it was just a billing error, but the Powers that Be have still revealed their true colors. And you have been forewarned. <u>Outcome</u>: Don't wait for an apology.

For STRATEGY questions. Conformity! This is a situation in which you are pressured to go along with the masses on their latest binge or be hammered into the ground until you submit. Peer pressure is a dangerous

thing, whether or not its intentions are good. At all costs, resist it.
<u>Outcome</u>: The blowhards have a way of blowing off.

BONUS ANSWERS FOR CHANGING LINES

Line 6: Rise from your knees. Your time of penance or oppression ends. Come back now among the living and do your work openly.

Line 5: Cast your private vote. When the curtains are drawn, you get the final say on who goes . . . and what stays.

Line 4: Render unto Caesar. Give the Powers that Be the things that keep them off your back. Then go on with your private life.

Line 3: Go through the motions. Keep up the pretenses while you plot your escape.

Line 2: Pretend to be sincere. Keep a straight face while you turn what is politically correct back upon itself.

Line 1: Drop to your knees. The only way out of this one is to give in. Repent. Apologize. Give in to conformity this time . . . at least for now.

THE STORM BREWING

WIND/THUNDER

Wind over Thunder. *Think about it.* This is a diagram about things that increase in intensity . . . like a storm brewing off in the distance and growing louder and louder as it approaches. Having drawn the sign of The Storm Brewing, you had better batten down the hatches and get ready to ride out the coming days and nights. Things will look better only after they have taken a turn for the worse. Prepare to watch and wait for the coast to clear.

For WORK questions. On Your Marks! All hell is about to break loose! And heads may even roll out the door before it's all said and done. But in the aftermath, you can look forward to an increase in benefits at least, if not in stature. Be a survivor. <u>Outcome</u>: What is left at the end of the day is more or less equally dispensed.

For LOVE questions. Get Ready! The lid's about to blow off the toothpaste again! (And who rubbed shaving cream on the towels this time?) Looks like you're in for a night of Truth or Dare. Try not to draw blood. Avoid saying what you will later regret. <u>Outcome</u>: Take two aspirins and call each other in the morning.

For MONEY questions. Get Set! It's going to be a night unfit for man or beast. But—ironically enough—in the wake of natural disaster, benefits accrue to you and dividends are dispensed. Your net assets increase. This could be the best thing that ever happened to you. <u>Outcome</u>: The government might even give you a handout. (But I wouldn't count on it.)

For STRATEGY questions. Duck! This situation involves a clear threat—but not a present danger—to your well-being. The National Weather Service has issued a warning. (But when was the last time they were right?) At any rate, you go out at your own risk tonight. <u>Outcome</u>: Hermits and thrill seekers have their work cut out for them. Both benefit from atmospheric disturbances.

BONUS ANSWERS FOR CHANGING LINES

Line 6:   A severe thunderstorm watch is called off. The excitement's over for now. The fireworks have fizzled . . . this time.

Line 5:   Better assume the prenatal position. Looks like you're caught unawares. Pull the blankets over your head.

Line 4:   Better hold on to your hat. The things that are coming your way could knock even your socks off.

Line 3:   Travelers are advised to be careful. For in strange places you can never be sure of the weather . . . or the rules.

Line 2:   In the event of . . . seek shelter immediately. Come in from the cold. Stay out of the damp. Cuddle up with someone you love.

Line 1:   A severe thunderstorm watch is in effect. Conditions are right for sudden changes of the intimidating kind. Brace yourself.

THE DRIVING RAIN

WIND/WATER

Wind over Water. *Think about it.* This is a diagram about things that are set apart . . . like sheets of rain being blown across the sea . . . like the whitecaps churning in the wind. Since you have drawn the sign of The Driving Rain, you are no doubt feeling a bit alienated. Something or someone has pushed you aside. Possessions have been dispersed, perhaps. Or a feeling of security has suddenly dissipated. You feel like the rug has been pulled out from under you. You feel like you've been stabbed in the back. The only thing left to do is stage a comeback.

For WORK questions. A Wet Blanket! Somebody wants to rain on your parade. It puts a damper on things, for sure. But—the truth to tell—these are only scattered downpours. Which means there is still a reason to hold out hope and trust in tomorrow. Outcome: The show must go on.

For LOVE questions. A Cold Shower! This relationship has gotten a little too close for comfort, it seems. A time-out is called by one of you. And a few tears are shed—perhaps in the bathroom. It's nothing you can't get over. And it's nothing you can't live through, forget, or forgive. Outcome: The question is, do you want to get over it?

For MONEY questions. Early Withdrawal! Funds are distributed from an interest-bearing account. But premature withdrawals carry a stiff fine, and a big chunk of it goes out in taxes. Oh well, it was all just on paper anyway. Take out what you need for the current hardship. Outcome: Put it back in when you can.

For STRATEGY questions. Fallout! This situation involves forces outside yourself. Things simply blow apart, crash down, or disintegrate. You are sure to feel the fallout. At the very least you are set on edge or made to see red. Your plans are put on hold. Your schedule is interrupted. You feel upset. Outcome: The only thing left to do is cry in your . . . 2% milk.

BONUS ANSWERS FOR CHANGING LINES

Line 6: The question is gone with the wind. You already know what the answer is. And frankly, my dear . . .

Line 5: Take a long last look. Say your fond farewells to the way things were. And sail off into the sunset.

Line 4: Rub your bleary eyes. What's done is done. What's past is gone . . . even if not forgotten. Should auld acquaintance . . .

Line 3: Blow your nose in a handkerchief. And consult Line 3 in your resulting hexagram.

Line 2: Keep a stiff upper lip. And no matter what happens, don't let them see you cry, tremble, or sweat.

Line 1: The answer is blowin' in the wind. And besides, some questions simply shouldn't be asked . . . at least not at this time. Try again later.

THE WARM FRONT

WIND/FIRE

Wind over Fire. *Think about it.* This is a diagram about things that are warm and welcome to the touch . . . like an unseasonable breeze coming suddenly north. Since you have drawn the sign of The Warm Front, it is clear you are in store for a warming trend—but more important, a few hugs. You feel warmly toward others. And they feel warmly toward you. Even if the words go unspoken, the feelings find expression in small ways. Some things do not need to be said to be understood . . . this is one of them.

For WORK questions. The Team! There are warm feelings in the workplace. A little proverbial stroking is going on, in fact . . . a little friendly pat on the back . . . or a warm handshake. It's nothing more and nothing less than that. But it makes all the difference. <u>Outcome</u>: Who would you rather work for?

For LOVE questions. The Household! Warm feelings invade the home front. Friends, relatives, and pets assemble for a "family" gathering. Not that everything is always peachy-keen among you, but you have your moments. And this is one of them. <u>Outcome</u>: Nice to see them come, nice to see them go. Make time for family.

For MONEY questions. The Members! A bunch of you get together by going in on something. Everybody chips in—some more than others—but everybody makes out in the end. It's more fair than square. But what the hay. It's a beautiful day out there that's just a'wasting. <u>Outcome</u>: Come on in. The water's fine.

For STRATEGY questions. The Network! This is a situation that involves feeling connected to other people . . . and feeling all warm and cuddly inside. Phone lines and computers may be involved, or maybe you actually still see people face-to-face. It's often a question of time, distance, and money—but what of these? <u>Outcome</u>: The family drifts apart and yet remains close.

BONUS ANSWERS FOR CHANGING LINES

Line 6: Turn to your extended family. Friends and acquaintances help you out right now . . . and the family approves.

Line 5: Make a couple of calls. Track down a few leads. Reestablish old contacts. Rehash old times.

Line 4: Join a couple of clubs. Get active. Be involved. Get interested. Expand your contacts. Extend your reach.

Line 3: Stay in touch with people from the past. Those who "knew you when" will always be a part of who you are. Don't be a stranger.

Line 2: Get to know the people you work with. Find out what you're up against and who you're in with.

Line 1: Turn to your immediate family. No one knows better right now than the people you grew up with. Blood is thicker . . .

THE CLOUDS GATHERING

WIND/MOUNTAIN

Wind over Mountain. *Think about it.* This is a diagram about things that make slow but steady progress . . . like the clouds gathering their forces behind the hills. Having drawn the sign of The Clouds Gathering, you, too, are developing—in your own way, on your own schedule, and in your own good time. Right now you need to gather your strength for an ensuing period of growth. Eat right, sleep well, work out, or psyche up—whatever it takes to give you an energy burst. You're going to need it.

For WORK questions. Slow & Steady! The going is not easy, but the view from the top is said to be worth it. You make your even progress up this slope by watching your step and placing your confidence in the right footholds. Easier said than done, I'd say. But keep plugging . . . and keep believing. <u>Outcome</u>: How you got there determines what you do when you get there.

For LOVE questions. Step by Step! Things are starting to happen in this relationship, even if the going is a little slow. Keep the tempo nice and easy. This relationship develops more fully when it lingers longer. Let it grow. <u>Outcome</u>: The opening act is only a buildup to the main event. (Better catch your breath at intermission.)

For MONEY questions. Little by Little! Material possessions are built up over time. Cash reserves are set aside for a rainy day. A few pennies are pinched. A few credit cards are cut in half. And wealth is eventually accumulated. But even then . . . <u>Outcome</u>: Only you can decide what's worth doing with your own money . . . and what's worth doing without.

For STRATEGY questions. Nice & Easy. You are in a situation that requires you to go through all the steps—one at a time—before you can achieve the end result. Develop your skills and techniques. Practice your resolves. And go nice and steady on your course. <u>Outcome</u>: By the time you arrive where you are going, they will be waiting for you.

BONUS ANSWERS FOR CHANGING LINES

Line 6: You climb over a brick wall. There is one more hurdle behind you. What will you do for an encore?

Line 5: Implement Phase 1. Make your initial moves. What needs to happen next depends on getting feedback from early attempts.

Line 4: Make a game plan. Map out some strategies and tactics. But play it by ear in the end.

Line 3: Sleep on it. Give your thoughts a rest, and let the answer come to you . . . when you're least expecting it. Eureka!

Line 2: Stop, look, and listen. The signs are there. But only you can (and must) read them for yourself.

Line 1: You come to a brick wall. Progress halts for a moment of silence while you consider your next move. Good luck.

THE SWIRLING MIST

WIND/MIST

Wind over Mist. *Think about it.* This is a diagram about looking deeply into something cloudy . . . like the center of a passing patch of fog. Having drawn the sign of The Swirling Mist, it is clear you are attempting to get to the heart and soul of a matter. You are peering into the murky depths of your own emotions, perhaps. Or you are gazing into your crystal ball to see what the future really, truly holds. The best you can hope for is a flash of truth that suddenly reveals all—both good and bad. But these inner workings tend to favor fleeting impressions that are subject to interpretation. It's all in the eye of the beholder. Behold.

For WORK questions. Sincerity! You need to decide what it is you really want to do, if not for a living, then for your life's work. Look in the want ads for ideas . . . but first look deeply into your own eyes. What is it you love to do more than anything else? C'mon now, tell the truth. <u>Outcome</u>: Now that you have found your mission, pursue it in your own way.

For LOVE questions. Understanding! Sometimes you think you know them better than they know themselves—but the same can be said by them of you. It takes a three-way mirror to reveal the facts. But it takes a magic mirror to see the truth lying in this heart. <u>Outcome</u>: To understand the other, first learn to see the self.

For MONEY questions. Truthfulness! What is going on under the surface of these transactions is anybody's guess. But one thing is certain: the face value is not a measure of true worth. Nor is the inscription on the money accurate of the kind of work it does. <u>Outcome</u>: Believe what you will . . . but trust in your own hunches.

For STRATEGY questions. Insight! This situation requires you to investigate below the surface of something. Use hindsight, foresight, and even your side mirrors if you like. (But remember, objects are closer than they seem, and everything is backwards.) <u>Outcome</u>: The truth of this matter lies within your own jurisdiction.

BONUS ANSWERS FOR CHANGING LINES

Line 6: What you feel is what you get. Take a friendly word of advice . . . from your intuition.

Line 5: Read your own body language. What is it you know inside? What is your mind trying to tell you?

Line 4: Look at their shoes . . . and then at your own. Whose would you rather be in?

Line 3: Shake their hand. Hello. So long. Way to go. Put 'er there. How do you do? The right sentiments come to you.

Line 2: Look them in the eye. Read what they are thinking in the look you get back.

Line 1: What you see is what you get. Consider carefully both what you look at and what you look for.

THUNDER

Thunder Signs

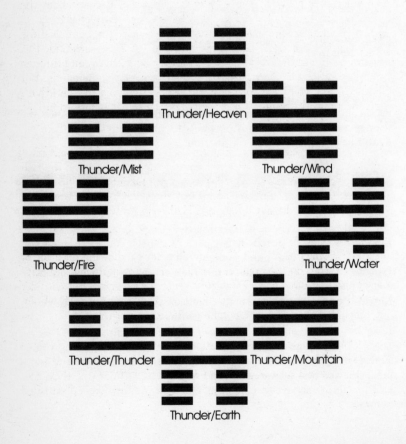

Thunder/Heaven

Thunder/Mist

Thunder/Wind

Thunder/Fire

Thunder/Water

Thunder/Thunder

Thunder/Mountain

Thunder/Earth

THE GREAT THUNDER

THUNDER/
HEAVEN

Thunder over Heaven. *Think about it.* This is a diagram about the things that are powerful . . . like a mighty clap of thunder high up in the sky. Having drawn the sign of The Great Thunder, it seems as if the Powers that Be are really ticked off this time. You are surrounded by powerful people who want to have their own way with, by, and through you. They push you. You push yourself to meet their demands. But sometimes, too, you push back—or at least are tempted to—and that's when the fireworks begin. Whatever happens here, it is sure to be . . . explosive.

For WORK questions. High & Mighty! The corporate tower is rumbling again. Thunder comes from behind the closed doors. And the fallout goes right on down the line. Brace yourself for some low blows. But remember, you are in ultimate control of the quality of the work that gets put out . . . or doesn't. <u>Outcome</u>: Hell hath no fury like a disgruntled worker.

For LOVE questions. Vim & Vigor! Someone's showing off a bit or trying to get your undivided attention. The snapping of fingers and clapping of hands are involved. Take these signs at face value. But consider your position: You say when. You say how. And you say with whom. <u>Outcome</u>: Hell hath no fury like an unconsenting partner.

For MONEY questions. Shirt & Tie! They will be expecting you to answer when they ask the questions of you. And if you want to see a dime, you had best submit. But never forget that without you, they, too, would be up . . . the creek. <u>Outcome</u>: Hell hath no fury like a dissatisfied customer.

For STRATEGY questions. Great & Powerful! This situation puts you up against some heavy hitters and maybe even a prima donna or two. It's best to hold your own tongue while another mouths off. But there is power, too, in silence. Strength comes from waiting for the right moment—in knowing when to push forward . . . and when to pull back. <u>Outcome</u>: Hell hath no fury . . .

BONUS ANSWERS FOR CHANGING LINES

Line 6:   Big backs off . . . but it is usually with bravado. Be a good sport. Try not to rub it in.

Line 5:   The riot act gets read . . . but it only tends to escalate the problems. It's time to choose sides.

Line 4:   Rules get changed . . . but it is the rule followers who must adjust. Fall in line, or else take a final stand.

Line 3:   Guilt gets heaped . . . but only the guilt-ridden react. Give no more blame than you are willing to accept.

Line 2:   Blame gets laid . . . but usually on a scapegoat. Keep your own nose clean and your own billy goat's gruff covered.

Line 1:   Big uses force . . . but not always to its own advantage. Play along and see what it gets you.

THE HOLLOW THUNDER

THUNDER/
EARTH

Thunder over Earth. *Think about it.* This is a diagram about things that rattle and hum . . . like the lulling roll of far-off—almost inaudible—thunder, the dull ringing in your ears on a clear and starlit night. Having drawn the sign of The Hollow Thunder, you are "at one" with the Music of the Spheres. You are tuned into the right channel. And you are set to the proper wavelength. You are homed in on the frequency of the world in motion. The emptiness you feel is the tip-off. When you feel calm inside, you will know the moment of truth has arrived—and it is good news.

For WORK questions. Harmony! Management is a low, reassuring voice that keeps its distance. The tempo in the workplace is nice to dance to. And everything and everybody is in sync. You have found the perfect job . . . for you. Congratulations! <u>Outcome</u>: The Powers that Be are looking out for you. Say thanks.

For LOVE questions. Happiness! Oh, it's not as if there isn't a little healthy grumbling once in a while or a distant longing from time to time. But all in all—and when all is said and done—you couldn't ask for a better companion. Come on, admit it! <u>Outcome</u>: The Powers that Be have blessed you. Say something nice.

For MONEY questions. Contentment! So your bank account is not Fort Knox. And your house doesn't overlook Central Park. There comes a time when enough is enough . . . and, besides, it just doesn't get any better than this. <u>Outcome</u>: The Powers that Be have shined on you. Be gracious.

For STRATEGY questions. Rejoicing! This situation is a cause for nothing but celebration. The only storm there is is a dud in the distance. All's right with your world . . . at least for the moment. Rejoice in it! <u>Outcome</u>: The Powers that Be have spoken a word in your favor. Hip! Hip! Hooray!

BONUS ANSWERS FOR CHANGING LINES

Line 6: This is your finest hour. Sit back. Put your feet up. Enjoy the feeling. Hang on to it as long as you can.

Line 5: You have all the time in the world. Hurry less. Laugh more. Get there in one piece.

Line 4: You have food, clothing, and shelter. Eat, drink, and be merry. Make love.

Line 3: You have each other. Stay close enough to remain in touch. Appreciate what you've got.

Line 2: You have your work. Throw yourself into it, but keep one eye on the clock. And cut out early once in a while.

Line 1: This is the moment you have waited for. So what are you waiting for?

THE TRAILING THUNDER

THUNDER/WIND

Thunder over Wind. *Think about it.* This is a diagram about things that are persistent . . . like the thunder rumbling as it fades away . . . like the far-off hum of cars on the interstate . . . or the train rattling in the distance. Having drawn the sign of The Trailing Thunder, you, too, must persevere and be relentless. It is only by continuously acting out your own story that you fulfill your true destiny. Look for the blinding light inside of you, and trail along after it. Steer where the light leads, and you will not get lost.

For WORK questions. Keep Plugging! There will always be rumors about what is "really" going on. And there will always be things actually happening behind the scenes. Don't let it distract you. Continue on your own straight path. And not to panic . . . <u>Outcome</u>: The storm passes as quickly as it comes. A period of anxiety is over.

For LOVE questions. Remain True! There are laws of human nature involved here, and cycles larger than life. Boys will be boys, girls will be girls, and you must be you—regardless of the label. Stick to your guns. <u>Outcome</u>: After the storm passes, the sky clears. And you are free to emerge from your hiding place.

For MONEY questions. Roll Again! Lady luck may not always be at your elbow, but when fortune turns, you will sure want to be there. Put yourself in situations where the odds are in your favor. Then play the cards you're dealt. <u>Outcome</u>: Sometimes you win, sometimes you lose— but it all evens out in the end, or so they say.

For STRATEGY questions. Persistence! This is a situation that requires you to hang in there. Be who you are. Do what you do. Go after the light you see. And let the rest believe what they will. No one knows what is going to happen, or who needs to be there when it does. <u>Outcome</u>: Ready yourself. Your time is surely coming.

BONUS ANSWERS FOR CHANGING LINES

Line 6: Be true to yourself . . . but not overindulgent. Keep all things in balance, both inside and out.

Line 5: Prepare for the task. Steady things. Ready things. Time things out in advance. Make a schedule.

Line 4: Take a few risks. Put your money where your dreams live. But most of all invest your time wisely.

Line 3: Indulge your passions. Explore your desires. Enjoy yourself. Make use of your idle hours.

Line 2: Pursue your hobbies. Follow your interests. Use your free time to do something you really want to do.

Line 1: Be sure of yourself . . . but not overconfident. Keep all things in proper balance.

THE THUNDERBOLT

THUNDER/THUNDER

Thunder over Thunder. *Think about it.* This is a diagram about atmospheric disturbances . . . like a bolt of lightning jagging down to the ground—lighting up the night and making your hair stand up on end. Having drawn the sign of The Thunderbolt, you should prepare yourself for a shock. A piece of news reaches you that bowls you over. An experience takes you on a roller coaster ride. Or you come a little too close for comfort to a danger zone.

For WORK questions. Revelations! The news is shocking . . . sending waves through the company. The implications go all the way from the top to the bottom. Doors slam. Teeth gnash. Fists clench. And it seems like the end of the world. But of course, it's not. <u>Outcome</u>: Truth can be stranger than fiction, especially when it's laced with lies.

For LOVE questions. Excitement! This relationship makes you tingle from head to toe. It rattles you, rolls you, takes you to new limits, and gives you a thrill a minute. It will also shock the living daylights out of you, if you give it half a chance! Exercise caution. Take necessary precautions. <u>Outcome</u>: An accident is avoided if you exercise common sense.

For MONEY questions. Panic! Money matters occur with some commotion. Sudden trading takes place. Or the rate of foreign exchange fluctuates (again). But by the time you hear the news, the opportunity is over. Write this one off. <u>Outcome</u>: Better luck next time.

For STRATEGY questions. Crisis! The situation requires you to think fast and on your feet. If you see the sky about to fall—by all means get out of the way. Soon you will have the opportunity to pick up the pieces. But first there is a little commotion to get through. <u>Outcome</u>: One, two, three . . . DUCK!

BONUS ANSWERS FOR CHANGING LINES

Line 6: You are the last to learn. Take a message from the things that reoccur.

Line 5: Run as fast as you can . . . either forward (charge!) or in the opposite direction (retreat!). Go as the spirit moves you.

Line 4: Cover your own tracks. Protect your own flanks. And maneuver into an advantageous position.

Line 3: Think 10 minutes ahead. But act on the instant. And be prepared to stop on a dime.

Line 2: Listen to a friend of a friend of a friend. But decide the truth for yourself.

Line 1: You are the first to know. Accept a confidence. And keep a promise.

THE YOUNG THUNDER

THUNDER/WATER

Thunder over Water. *Think about it.* This is a diagram about coming of age . . . like the thundering river that has not yet worn its way free and clear, but is still in the process of transformation. Having drawn the sign of The Young Thunder, you, too, are now in the act of breaking clear of your past restrictions. You are testing your voice, building up your muscle, and getting ready to release a ton of energy in the process of personal transformation. It's time to get out there on your own. This is the start of something new . . . and big.

For WORK questions. Shoot the Rapids! The future unravels like a continuous, coursing stream; but there are many channels, forks, and tributaries to explore along the way. In setting out on your own, you must make your own decisions and take your life into your own hands. <u>Outcome</u>: It is time to draw your own map of the wilderness and set your own course.

For LOVE questions. Untie a Knot! Whether it seems like the right time or not, the apron strings are about to be cut. A free spirit simply can't be held down for very long or kept forever in one place. The knot that once was tied tight is loosening again. <u>Outcome</u>: It is time to let go of someone . . . or get loose yourself.

For MONEY questions. Free Things Up! These are liquid assets you're dealing with. Money that was tied up in something is about to mature, pay off, or become available. Tangible items are turned into cash. Perhaps something is sold off or an inheritance is advanced. <u>Outcome</u>: It's time to count the take.

For STRATEGY questions. Liberate! This is a situation in which past complications or entanglements are suddenly overcome in a great rush of forward progress. You find yourself compelled, propelled, and thrust forward . . . perhaps into the spotlight. You are free and clear now to do what you want and to say what you think. <u>Outcome</u>: Welcome to the world that ought to be.

BONUS ANSWERS FOR CHANGING LINES

Line 6: The wheels of chance are spinning. And you will soon know where they stop. Say hello to your new tomorrow. This is it.

Line 5: An opportunity presents itself. Stare it in the face before you decide if it's for you. Separate truth from hype. Accept or reject.

Line 4: An account is settled. An old score is erased. You are a free agent again. Make a new wish. Select a new choice.

Line 3: A door shuts. But it was time to be closed. Door #2 opens up—and Door #3. Consider your options. Weigh the choices.

Line 2: A window opens. Take the opportunity to stick your neck out. Take the dare. Accept the challenge. Risk it.

Line 1: The wheels of change are turning. Say good-bye to the past. You will know soon enough what it was all leading up to.

THE THUNDER BALL

THUNDER/FIRE

Thunder over Fire. *Think about it.* This is a diagram about things that have achieved their ultimate manifestation . . . like a ball of fire rising from a lightning bolt. Having drawn the sign of The Thunder Ball, it is clear you are approaching a high point in your life. You are realizing your full potential. You are achieving your zenith. Or you are receiving a just reward for things you did in the past. At last your efforts pay off. At last Lady Luck shines on you. Congratulations! You've made it.

For WORK questions. Prosperity! Business is going great guns again, and you are making a substantial contribution to the bottom line. Your accomplishments here will not go unnoticed. For where there is fire, there are also smoke signals . . . and bosses who can read them. They know who you are. They know what you can do. And you are in their plans. <u>Outcome</u>: Power.

For LOVE questions. Abundance! This is an enriched and enriching relationship that literally explodes with enthusiasm. You have been struck as if by Cupid's arrow. And you are hopelessly, madly burning with desire for each other. What more can I say? . . . <u>Outcome</u>: Nirvana.

For MONEY questions. Riches! It's manna from heaven for you this time. But it's not as if you don't deserve a break. Consider yourself paid back with interest for an investment you made in the past. What will you do with it all? What a great problem to have! <u>Outcome</u>: Utopia.

For STRATEGY questions. High Point! This situation finds you lucking out in something of great importance to you. It's not that you haven't worked for it, mind you, but the results are even better than you ever hoped. You have simply outdone yourself this time . . . and been in the right place at the right time. <u>Outcome</u>: Sweet success.

BONUS ANSWERS FOR CHANGING LINES

Line 6: Swift progress occurs. Measure your advances in leaps and bounds. Rapid growth can be projected.

Line 5: An effort pays off. Measure your advances in percentage points gained or shares accumulated.

Line 4: A mortgage is burned. Measure your advances against the going rate and comparable prices.

Line 3: A favor is returned. Measure your advances in points scored or credits earned.

Line 2: A reward is offered. Measure your advances in dollars, cents, and return on investment.

Line 1: Sure progress is made. Measure your advances against a yardstick of your own making. How did you do against your goals?

THE RECEDING THUNDER

THUNDER/MOUNTAIN

Thunder over Mountain. *Think about it.* This is a diagram about things that occur in a sequence or series . . . like the fading echoes of the thunder moving away into the distance. Having drawn the sign of The Receding Thunder, you can look forward to a series of small successes. It is little by little and day by day, but definite progress is made, even by things that themselves are small. An existing pattern may be involved. Do things in order. Complete each step that is required before you move on. Get to know the sequence. Get into the rhythm. And if all else fails, make a game of it.

For WORK questions. Details! Your work has a microscopic element. It's all in the details. If there's a bad number somewhere, it's garbage in, garbage out. Yet you thrive on making all these little things add up into the Big Picture. Take your time. Do it right the first time. <u>Outcome</u>: Pay attention to your math.

For LOVE questions. Little Things! It's the small things that tend to count the most in a relationship. In this case, it is by succeeding in what is small that you will yet succeed in what is great. It's not how fast you get there that counts. The how, why, and wherefore are as important as the when. <u>Outcome</u>: Take it one step at a time.

For MONEY questions. A Little at a Time! You will achieve your financial goals dollar by dollar and bit by bit. Put a little aside each month. Or pay a little extra on your cards. The past can be put behind you if you set interim goals. <u>Outcome</u>: Chart your progress and performance over time.

For STRATEGY questions. Smallness to the nth degree! This situation favors those who appreciate the fine points. Success here depends on handling the small things right. Tend to the details. Work on the fine points. <u>Outcome</u>: Take a micro rather than a macro view.

BONUS ANSWERS FOR CHANGING LINES

Line 6: Small wins out. Workers . . . triers . . . believers—each makes a difference. Work. Try. Believe.

Line 5: Small accomplishments add up. It's one thing after another— or one thing on top of another—and it all counts in the end.

Line 4: Small succeeds in small things. But success is success, and nothing tastes sweeter, regardless of the impact.

Line 3: Small tries harder. It is no guarantee, of course, but it's always worth a shot. So do your best.

Line 2: Small gets by. It is not much. And yet it is enough to see you through for a little while.

Line 1: Smallness at the forefront. It is the little things that count most, at least right now.

THE OLD THUNDER

THUNDER/MIST

Thunder over Mist. *Think about it.* This is a diagram about things that are muffled . . . like the sound of thundering waves coming to the ear through a thick mist . . . like memories that are growing distant. Having drawn the sign of The Old Thunder, it is clear that you are having that old, familiar feeling again. A voice may actually call from out of your past. But more than likely it will be a voice in your head going off . . . like a distant alarm clock. This is your wake-up call, my friend. It's time to revisit the past if you want to learn the future.

229

For WORK questions. Old Home Week! You will get together with people from a former life. Old workmates make a sudden reappearance on the scene. Or you suddenly bump into someone you used to work with. What a coincidence! Take time to get reacquainted . . . and reoriented. Outcome: You continue where you last left off.

For LOVE questions. Going Home Again! A family gathering is involved, quite possibly the marriage of a young woman to her young man. The event recalls many a thing in you and reawakens an old feeling that has been sleeping on the job. You may only be young once, but you are never too old to fall in love. Outcome: Relationships are kindled . . . and rekindled.

For MONEY questions. Reviewing the Record! As you sort through your finances, you will know if you have overspent by whether or not the line items bring smiles or tears to your face. The money went where it did, but was it worth it? Learn something from your memories. Outcome: Resolutions are made . . . broken . . . and reevaluated.

For STRATEGY questions. Going Back! This situation requires you to review the past. Sometimes you have to watch the same video several times to get the nuances of the film and see how it all fits together. The same is true here. In your rush to move forward, take time to look back. Outcome: The lesson you were meant to learn eventually is in your reach right now.

BONUS ANSWERS FOR CHANGING LINES

Line 6: This is a marriage of the souls. Two destinies collide. This is simply meant to be.

Line 5: This is a marriage of the hearts. Two lives and lifelines intersect. Everything comes together at last.

Line 4: This is a marriage of the funds. Two accounts are merged. Joint assets are encouraged.

Line 3: This is a marriage of the bodies. Two life forces unite. Physical contact is favored.

Line 2:   This is a marriage of the minds. Two thought patterns come into sync. Mutual interests are the key.

Line 1:   This is a marriage of convenience. Two things come together for mutual advantage. Joint ventures are favored.

WATER

Water Signs

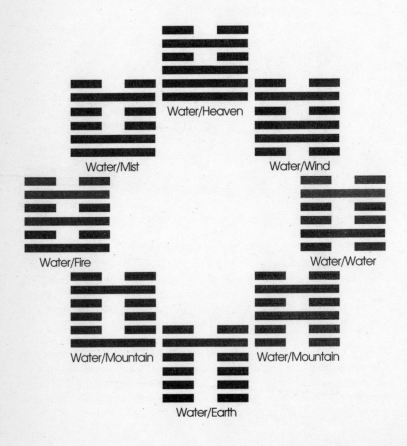

Water/Heaven

Water/Mist

Water/Wind

Water/Fire

Water/Water

Water/Mountain

Water/Mountain

Water/Earth

THE MILKY WAY

WATER/HEAVEN

Water over Heaven. *Think about it.* This is a diagram about things that take time . . . our galaxy on its slow sweep through the cosmos, stretching like a river through our own skies. Having drawn the sign of The Milky Way, you, too, will have to bide your time. For the Universe is in no hurry to get where it is going. And things can only happen as they should when given the time they need. This a time for patient—intentional—waiting for the things that are meant to be.

For WORK questions. Standing in the Wings! You have been preparing to make your move for quite some time—or so it seems. You are biding your time. You are waiting for your cue. It is the only thing you *can* do right now. But . . . <u>Outcome</u>: Time can be counted upon to pass.

For LOVE questions. A Trial Period! You decide to give this relationship its chance. You need to get a feel for each other. You need to find out what it would be like to go through life together . . . or apart. It is a calculated risk. But one way or another . . . <u>Outcome</u>: Time reveals the hidden truth.

For MONEY questions. Biding Your Time! Income flows in . . . and income flows out in a steady stream and consistent rhythm. Sometimes you buy, sometimes you sell, and sometimes you do neither. This is a time to wait cautiously. Hold on to what you've got for now. <u>Outcome</u>: When the moment is right, you will know.

For STRATEGY questions. Calculated Waiting! This situation requires you to put yourself intentionally into standby mode. There is no better course of action to take at this time. Sit back and go with the flow. Stand by and wait patiently. These things happen in their own time. <u>Outcome</u>: You'll get there eventually.

BONUS ANSWERS FOR CHANGING LINES

Line 6: Trust in the future. Await the signs of change as you pass the time. Things will look better tomorrow—I promise.

Line 5: Hang on . . . but only to the things of enduring importance and lasting benefit. All else can be left behind.

Line 4: Hold out. Remain firm in your beliefs, convictions, ideals, and dreams. And whatever you do, don't give up now.

Line 3: Give it a chance . . . to simmer . . . to gather strength . . . to sink in. These things cannot be rushed.

Line 2: Fear not. There is no use in being either worried or anxious about things that you cannot foresee, foretell, or influence.

Line 1: Hope for the best. Await news of an encouraging nature. Remain optimistic.

THE ANCIENT RIVER

WATER/EARTH

Water over Earth. *Think about it.* This is a diagram about things coming together . . . like the fresh waters flowing endlessly along their old and timeworn path. Having drawn the sign of The Ancient River, it is clear you are involved in a common effort with others. You are involved in a common cause. You are aiming to achieve a common goal. For it is only by combining your individual strengths now that you gain the power to fulfill your common purpose . . . and your collective destiny. The key word is cooperate.

For WORK questions. Strategic Alliance! You just can't do it all by your lonesome. But don't overlook the fact that there are others in the very same boat! If you can just get your heads together, you may yet be able to bridge the gap. Give and take in order to gain. <u>Outcome</u>: Two heads are bigger than one.

For LOVE questions. Equal Partnership! By combining your wages and deductions, you may yet get a tax break. But if the partnership ends there, it will never last. This relationship gains its very lifeblood from eating, breathing, and sleeping together. This is what forms the bond. So put your checkbooks aside. <u>Outcome</u>: Quality and quantity each play a role.

For MONEY questions. Combined Forces! Through a process of merger and consolidation, the bottom line looks like it could be improved. But in making your assessment, consider more than the math. Weigh equally the human factors. *Outcome*: Two wrongs do not make a right.

For STRATEGY questions. United Energies! This situation finds you suddenly sharing the same riverbed . . . getting "into bed" with someone else . . . maybe even sharing the covers. In merging your forces with another, you must inevitably sacrifice a little piece of yourself. A small concession is worth the price. <u>Outcome</u>: The whole is greater than the sum of its parts.

BONUS ANSWERS FOR CHANGING LINES

Line 6: This is a consummated union. But more important, it's enduring. This is one that lasts a lifetime. Best wishes.

Line 5: It takes a few years to pay off. Three to five years should be enough to tell if it can live up to its promise.

Line 4: It takes a few seasons to test. Give it a full year just in case, and then make your decision.

Line 3: It takes a few months to gel. In the meanwhile, let things run their natural course. Within three Full Moons you'll know.

Line 2: It takes a few weeks to get settled. Neither push nor rush these things at first. Give them a chance to take hold.

Line 1: This is a conceivable union. Consider what will spring from it . . . why? . . . how? . . . when? . . . and where?

THE DRINKING WATER

WATER/WIND

Water over Wind. *Think about it.* This is a diagram about the things that spring up . . . like water bubbling from the bottom of a well . . . like a bit of news that reaches your ear. Having drawn the sign of The Drinking Water, you can expect a close encounter with some chatty people at the water fountain or the coffeepot. At any rate, a fresh piece of gossip or the tail end of a rumor makes its way to you. Oh, it's just some variation on the same old story, and yet the details never cease to surprise us. Listen with a cautious ear—and an eye for entertainment value. You can never really know another person's story—let alone figure out the moral.

For WORK questions. The Source! A tasty tidbit makes the rounds, but before you believe everything you hear, better track down the source of the whisper. There is a truth to be learned from this. And it's about jumping to conclusions. <u>Outcome</u>: People will talk, but they seldom listen and rarely learn.

For LOVE questions. The Wellspring! Tears come to the eyes, but are they from laughter, sadness, or pain? The news brings a chuckle to the grapevine. But remember the victim. Only one heart knows the whole truth. Is it yours? <u>Outcome</u>: No one else can ever really understand.

For MONEY questions. The Tap! Money comes in a steady stream, as if from a secret source—or so it seems to everybody else. You know better, of course. But why would you let on? Let them think what they will. And let them say what they want. <u>Outcome</u>: Keep your secrets to yourself. Laugh all the way to the bank.

For STRATEGY questions. The Well! This situation requires you to deal with things happening below the surface or behind your back. The facts of a matter are one thing—they bubble up. But facts do not always reveal the God's honest truth. Get your news from the horse's mouth. Even so . . . <u>Outcome</u>: Don't believe half of what your hear.

BONUS ANSWERS FOR CHANGING LINES

Line 6: Call it as you see it. Make a judgment call. Reach a decision. Bring things to closure, once and for all. And speak no more of it.

Line 5: Keep your mouth shut. What is said, done, or determined is not to leave the room. Your lips are sealed.

Line 4: Tell no one else. Let these things go no further than your own two ears. Keep a confidence. Be a confidant.

Line 3: Swear each other to secrecy. Mind your own business. And keep your word—no matter how tempted or tricked.

Line 2: Get it from the horse's mouth. Discount secondhand knowledge. Steer clear of hearsay.

Line 1: Tell it like it is. Relate the facts. Express your opinions. But seek out the truth in the heart where it lives.

THE WHITE WATER

WATER/THUNDER

Water over Thunder. *Think about it.* This is a diagram about things that struggle at the start . . . like the thundering rapids roaring down their course. Having drawn the sign of The White Water, you, too, are going through a time of deep endeavor and temporary excitement. You may even feel out of control. It's just a passing thing, of course. In fact, you'll laugh about it someday. So for now, you might as well enjoy the thrill of these events as they unfold. It gives you much to talk about later. Wow-ee! What a ride!

For WORK questions. Learning Curve! You are new to this. And there are many twists and turns to figure out on this job. It is like one of those water park slides: You're coming up over the edge of the chute with your arms up over your head . . . and then all of a sudden you find yourself screaming! Yet in the end . . . <u>Outcome</u>: You want to do it all again!

For LOVE questions. Opening Stages! Even though you are each exactly what the other's computer profile matched, this relationship—like all—must struggle for its surge and spark. Shoot these rapids for what they're worth. But reserve your option to bail out. <u>Outcome</u>: Lucky you thought to wear your life vest.

For MONEY questions. Run for the Money! It looks like an opportunity to get ahead fast. But you'll have to hustle if you want to make a fast buck on this deal. What appears to be aboveboard may yet turn slippery . . . or leave you floating adrift. Be prepared to get a little wet—at least behind the ears. <u>Outcome</u>: There's no substitute for experience.

For STRATEGY questions. Struggling it Out! This situation pits you against the Forces of Nature. There are both false hopes and false starts in this world. And in your effort to rush forward, you'll have to learn quick and react fast. You'll either sink or swim, my friend. For this is a test. <u>Outcome</u>: Live and learn.

BONUS ANSWERS FOR CHANGING LINES

Line 6: Ten bucks says you *can* do it. Some things are mostly a matter of faith. Feel good about yourself, and take the plunge.

Line 5: Dive off the high board. Now is your chance to make a big splash. Tuck your head. Point your toes. Hold your breath.

Line 4: Race you to the end of the pool! The dare is made now. So what do you say?

Line 3: Jump in the deep end. But only if you already know how to swim.

Line 2: How long can you hold your breath? With every challenge comes a moment of suspense. Is this test even worth passing?

Line 1: Five bucks says you chicken out. Bouck-buck! (Perhaps you should!) At least give it a second thought.

THE DEEP

WATER/WATER

Water over Water. *Think about it.* This is a diagram about things that are dense, dark, and lonely . . . like the icy depths of the deepest seas. Having drawn the sign of The Deep, it is clear that you are in over your head. But take heart. There are external dangers to be sure—and pitfalls aplenty in this world—but the greatest threat invariably comes not from without, but from within. That is also where the answer to this problem lies. You'll have to look below the surface in order to figure this one out.

For WORK questions. Deep Doo-Doo! No one needs to tell you—for the signs are as clear as the spray from the fan—things are in a downward spiral. Things have sunk to new depths. And so have you. You are in it up to your BVDs. <u>Outcome</u>: To change things, first change yourself. It is the only way out.

For LOVE questions. Deep Feelings! Something deep, dark, and secret is about to surface. Erratic emotions, pent-up hormones, primal urges, and temporary insanity all combine to put you in a glassy-eyed mood. When the two of you get together it is like opposite currents competing. This is a game without set rules. <u>Outcome</u>: You will have to weigh the odds and options for yourself.

For MONEY questions. Deep Debt! The house is a money pit. The car is a lemon. The boat is like pouring money down the sink. And the RV sucks gas like an oil well. Where does it all end? The deeper you sink, the deeper it gets. <u>Outcome</u>: Learn to separate your needs from your caprices.

For STRATEGY questions. Deep Recesses! This situation is more like an emerging feeling rather than a particular event. You are up against something difficult to fathom or hard to imagine, let alone worm your way out of. These are simply uncharted waters you have entered. Survey the scene. <u>Outcome</u>: You must discover your own way out.

BONUS ANSWERS FOR CHANGING LINES

Line 6: Let this be a sign unto you. Proceed with caution . . . but also with conviction. And pay attention to your dreams.

Line 5: Send up a flare. Signal for help if and when you need it. Ask for a leg up or a hand out.

Line 4: Jettison excess baggage. You will make better progress if you travel light. Unload past biases and worn-out beliefs.

Line 3: Cling to your flotation device. Help comes to the rescue . . . but not always right away. Conserve your strength in the interim.

Line 2: Bail out while you still can. This is your chance to exit gracefully. Don't even think about lingering on.

Line 1: Let this be a warning to you. Read the signs like a flashing yellow light—but when you see it, slow down this time.

THE BOILING WATER

WATER/FIRE

Water over Fire. *Think about it.* This is a diagram about things that are practically finished . . . like hot water about to boil away into steam. Having drawn the sign of The Boiling Water, it is clear that you are coming to a turning point in your life. Things are ending and beginning for you at one and the same time. One stage, phase, or era is over now, and you are in the process of crossing over into a new set of terms and conditions. One last thing remains to be finished . . . the transition.

For WORK questions. Intuitive Leap! Add up all the numbers. Study all the facts. Review all the results. But then get away from it all. Put the lid on it and let it simmer. Conclusions have a way of bubbling to the surface. Catch them before they evaporate! <u>Outcome</u>: The answer comes to you in a hot bath.

For LOVE questions. Hot Water! A face turns the color of a boiled lobster. Someone's really done it this time . . . been caught red-handed, I'd say. What's done is done, of course. And what heats up usually cools back down again. But better be prepared to think quick. <u>Outcome:</u> Now that you have finally come to it, it's time to cross *that* bridge (even if it is burning).

For MONEY questions. Day of Reckoning! This is one of those things you can only understand once it's all over, done with, behind you . . . and too late. At the end of the accounting period, strike a balance, close the books, open a fresh spreadsheet, and wipe that sheepish grin off your face. Do better next time. <u>Outcome:</u> Equilibrium has a way of making a comeback.

For STRATEGY questions. After It's All Over! This situation involves a series of relatively small events adding up to the inevitable conclusion, the Grand Finale. But by this point, it's as much as already over . . . except for setting the fireworks off. <u>Outcome:</u> T minus 10 and counting.

BONUS ANSWERS FOR CHANGING LINES

Line 6: The moment passes. Everything builds up to a certain point but then evaporates into thin air. Write it off and start anew.

Line 5: Kiss and make up. Reconcile your differences before striking out again. Take another turn at bat. Cast another hexagram.

Line 4: Learn your lesson. Take time now to debrief and conclude. What will you know better next time? What have you learned?

Line 3: Think up a good line . . . to kick things off, or wrap things up. Adopt a motto. Coin a slogan to live your life by.

Line 2: Prepare mentally. Psyche up by clearing your mind of worries and distractions. Count backwards from a hundred. Learn to relax.

Line 1: The moment is at hand. You've worked, waited, wondered, and worried. Now the suspense is coming to its end.

THE RAINWATER

WATER/MOUNTAIN

Water over Mountain. *Think about it.* This is a diagram about things that are slippery when wet . . . like rain-slick mountain trails. Having drawn the sign of The Rainwater, you can expect some slow going now. Though the Forces of Nature do not intend to hinder your progress—and it is "nothing personal"—the result is the same. The distance you will cover at this time is simply much less than you had planned. There is a certain amount of lost time you can make up for later. But some opportunities are lost for good. Adjust your plans and expectations accordingly.

For WORK questions. A Difficult Task! It's nothing about you in particular. This is just a hard assignment that would stymie the best of them. Consider yourself in good company. These first steps may seem unsure or faltering. But ruling out dead ends is useful too. <u>Outcome</u>: After eliminating the obvious, consider the improbable and unlikely.

For LOVE questions. Difficulty in Walking! What can I say? The rain-streaked windows have fogged up again. There's nothing much else to do on a cold, desultory day except . . . make a day of it. This relationship takes its time to get there, but who's complaining? <u>Outcome</u>: It's a tough job, but someone's got to do it.

For MONEY questions. Slip-Sliding Away! The estimates, it seems, were just that! Things always cost a little more than you thought . . . but really! Hopefully you built in a little margin for error and you left a little cushion in the bank. Have wheels, will travel—but otherwise, what are you gonna do? <u>Outcome</u>: They've got you by the Michelins on this one.

For STRATEGY questions. Slow but Sure! This is a situation that demands your full concentration and complete attention span. The going may well be slow and hesitant—maybe even stumbling and bumbling. But you are in it for the duration. And you have no choice but to push ever onward and upward. <u>Outcome</u>: Some headway is made.

BONUS ANSWERS FOR CHANGING LINES

Line 6: Run the gamut. There is a mental test to be passed. Draw from both your knowledge and experience.

Line 5: Cope with the coincidence. Random events sometimes play into your hand or foil your best-laid plans. Either way, you learn.

Line 4: Deal with the accidental. Consider something off-the-wall or unforeseen at the start.

Line 3: Exhaust the possibilities. Eliminate the options one by one. Try out even the unlikely combinations.

Line 2: Explore the maze. There are both blind alleys and dead ends here. Use trial and error to find your way.

Line 1: Run the gauntlet. There is a physical challenge to be passed. Muster both your strength and courage for this test.

THE MORNING DEW

WATER/MIST

Water over Mist. *Think about it.* This is a diagram about the things that you feel in your bones or that get under your skin . . . like the dampness of a wet morning. Having drawn the sign of The Morning Dew, you have come up against some physical limitations. Joints and muscles may be involved—or maybe you're just having a knee-jerk reaction to something. At any rate, there is a distraction that turns your thoughts inward and your focus onto your own well-being.

For WORK questions. Rules & Regulations! New policies and procedures go into effect, despite their counterproductive aspects. It tends to cramp your style and alter the entire mood. What is the benefit of tolerance? What is the price of compliance? <u>Outcome</u>: Consider working at home.

For LOVE questions. The Facts of Life! The sunrise can be just as spectacular as the sunset—I know. But how many all-nighters have you got left in you? Listen to what your body is telling you. <u>Outcome</u>: The flesh is willing to restrain, but the free spirit has a mind of its own.

For MONEY questions. Jerked Around! Why is it those who control the purse strings think you are their puppet? Haven't they already determined enough about your life by setting your standard of living? How about giving your own knee a jerk? <u>Outcome</u>: Develop alternative revenue streams.

For STRATEGY questions. Branching Out! This situation is like bamboo. Your life is divided into distinct segments separated by knotty transitions. There are periods of wet and dry, with dampness and swelling in between. You are at one of these junctures. <u>Outcome</u>: It is time to mark a turning point.

BONUS ANSWERS FOR CHANGING LINES

Line 6: The Powers that Be have decided. The only recourse left is petition and defiance.

Line 5: The road to hell is paved with good intentions. A truly good end demands truly good means, or else it is all vanity.

Line 4: The quality of virtue is not strained. Show mercy, compassion, and forgiveness to your fellow human beings.

Line 3: A little knowledge is a dangerous thing. Consider all angles before you jump to conclusions.

Line 2: One man's virtue is another man's vice. And without diversity there is no balance.

Line 1: The surgeon general has determined . . . But it's not how long you make it, it's how you make it long.

FIRE

Fire Signs

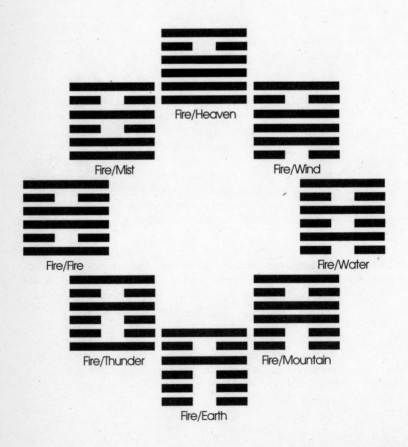

Fire/Heaven

Fire/Mist

Fire/Wind

Fire/Fire

Fire/Water

Fire/Thunder

Fire/Earth

Fire/Mountain

THE SHOOTING STARS

FIRE/HEAVEN

Fire over Heaven. *Think about it.* This is a diagram about common destinies . . . like a storm of meteors riding out their nights together—in a streak of jagged light. Having drawn the sign of The Shooting Stars, it is clear that your life is carried out in the company of loyal companions. Compared to a relatively stark, empty, and lonely Universe, you possess great abundance. You have both friends and acquaintances. And you travel in good company. Count your blessings.

For WORK questions. Intangible Assets! There is something good about this job that's hard to pinpoint or pigeonhole. It's not just the work—it's the company. Not everything can be measured in dollars and cents. If you must count something . . . <u>Outcome</u>: Count on your friends.

For LOVE questions. Great Eyes! When you look into the depths of these baby blues all else will cease to matter but the spark and sparkle from deep inside. She has a great personality. He's an interesting character. And together they possess all that matters. <u>Outcome</u>: Strut your stuff.

For MONEY questions. Rich Relatives! You find yourself in a pocket of prosperity. But more than likely it's the poor cousins you can really count on in a pinch. At any rate, you are lucky to have the choice. Blood is thicker than water. <u>Outcome</u>: Make a wish upon a star.

For STRATEGY questions. Great Having! This situation involves great wealth in the things that matter. Money in vast amounts may be a part of it—but if so, you will truly have everything. Mostly you have companionship. And you are blessed in the things that truly matter. <u>Outcome</u>: You stick together.

247

BONUS ANSWERS FOR CHANGING LINES

Line 6: You share a common future. Build it together and share the responsibility for how it all turns out in the end.

Line 5: It's like money in the bank. You can almost count these chickens before they're hatched. (But I wouldn't if I were you.)

Line 4: It's all in the blood. Everything is relative here. You share a common past even if not a common heritage.

Line 3: You just naturally hit it off. What you have in common is worth the price of tolerating what you do not.

Line 2: You can be yourself here. What is "good" and what is "bad" strike an even balance in this perfect relationship . . . for you.

Line 1: You share a common past. Hold on to your memories. Build on the past foundation. Go forward together.

THE BRUSHFIRE

FIRE/EARTH

Fire over Earth. *Think about it.* This diagram is about progress through chemistry . . . like the fire clearing the way by altering everything in its path. Having drawn the sign of The Brush Fire, you can expect sure, swift progress now. But before building something new, remember it often takes an act of destruction to level the ground first. Weigh carefully what you tear down in the name of progress . . . and what you save. Choose wisely, my friend. You make the call.

For WORK questions. Fire Drill! The faces are the same in the workplace, but the titles have all been switched around. A fire of sorts spreads through the file room, and all the old stuff is shredded and burned. A new company name is christened. And you're back to square one. But . . . <u>Outcome</u>: It's just a reinvention of the wheel.

For LOVE questions. Six-Alarm Blaze! Uh-oh, my pretties! This one's going up in flames. Or is that your socks on fire? I can't tell whether you're clearing the way for a new fling or getting a head start on this one. At any rate, it's a smoker. Handle with care. <u>Outcome</u>: You be the one to decide.

For MONEY questions. False Alarm! You know all that money you haven't been circulating? That little nest egg you have tucked away in a safe place? Those Keoghs and IRAs and certificates of deposit and U.S. savings bonds? Well, nothing's ever really safe, but if I were you, I'd . . . let them mature. (Fooled you, didn't I?) <u>Outcome</u>: Keep your money in the bank.

For STRATEGY questions. Dial 911! This is a situation that progresses rapidly, and before you know it, things have spread out of control. You'll need to leap into action at the first sign of crisis and take decisive steps to save your . . . personal effects. <u>Outcome</u>: Drastic change precedes swift progress.

BONUS ANSWERS FOR CHANGING LINES

Line 6: The temperature's falling. Watch the digital readouts carefully. Dress in layers, and light a fire.

Line 5: Looks like it's time to cool down. Better throw some cold water on this one. Count to 10 before you speak.

Line 4: Looks like things are cooking now. Keep an eye on the clock and make sure nothing boils over.

Line 3: Looks like it's starting to smolder. Better keep a lookout for further developments (which are about to happen fast).

Line 2: Looks like it's heating up out there. Wear as little as possible, but be careful not to get burned.

Line 1: The temperature's rising. Monitor the signs of coming trouble. Watch for danger signals and warning lights.

THE LICKING FLAMES

FIRE/WIND

Fire over Wind. *Think about it.* This is a diagram about cooking things up . . . like the fire of a gas range licking the bottom of the pot. Having drawn the sign of The Licking Flames, it would seem you're cooking up a little something for yourself. Or is it food to impress the boss? Food to feed a little cold? Food for the soul? At any rate, simmer till done. And let stand a few minutes before serving. Happy deliverance! Happy Thanksgiving! Dig in.

For WORK questions. Potluck! You can look forward to a little morale booster in the workplace. Either everybody brings in a hot dish or somebody stands up and gives a pep talk. It's food for thought, all right, but . . . Outcome: Why are you still hungry at the end of the day?

For LOVE questions. Peking Duck! With your busy schedules, who has time to cook? Order carryout for two, and spend a quiet evening cuddled up in front of the fire. Outcome: Pay attention to what your fortune cookie says. (Or, better yet, use your chopsticks and consult the I Ching together.)

For MONEY questions. Chateaubriand! Don't look now, but your dinner's on fire! Or is that why it costs a hundred bucks a plate? What can I say? Eat your heart out if you can afford it! But if I were you, I wouldn't dare ask for an ashtray. Outcome: What can I get you for dessert? Choose your own poison, and let others choose theirs.

For STRATEGY questions. The Back Burner! This is a situation that requires a slow-cook method. There is simply no way to rush through the process and expect the stew to turn out. In this case the process is as important as the ingredients. Use the Crockpot. Outcome: Some things are worth waiting for. Some things are worth giving up other things for . . . and this is one worth the sacrifice.

BONUS ANSWERS FOR CHANGING LINES

Line 6:   It's your own recipe now . . . and something you can be proud of claiming. Go on, indulge yourself.

Line 5:   Throw in a few things of your own. But don't vary too many ingredients at once. Give it the old taste test. And then decide.

Line 4:   Follow the instructions . . . but not to the point of doing something dumb. Life is a thought process. Think things through.

Line 3:   Measure precisely. But remember, formulas and statistics are not always accurate. You may need to innovate and improvise.

Line 2:   Don't forget the secret ingredient. Don't be afraid to add a little magic touch of your own. Spice up your life.

Line 1:   It's an old family recipe. But what worked in the past may not always hold true. Update. Adjust. Validate. Confirm.

THE FIRE BREAKING UP

FIRE/THUNDER

Fire over Thunder. *Think about it.* This is a diagram about things that are subject to reform . . . like the wood that is burned . . . like the fire breaking up, crashing in upon itself. Having drawn the sign of The Fire Breaking Up, you feel like the world is changing around you. And these changes may be hard for you to swallow. Someone may even be trying to force them down your throat. As always, the will of the few is carried out only with the consent and help of the many. Your best friends are turned against you.

For WORK questions.   Open Wide! Someone is attempting to make you swallow some half-truth. Still, everyone else is jumping on the bandwagon, so you're faced with a choice. Either stand alone or give in to the tide of popular opinion. <u>Outcome</u>: Consensus based on fear is the easiest to achieve. If you can't beat 'em, join 'em?

For LOVE questions. Bite the Bullet! There may be a little physical "discomfort" here at first. (But fortunately the feeling you describe as anguish is just all in your head.) "We're really only here to help you," said the inquisitor. <u>Outcome</u>: Hatred builds consensus faster than love. Do unto others . . . ?

For MONEY questions. Bend Over! There's a new tax proposal up on the Hill . . . and a whole new bunch of reforms. But is that a great big bite coming out of the budget? . . . or an even bigger piece out of your pay? <u>Outcome</u>: Silence builds its own consensus. Read my lips . . . ?

For STRATEGY questions. Crushing the Resistance! This is a situation in which one extreme is replaced by another through a violent process. But don't be fooled. The threat here is often sugarcoated, and the damage done leaves no scars . . . except on the inside. <u>Outcome</u>: Peer pressure is the oldest trick in the book. Beware the popular cause.

BONUS ANSWERS FOR CHANGING LINES

Line 6: Made in Germany? Who would have thought it? Things come full circle again. But does the past ever really repeat itself?

Line 5: Made in Cuba? I guess you could say it's time to hand out cigars. Past conflicts are at last resolved. (Got a light?)

Line 4: Made in Moscow? Ideals trade places. New converts are won. New players are found. But old ways die hard.

Line 3: Made in the People's Republic? Look for the union label. Roles and responsibilities shift. Find bargains offshore.

Line 2: Made in Japan? You get what you pay for, but in this case at least the price is right. Good things come in tiny boxes.

Line 1: Made in America? The quality goes in before the ads go out. Caveat emptor. (Better sign up for the maintenance deal.)

THE GREEN-WOOD FIRE

FIRE/WATER

Fire over Water. *Think about it*. This is a diagram about things that are not quite ready yet . . . like firewood that hasn't been aged properly. Having drawn the sign of The Green-Wood Fire, you are involved in something that is sputtering and smoking—and can't quite get started on its own. The problem is, you are jumping the gun. It's not time for these things to happen yet. And you can't force them. A season of curing is involved. Give it time.

For WORK questions. Almost, but Not Quite! Things remain unsettled in the workplace for yet another season. A few things need to be worked out or corrected in the weeks and months ahead. I'd give it another calendar quarter to shake out. Keep things under wraps till then. <u>Outcome</u>: You have a fire lit under you.

For LOVE questions. Not Yet Across! You've come quite far in this relationship, but still there is a final line to cross . . . there is a final phase to go through or a last point to resolve. I'd give it at least a month to six weeks to work itself out. Put it on the back burner for now. <u>Outcome</u>: The truth of a matter is realized after a trial period.

For MONEY questions. Not Yet Realized! Some money is sitting out there with your name on it, but you've got to do something yet in order to get it. Bills that others owe you remain outstanding for still another 30 days net due. You may have to go after accounts receivable in order to improve your cash flow. <u>Outcome</u>: In the end, you get what you're due . . . or at least what you have coming to you.

For STRATEGY questions. Before It's All Over! This is a situation that requires you to keep working on something you thought was already resolved. There will be a few parting shots before the bitter end has actually arrived. Things drag on and out—maybe even for as long as a full

253

year. But it is only their natural process. <u>Outcome:</u> Having started, there is no stopping now. Sit tight.

BONUS ANSWERS FOR CHANGING LINES

Line 6: Your business is finished. Finally! Now's your chance to take a little break. Here's to a refreshing change of pace.

Line 5: Wait and see. You have done all you can do but fret. And why do that? Let it go. It will all happen soon enough.

Line 4: Go after what's coming to you. Call in your markers. Demand your rewards. Chalk up some points. Even the score.

Line 3: Write the last chapter. What does it all add up to? What have you learned? Why? And what does it prove?

Line 2: Finish what you've started. Tie up loose ends. Wrap up work in progress, and then move on.

Line 1: You have unfinished business. Tend to it now. Get it out of the way.

THE ETERNAL FLAME

FIRE/FIRE

Fire over Fire. *Think about it.* This is a diagram about things that were simply made for each other . . . like two flames merging to form a single, enduring light. Having drawn the sign of The Eternal Flame, it is clear that your destiny involves a labor of love. For in the single, solitary act of going about your own business, you have caught up with the thing you adore. Callings, soul mates, and life's works are involved. Two hearts beat as one. Two missions collide. Two souls unite.

For WORK questions. Two Peas in a Pod! There's just a magical sort of synergy to this team effort. It's as if the minds have melded. You share a common vision of who, what, when, where, how . . . and why. And your ideas set each other on fire. <u>Outcome:</u> You share a burning passion.

Fire Signs

For LOVE questions. Two Moths at the Flame! Your attraction for each other is compelling. Two lost souls bump into each other—after all these years! The result is rather gravitational. You dance around the light that drew you to the same place at the same time. <u>Outcome</u>: You share a burning obsession.

For MONEY questions. Two Covetous Old Sinners! Extended purchasing power and bottomless unmet needs come together in this picture of the perfect consumer. But with every luxury comes a new necessity . . . to maintain, update, and replace. Buyers and sellers hit it off. <u>Outcome</u>: You share a burning compulsion.

For STRATEGY questions. Two Lights in the Darkness! This is a situation that involves a candle burning at both ends. Two life forces are on a collision course with destiny. The truth—as always—lies between their two extremes. But together these two entities glow—as if forever—with a combined light. <u>Outcome</u>: You share a burning desire.

BONUS ANSWERS FOR CHANGING LINES

Line 6: You belong to someone. Take this commitment seriously. Trust each other fully . . . honor and forgive.

Line 5: You come from similar backgrounds. Take solace in your mutual experience. Here's to a lifetime of shared adventures.

Line 4: You share similar interests. Shoot the breeze and exchange a few tips. You'll hit it off immediately.

Line 3: There is a mutual physical attraction. Or is it love at first sight? I guess there's only one way to find out.

Line 2: You have the same general idea. Conduct a meeting of the minds and see what comes of it.

Line 1: You report to someone. Ask plenty of questions. Prepare plenty of answers. And work toward the same goal.

THE SIGNAL FIRE

FIRE/
MOUNTAIN

Fire over Mountain. *Think about it.* This is a diagram about signaling for help . . . like the fire set intentionally on a high hill to attract attention. Having drawn the sign of The Signal Fire, it is clear that you are about to send up a few flares yourself. Time, distance, and travel are involved. And there is a distinct possibility you may even get lost along the way. If so, trust in the kindness of strangers. Look for the candle burning in the window. And in an emergency, guide your fellow travelers out of harm's way.

For WORK questions. Roughing It! Your work takes you on the road, but perhaps not in the style to which you are accustomed. Still, the change in scenery—and the break in routine—will help you see things in a new light. Strangers you meet along the way add to your perspective. Strike up a conversation. <u>Outcome</u>: If you get lost, ask for directions.

For LOVE questions. Roaming! Two strangers meet under remote circumstances and sheer coincidence . . . or is it? Perhaps you are hitchhiking around Europe, kicking around Mexico, or just shopping at the supermarket. At any rate, you bump into a perfect stranger. And the rest is history. <u>Outcome</u>: You share an adventure.

For MONEY questions. Wandering! Your money has the urge to go! And in this case, you can and should take it with you. This is a time for expanding your horizons and having an adventure or two. But real thrills never come cheaply. Take plenty of cash, traveler's checks, and good old American Express. Otherwise . . . <u>Outcome</u>: Travel lightly.

For STRATEGY questions. Traveling Abroad! This is a situation that finds you leaving your home turf and venturing out into the wide world. Take your time. Ask for guidance. Along the way your path will come across many whom you might not otherwise have met. Get to know them. But most of all, enjoy the scenery. <u>Outcome</u>: The road-weary traveler returns home with empty pockets and a head full of new ideas.

BONUS ANSWERS FOR CHANGING LINES

Line 6: Strange bedfellows. Though highly unlikely and doubly improbable, the unexpected occurs this time, in defiance of all odds.

Line 5: Stranger in a strange land. Everything is new, unfamiliar, and odd. But in time, you'll know it like the back of your hand.

Line 4: Stranger things have happened. Nothing should surprise you by now, and yet . . . Here you go again.

Line 3: Stranger than fiction. The truth is more interesting in this case than the packaging. Watch out for little white lies.

Line 2: Strange feelings. It's difficult to put a finger on it—or words around it. You have to trust your own instincts.

Line 1: Strangers in the night. There is a meeting, and an exchange of some kind . . . then a going in separate directions again. Could it be coincidence?

THE GUIDING LIGHT

FIRE/MIST

Fire over Mist. *Think about it.* This is a diagram about things that light the way . . . like a torch piercing the darkness . . . like a flashlight revealing the path . . . like the line of a searchlight cutting the thick mist. Having drawn the sign of The Guiding Light, it is clear you are looking for direction in your life. Fear not. Help is on the way. For though the quest is not straightforward nor the path definite, the end is certain. But know this: When the light reveals the way, you must be willing to follow. The choice is always yours.

For WORK questions. In the Dark! I don't know what it is exactly, but you're feeling like an outsider all of a sudden. The workplace just seems to be closing in on you, until you can't see the point anymore. Take a hint. Seek career guidance. <u>Outcome</u>: A new opportunity presents itself. But will you bite?

For LOVE questions. Left Out! A pall of silence has fallen between you two. Or a veil of secrecy has been dropped around you. You feel as if you are walking underwater. But at last the answer comes to you in a blinding revelation. <u>Outcome</u>: You see it all for what it is. And now you are free to reach your final decision.

For MONEY questions. Shady Deal! This opportunity either seems too good to be true . . . or actually is! A real joint venture involves both parties sharing the expense and taking an equal risk. A little light needs to be shed on a contract or legal document. <u>Outcome</u>: All you really need to know is written in the fine print. Read it carefully.

For STRATEGY questions. Tunnel Vision! This is a situation that leaves you feeling lost. It is as if you are walking through a dark tunnel with no end in sight. But suddenly you see the light. How could you choose not to follow it? And yet it is a big decision. <u>Outcome</u>: The writing is on the wall, but you must read it for yourself.

BONUS ANSWERS FOR CHANGING LINES

Line 6: Two households both alike in dignity . . . The point is, it is better to combine forces than to feud.

Line 5: Hide and seek. Lie low while you sort things out for yourself (and until it's safe to come out).

Line 4: Hunt and peck. Search for the keys that unlock the hidden message. Speak in secret codes.

Line 3: Lift and separate. Dissect the whole. Label the pieces. Then reassemble.

Line 2:   Divide and conquer . . . but first build consensus among your
          equals.
Line 1:   A house divided against itself . . . The point is, it is better to
          stick together than to fight each other off.

MOUNTAIN

Mountain Signs

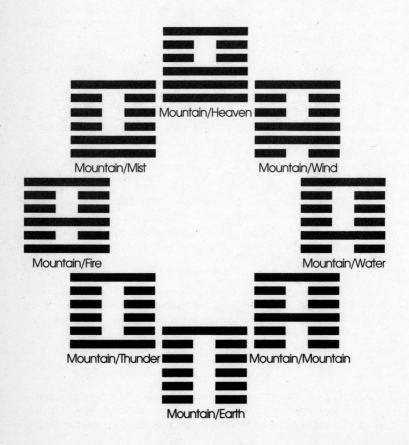

Mountain/Heaven

Mountain/Mist

Mountain/Wind

Mountain/Fire

Mountain/Water

Mountain/Thunder

Mountain/Mountain

Mountain/Earth

MOUNTAIN OF THE GODS

MOUNTAIN/HEAVEN

Mountain over Heaven. *Think about it.* This is a diagram about things that have great ambition . . . like the peaks of the mountains reaching toward the sky—toward the heavens and toward God. Having drawn the sign of the Mountain of the Gods, you are in the process of building up your courage and gathering your strength for a major undertaking. This is a test that involves both the physical and the mental. Body and mind come together in this heroic effort where, as a mere mortal, you match your wits against the Powers that Be.

For WORK questions. Big Is Tamed! It is the single, solitary climber who—with flexibility, staying power, and commitment—manages to conquer the mountain. And in this scenario, it is the "little guy" who wins out over the big corporation. <u>Outcome</u>: Maneuver your way unseen at the feet of the mighty.

For LOVE questions. The Bigger They Are! You may be out of your league. But just because a situation is challenging doesn't mean you can't give it a shot anyway. It is the strong, silent, and difficult-to-read who often are the most worth reaching. Go after the one you want. <u>Outcome</u>: Aim for the skies.

For MONEY questions. Big Bucks! The gap between rich and poor is wide—but there's plenty of ground for maneuvering in between. If you want to make it to the top of the pay scale, you can do it. But the days will be long, and the work, grueling. You'll also have to make some sacrifices and take some risks along the way. <u>Outcome</u>: There is no such thing as a free lunch.

For STRATEGY questions. Potential Power! This is a situation that involves something larger than life—a great challenge, an ambitious goal, or high expectations. Great resolve is required to reach the heights you have targeted. But for those with commitment and endurance, the reward is worth the price. Make your plans. Map out your trail. Focus on tactics. <u>Outcome</u>: You have the power to move mountains.

BONUS ANSWERS FOR CHANGING LINES

Line 6: Repeat the lessons of the past. Do these things until you get them right or at least until you learn the moral of your story.

Line 5: Big becomes small again. No power base lasts forever (thank God!). Await the passing of greatness.

Line 4: Big has its price. Make your best, last, and final offer . . . but better make it good.

Line 3: Big has a soft spot. Appeal to the heart of the lion that roars. Remove a splinter from the foot of the beast.

Line 2: Big gets fat and lazy. Be careful about assuming that things will go on like this forever.

Line 1: Learn the lessons of the past . . . especially your own past. What has somebody been trying to tell you?

VALLEY OF THE SHADOW

MOUNTAIN/EARTH

Mountain over Earth. *Think about it*. This is a diagram about things that cast a pall over other things . . . like the long shadow of the mountain creeping across the valley floor. Having drawn the sign of the Valley of the Shadow, you are experiencing a sinking feeling. Day by day subtle changes alter larger things. Until one day the past is gone forever, even if not for the good. The world as you know it is fading away. No wonder you feel blue.

For WORK questions. Collapse of Power! The Powers that Were are no longer the Powers that Be—even if you really can't tell the difference in the new and old regimes. What was God's truth in the past no longer even counts. It's a whole new ball game. But where are the bases? And who's on first? <u>Outcome</u>: Out with the old, in with the new—and up with the next batter.

For LOVE questions. Falling Out! This relationship undergoes a superficial change, accompanied by a change of heart. The shadows of the past tend to come back to haunt you. Gather your memories and divide the photographs. The sun is setting on an era. <u>Outcome</u>: Get ready to begin again.

For MONEY questions. Erosion of Assets! Even that which appears solid is not unshakable. Funds that seem to be building up may actually be shrinking in constant dollars. Creeping inflation has its long-term price, and there are no sure bets or secure hedges. <u>Outcome</u>: In tomorrow's money, things will be a bargain at today's prices.

For STRATEGY questions. Strip Back! This is a situation that requires you to slough off the things that you no longer need or have no further use for. The shadow erases what a former light has cast. But a new dawn is coming fast. Be ready to make headway tomorrow. <u>Outcome</u>: What shall you write on the blank slate?

BONUS ANSWERS FOR CHANGING LINES

Line 6: The playing field is level once again. Map out your winning strategy. Learn a new position.

Line 5: The opportunities are opening up. As they come knocking, one by one, you will have to decide.

Line 4: The rules are changing. Now's your chance to help define the new ones. Be fair about it.

Line 3: The look of things is altering. Consider your own appearance. Fit in now by standing out.

Line 2: The context is changing. Find your newly defined role. Refit yourself into the new scheme of things.

Line 1: Things are deteriorating fast. It's time to look out for yourself. Plan what you want tomorrow to look like.

THE SMOKING VOLCANO

MOUNTAIN/WIND

Mountain over Wind. *Think about it*. This is a diagram about things building up again . . . like the mountain about to restructure itself in a burst of molten rock. Having drawn the sign of The Smoking Volcano, it is clear that you yourself are going through a period of regeneration. This is a time of recovery and renewal. Physical, mental, psychic, emotional, or spiritual factors are involved—maybe all of the above. You are changing. You are evolving. You are growing again.

For WORK questions. Services to Render! Either planned or natural obsolescence works its way on things. This is a time that favors repairs and replacements. The old breaks down or blows up. But where there is smoke, there are new sales to be made and profits to be had. Create something new to replace the worn-out. <u>Outcome:</u> Gain comes following an initial loss.

For LOVE questions. Services to Perform! A period of illness precedes a period of recuperation and ultimate healing. In the interim, mineral baths and herbal tea may be in order. Or try a hot water bottle. Take the other's pulse and temperature. Monitor the vital signs. <u>Outcome:</u> Here's to a speedy recovery.

For MONEY questions. Duties to Perform! This investment is a fixer-upper if I've ever seen one. There's a great deal of sweat labor involved. But in the end, your hard work will show both on the surface and on the bottom line. <u>Outcome:</u> Rehab the old into something brand-new. Refinish. Refurnish.

For STRATEGY questions. Roll to Play! This is a situation that involves a dirty job . . . but someone's got to do the cleanup and start the rebuilding effort. You might as well roll up your sleeves. In the end you'll wonder how you did it . . . but be glad you did. <u>Outcome:</u> Psyche up for the coming recovery.

BONUS ANSWERS FOR CHANGING LINES

Line 6: No gain, no pain. Nothing comes from nothing. But in this case, nothing is won . . . and nothing is lost.

Line 5: Just do it. When all else fails to motivate you, crack down on yourself. (Nobody said it had to be fun.)

Line 4: Will yourself. Muster your determination and inner resolve. Make a commitment to yourself. Push.

Line 3: Endurance counts this time. Hang in there . . . keep plugging . . . and all that rot. Try, try again.

Line 2: Two steps back, one step forward. The farther you go, the behinder you get. It's progress, all right—but mostly in reverse.

Line 1: No pain, no gain . . . or so they say. Invest time, money, and effort in the things that produce the payoff you want.

THE MOUTH OF THE VOLCANO

MOUNTAIN/THUNDER

Mountain over Thunder. *Think about it!* This is a diagram about the stomach growling . . . like the mountain that is starting to speak in angry tongues—as if demanding an offering. Having drawn the sign of The Mouth of the Volcano, you are hungering after something yourself— some kind of spiritual nourishment, no doubt. Whatever it is you find in the process, be prepared! It may be a little hard to digest at first. Some personal sacrifice may be involved in this soul-search. Call upon your Guardian Angel . . . and your Spirit Guide.

For WORK questions. Open Jaws! Where the dead-at-heart lie down on the job, the vulture circles. And it is only a matter of time until the Powers that Be clamp down hard (again). Watch out or else you could become the next human sacrifice of downsizing. Better yet, plot your escape. <u>Outcome</u>: At the last moment, there is a sudden reprieve . . . and a big choice to make.

For LOVE questions. Sudden Cravings! Uh-oh, pickles and ice cream for everyone! (Or is it strawberries Romanov?) Whatever your passion fruit . . . you're dying for a taste of it right now, and that tummy of yours is growling up a storm. Ah, what the heck. Indulge these whims. Feed this hunger. Nourish your soul. <u>Outcome</u>: You're eating for two now.

For MONEY questions. Deep Pockets! This scheme may seem rather like an open pit to the financially nervous. But as long as the dream hungers on in you, the investment is worth a calculated risk. How close can you get to the edge before vertigo grabs hold? Set your upper limit, but . . . <u>Outcome</u>: Put your money where your heart is.

For STRATEGY questions. Hungering After! This is a situation that finds you compelled to do something rather drastic. Your own innards egg you on here, and it is difficult to resist the tug and pull of these compelling forces. Both the body and the soul make their stirring, gurgling demands on you. And they will not be quieted until you have fed both. <u>Outcome</u>: Starve a fever, feed the soul.

BONUS ANSWERS FOR CHANGING LINES

Line 6: Give in to something. Baby yourself. Allow yourself a treat—just this once.
Line 5: Sacrifice your resistance. Give in to a matter of slight importance in order to gain much more than that which shows.
Line 4: Sacrifice your money. Do with less in the bank now in order to make good your future.
Line 3: Sacrifice public opinion. Quit worrying about what others will think of you. Do what you know is right.
Line 2: Sacrifice security. Nothing is quite permanent or safe. Give up some current lifeline in order to secure the long run.
Line 1: Give something up. A sacrifice is needed to get the things you want, need, or require. Hang something up.

THE RIVER GORGE

MOUNTAIN/WATER

Mountain over Water. *Think about it*! This is a diagram about things that are inexperienced . . . like the young river digging its way through the bedrock. Having drawn the sign of The River Gorge, it is clear that no matter how old you get, you retain some sense of innocence . . . optimism . . . youth . . . and trust. The world is big, new, and open to you. And you are always learning something new. Keep up the good work.

For WORK questions. Inexperience Counts! You may be new to the team or new on the job. At any rate you feel as if you have a lot of catching up to do to get up to speed. But your lack of on-the-job experience is actually a blessing in disguise, since you are not set in the old ways. Offer your unique perspective on things. <u>Outcome:</u> Try something that was ruled out in the past.

For LOVE questions. The Offshoot! They may well be the spitting image of you, but they have minds of their own. Yes, it would be nice if they could benefit from your experience. But then, they'd miss out on the thrill of learning for themselves. And besides, they keep you young. <u>Outcome:</u> The same old story is played out . . . but with a brand-new ending this time.

For MONEY questions. A Fool & His Money! So it's a whim! So it's a waste of money! How can you expect to learn the value of a dollar (and at today's rates!) unless you win some and lose some for yourself? Immaturity leads to maturity. But since the game is always changing, you must keep an open mind. <u>Outcome:</u> Ignorance quickly turns to knowledge . . . and there are always new lessons to learn.

For STRATEGY questions. Youth! One solution to the situation you face is no doubt obvious to those older and wiser. Seek their opinion if you like. Just remember nothing works quite the same way twice. So you will have to follow your own intuition in the end. <u>Outcome</u>: Experience is a good teacher, but no two situations are the same. Make your own choices.

BONUS ANSWERS FOR CHANGING LINES

Line 6: Go the way of your own experience. Learn from the things that happen to you. Reach your own conclusions.

Line 5: Gain fresh insights. Look at things from a new direction. Seek different opinions.

Line 4: Learn from your early mistakes. Apply your experience to the task at hand.

Line 3: Try things out for yourself. Give new things a test drive. Expand your horizons. Take a spin around the block.

Line 2: Suspend your disbelief. See the reality in your dreams. Imagine. Visualize. Allow yourself to be drawn into the story.

Line 1: Go the way of youthful innocence. Experiment. Experience. Grow in wisdom. Mature in confidence.

THE AUTUMN HILLS

MOUNTAIN/FIRE

Mountain over Fire. *Think about it!* This is a diagram about things that put on a good show . . . like the fall hills wearing their coat of many colors. Having drawn the sign of The Autumn Hills, it is clear that you, too, are a thing of beauty . . . and a joy forever. So put on your Sunday best or your Friday night duds—if you please—and head for a night out on the town. Days and nights like this come few and far between. If you only have one life to lead, you might as well catch a few of the dusk- to-dawns . . . a few glorious sunsets, a few moonlit nights, and a few golden sunrises.

For WORK questions. Dress for Success! If you want to get to the top, you'll have to play the part. In a world that buys the cover of the book, you really have no choice. Just make sure you can deliver what you promise. <u>Outcome</u>: It takes a big tree to stand out from the forest.

For LOVE questions. Beauty Is Skin-Deep! You can adorn these weary bones to your heart's content—and you might even snare a mate or two in the process. But what lasts is not the part that blows away in the smoke. She walks in beauty that glows with inner light. Still . . . <u>Outcome</u>: May this night last forever.

For MONEY questions. Designer Checks! It's just paper, you know! And nobody really cares about what's going on in the background of these monetary instruments. As long as your signature is in the right place and nothing has changed up in the address line, you're good for it, right? <u>Outcome</u>: What's money for?

For STRATEGY questions. Say Grace! This is a situation that involves an extravagance of some sort. But sometimes you've got to go out in style, and this is one of those times. Take a deep breath and haul out your wallet. You'll be glad that you did when someone says thanks. <u>Outcome</u>: Buy baubles, bangles, and beads.

BONUS ANSWERS FOR CHANGING LINES

Line 6: Cubic zirconium can be forever, too. It's the thought that counts and not the substance.

Line 5: Pearls go before swine. Share your treasures with those who will appreciate them.

Line 4: Clothes make the man . . . or so they say. Be neither impressed nor taken in by wolves in sheepskin.

Line 3: Nothing glitters quite like a gold band . . . especially if it's placed upon the third finger of the left hand. Best wishes to you both.

Line 2: Accessories make the woman . . . or so they say. Be neither misled nor bedazzled by the accouterments. Look, but don't touch.

Line 1: Diamonds are forever . . . like the stars that made them . . . and the love that shines on and on.

THE MOUNTAIN PASS

MOUNTAIN/MOUNTAIN

Mountain over Mountain. *Think about it.* This is a diagram about matters of principle . . . like the mountains keeping in their place and never shifting from their base. Having drawn the sign of The Mountain Pass, you, too, have come up against a matter that takes some getting around, living through, or passing over. Deep thought is the only answer. In stillness and solitude, the truth comes to you. And at last you know.

For WORK questions. Doing What Is Right! There is some moral decision associated with your work at this time. And you must decide where it is that you will draw the line. Does a little compromise sacrifice everything? Is it necessary sometimes to get around the rules? In moral matters, there is always some shadow of a doubt. <u>Outcome</u>: Hold on to your ideals, but face up to reality.

For LOVE questions. Resting on Principle! It may seem like it was a small thing to you, but the issue is certainly much larger. And now that some doubt has been cast, you will have your hands full making up for it. What was it all about? And what does it really mean? <u>Outcome</u>: Doing the honorable thing is not always the right thing.

For MONEY questions. Holding on for Dear Life! You find yourself on some pretty rocky financial ground. And you'll have to watch your footing. But if you can pay off a little principle, the interest payments will go down, too. Give your finances the respect they deserve. Hold on to your assets . . . and your honor. <u>Outcome</u>: The grass really is greener over this hump.

For STRATEGY questions. Following the Right! The situation you are in calls for you to look inward for a sign. The odds seem incredible (because they are!). But by returning to the basics, you can surmount

270

the obstacles you face. Pause. Reflect on your situation. Consider the options. Review your beliefs. But most of all, believe in yourself. <u>Outcome</u>: Stay true to your higher principles.

BONUS ANSWERS FOR CHANGING LINES

Line 6: See your way out. Work around your current limitations. Fill in the gaps. Take shortcuts wherever you find them.

Line 5: Make an exception. Bend the rules a bit for a good cause. Show mercy.

Line 4: Yield to your conscience. Do what the voice of reason advises.

Line 3: Watch your step. And mind your own business.

Line 2: Think before you act. What are the consequences? What is risked and what is gained from this?

Line 1: See your way in. Then work from the inside.

THE SHRINKING HILLS

MOUNTAIN/MIST

Mountain over Mist. *Think about it!* This is a diagram about things fading in the distance . . . like the hills obscured by the gathering mist. Having drawn the sign of The Shrinking Hills, you need to size things up again. What is large is suddenly reduced or humbled. What is firm and definite suddenly becomes intangible, indiscernible, and hidden. You have come down to the things that really count here. But you will have to wait for the smoke to clear to see what's left to count on.

For WORK questions. Reduction in Force! Layoffs are as likely as hirings in the business world. And it's always possible to tighten further an already tightened corporate belt. Some appear to lose at first, but when the smoke clears . . . <u>Outcome</u>: You are all just about as well off as before the purge.

For LOVE questions. Decline in Passion! Things have settled into a routine, it seems . . . and yet this dark cloud comes as a surprise and a new development. The fog that descends upon you now just as easily lifts, revealing the strength of your relationship. <u>Outcome</u>: Things are even more solid than they first appeared.

For MONEY questions. Temporary Reduction! You may have to take a voluntary cut in income or put in a day of unpaid labor in order to get through a looming crisis. You may even have to dig into savings or leverage your current assets until a period of gloom passes. But once you weather this unstable time . . . <u>Outcome</u>: There is a return to normalcy.

For STRATEGY questions. Tighten Up! This is a situation that requires you to pull in the reins a bit. Your world is shrouded right now, and it's difficult to see two steps in front of you, let alone farther into the distance. The best thing to do is bide your time . . . and abide in your efforts. Scale back and focus on the facts. The situation will be clarified shortly. <u>Outcome</u>: When the fog passes, you'll see things in their proper perspective.

BONUS ANSWERS FOR CHANGING LINES

Line 6: Take it easy. Nice and slow . . . ready, steady . . . Don't let it get you down.

Line 5: Hold your breath . . . lest what is gained is suddenly lost, or you wake to find it all a dream.

Line 4: Keep your fingers crossed. Make a wish. And hope for the best.

Line 3: Approach slowly. And be somewhat cautious of putting your trust in ephemeral things.

Line 2: Go quietly. There is really no other choice but to remain patient.

Line 1: Keep it simple. There is no need to be elaborate right now . . . or to elaborate a point to death.

MIST

Mist Signs

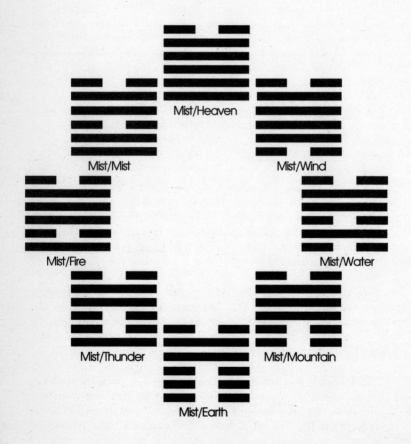

Mist/Heaven

Mist/Mist

Mist/Wind

Mist/Fire

Mist/Water

Mist/Thunder

Mist/Mountain

Mist/Earth

THE NORTHERN LIGHTS

MIST/HEAVEN

Mist over Heaven. *Think about it.* This is a diagram about things making a special appearance . . . like the long fingers of the aurora borealis streaming their occasional way through the skies. Having drawn the sign of The Northern Lights, it appears that you have come out of the darkness yourself. You have singled yourself out. You have revealed your true colors. Or you have made your own unique statement. The result is spectacular. People stand up and take notice. A finger is pointed at you. You are the center of attention.

For WORK questions. Visionaries! Rising stars burn out fast in their hurry to fix their place. But every once in a while, there is a glimmer of hope and a fresh vision of the future. Hook up with the one whose ideas ring true. Look, too, for the truth that burns inside you. <u>Outcome</u>: The future's in the bag.

For LOVE questions. Luminaries! This couple glows with a pure radiance. Your lives have intertwined. Your destinies have intermingled. Arm in arm you spread your span of influence now, by setting the good example. Be fruitful, but do not overmultiply. <u>Outcome</u>: This one has a fairy-tale ending . . . really!

For MONEY questions. Breakthroughs! A growing impression becomes a sudden inspiration. Your net worth spreads out. Equity builds. Investments come to term and pay off. At last you see your way clear. A buffer or a reserve is built up. Security is achieved. This is the good life. <u>Outcome</u>: Tomorrow takes care of itself.

For STRATEGY questions. Resolution! This is a time for realizing things, for coming to natural conclusions, and for reaching your true potential. Your direction suddenly crystallizes and takes shape. Decisions you made in the past pay off. Choices you could not bring yourself to make, suddenly are made for you. It seems as if this is the way things were simply meant to turn out. <u>Outcome</u>: Let it be.

BONUS ANSWERS FOR CHANGING LINES

Line 6: Bad rulers are overcome. Enjoy your sudden reprieve. Choose carefully which successor you will give your loyalty to.

Line 5: The past is all behind you now . . . and your good fortune has come to pass. Welcome to the future.

Line 4: The prospects are looking up. Remain confident, certain, and sure. Predestined things are taking shape for you.

Line 3: Your time has come to shine. Sit back. Relax. And be who you are. Just act natural.

Line 2: The foreseeable future is bright. Look hopefully ahead to a new era.

Line 1: Bad rulers are overthrown. Do your part to see justice prevail. Hold them responsible.

SCATTERED PATCHES OF FOG

MIST/EARTH

Mist over Earth. *Think about it.* This is a diagram about things that gather together . . . like the mists sweeping the earth and gathering mass. Having drawn the sign of the Scattered Patches of Fog, it would appear you are in the process of pulling yourself together. The pieces of your life are suddenly falling into place. Your act is coming together. Your strength is drawing up from the center. The emphasis is on family and friends here. Take a piece of good advice from someone who cares about—not only for—you.

For WORK questions. Assembly! The troops are called into the auditorium. Fresh notepads are placed in the training rooms. New skills are needed in the workplace. But not to fear. Even old dogs are capable of learning new tricks. <u>Outcome</u>: It's time to assess your strengths and minimize your weaknesses. Keep expanding your skills.

For LOVE questions. Family Gathering! Everyone blows into town for the holidays (or some other excuse) to catch up with one another and compare notes on old times. Some things never change, of course. But it's funny how each cloud makes its own way through the world, and how each life has a mission of its own to fulfill. <u>Outcome</u>: A passing meeting renews old bonds. Catch up on what's been going on.

For MONEY questions. Collecting! A little here . . . a little there—if you just added it all up once, perhaps the results of your investment would surprise you. At any rate, you have all you need for the moment and that's better than most ever get. Gather your liquid assets together and live within these means. <u>Outcome</u>: Community property laws apply. Share it all with those you love.

For STRATEGY questions. Get Together! This is a situation that involves gathering up everything you've got or everybody you know. By amassing things that share a common interest, great strength is achieved . . . and even greater synergy. In this case, the whole is greater than its parts. <u>Outcome</u>: Act in the collective interest.

BONUS ANSWERS FOR CHANGING LINES

Line 6:   Timing is part of it . . . but not all: Better late than never . . . better finished well than in on time . . . and best done right the first time.

Line 5:   Get some immediate feedback. Gauge your progress along the way and adjust your actions accordingly.

Line 4:   Set both your lower and upper limits, but aim for a range in the middle. Meet halfway on an issue. Come to the center.

Line 3:   Establish reasonable time frames. Neither push for everything at once nor defer any one thing forever.

Line 2:   Synchronize your watches. Ally with like-minded others and agree on a well-orchestrated plan.

Line 1:   Timing is everything. Plan the sequence of events ahead of time and keep to the schedule.

THE FOG BANK

MIST/WIND

Mist over Wind. *Think about it.* This is a diagram about the passing of greatness . . . like the massive fog bank stretching out to three horizons and moving up the coast. Having drawn the sign of The Fog Bank, you have the honor of living in times of greatness. You are watching history unfold around you. You are a witness to the great changes taking place. But know this: Everything you see is fleeting. All the more reason to feel honored at getting to see and be a part of the here and now.

For WORK questions. Times of Transition! The old ways of doing things have gone out of style, but the new ways have not yet materialized. Anything and everything is possible . . . at least for this moment. Things are still taking shape. They are still malleable. And you can still have a say in how they shape up. <u>Outcome</u>: Toss in your three cents worth.

For LOVE questions. Let the Good Times Roll! Things couldn't be going any better, or so it seems. First there was the moonlight on the water, and now this outside force that literally drives you into each other's arms. What a coincidence! <u>Outcome</u>: It couldn't have gone better if you'd planned it this way.

For MONEY questions. Critical Mass! When the conditions are right, you'll know it. A variety of forces need to come together to create this perfect opportunity. But when it happens there will be no time for second thoughts. It takes a split-second decision now. <u>Outcome</u>: Are you in? Or not?

For STRATEGY questions. Changing Times! This situation finds you smack dab on the verge of revolutionary changes. Things are happening minute by minute. And you can hardly keep up. Watch! Witness! Decide! Contribute! <u>Outcome</u>: There's no time like the present.

BONUS ANSWERS FOR CHANGING LINES

Line 6: Great things are passing. Something or someone bigger than life is about to rush by. Keep a lookout. At least get an autograph.

Line 5: What is the risk of hanging on? Being left behind by others. What is the risk of letting go? Being left to your own devices.

Line 4: What does the moment hold? Nothing but potential. What will you do with it? Whatever you please. Make a wish.

Line 3: Where will you be tomorrow? Consider where you have been and where you are now.

Line 2: What have you come to? A turning point? A crossroads? A bottom line? Suddenly it all comes down to a single choice.

Line 1: Great things are arriving. An idea whose time has come, comes. You know a good thing when you see it.

THE FOGHORN

MIST/THUNDER

Mist over Thunder. *Think about it.* This is a diagram about adapting to change . . . like the passing ships warned by the wail of the siren to take necessary precautions and make necessary adjustments. Having drawn the sign of The Fog Horn, it is unfortunately certain you are facing unseen dangers too. Your environment is changing rapidly around you. And it is impossible to tell the mist for the haze. Watch and listen for the warning signals. The only way to survive is to respond and adapt . . . quickly to the unforeseen.

For WORK questions. Changing Course! It may well be midstream, and this development may be nothing like what you bargained for. But this is the time when the fittest survive. It is not enough to stay on course, for you must not only keep your bearings but you must steer out of danger's way. <u>Outcome</u>: Good news for those who respond quickly and take the lead.

For LOVE questions. Minor Adjustments! Look before you blow the whistle. Talk it over with each other. Perhaps you got off to a bad start, but all is not yet lost. And there is plenty of room for maneuvering into a way of life you both feel comfortable with. <u>Outcome</u>: Steer clear of depth charges. Watch out for smoke screens.

For MONEY questions. Get Back on Course! Okay, it was a temporary lapse. But be glad of the warning. You must return to your resolve before you look back with regret on your excesses. Consider this a past-due notice. <u>Outcome</u>: Your prompt and immediate attention is required. Act by the deadline.

For STRATEGY questions. The Search! This is a situation that finds you feeling your way without much to go by. You will have to sharpen your senses—even those you don't use very much. Trust your ears, your nose, and—most of all—your gut. <u>Outcome</u>: React at the first sign of danger.

BONUS ANSWERS FOR CHANGING LINES

Line 6: Lead your followers . . . but do not lead them astray. Reward trust by taking responsibility. Be worthy of respect.

Line 5: Recruit others . . . but not just anyone. Select your confidants with care, and your companions with caution.

Line 4: Don't let things slip. But if a few things do fall through the cracks, you can always make up for it. Get on with it now.

Line 3: Put in the hours . . . but only to the point of diminishing returns. There is only so much productive time in a single day.

Line 2: Take up the slack . . . but not all of it, at least not by yourself. Do your part and lend a hand, but don't be taken advantage of.

Line 1: Follow the leader . . . but not blindly. Reserve your trust for those who treat you with the respect and consideration you deserve.

THE VAPOR

MIST/WATER

Mist over Water. *Think about it.* This is a diagram about making it through a period of difficulty . . . like a boat drifting through dense, impenetrable fog. Having drawn the sign of The Vapor, perhaps you are feeling as if your environment is just a little too close. There's not enough breathing space. Or visibility has been reduced. Why is it the inconsequential things always seem to get to us the most? Look deep within yourself first. Then you will see how you can thrive despite these adverse conditions. Quit complaining. Start contributing.

For WORK questions. Exhaustion! You can't go on putting in double and triple shifts over such a flimsy excuse. Yes, the situation is dire and you can't count on anyone quite like you can count on yourself. But your own safe passage depends this time on more than your own willpower and personal moral fiber. <u>Outcome</u>: Heave ho, my friend. Work toward the common good.

For LOVE questions. Weariness! It seems like you can't help but get on each other's nerves. It's the little things that are spoken about, but the truth is: One needs more space. And one requires less distance. There needs to be a meeting in the middle. Each side has to give. <u>Outcome</u>: Heave ho, my friend. Give in a little.

For MONEY questions. Burdens to Bear! Whether you are swimming in a sea of debt or in a green haze of money, eventually you feel you are drowning. And you can't catch your breath. It's time to grab on to something more substantial . . . like solid ground. Muster your courage. . . . <u>Outcome</u>: Climb out, my friend. Pull yourself up.

For STRATEGY questions. Repression! The situation you are in involves your own perceptions of things—which at this time are cloud-ed. You feel oppressed. You simply cannot see a break in the troubles that surround you. And you are in it up to your ears! But the answer is already known to you. <u>Outcome</u>: Reach out, my friend, by reaching in.

BONUS ANSWERS FOR CHANGING LINES

Line 6: A tree growing in an enclosure. It is time to overcome limitations of all kinds. It is time to branch out.

Line 5: A tree whose growth is stunted. It is time to make do on less. Make the most of what you've got.

Line 4: A tree that cannot spread its limbs. It is time to stop growing until things around you change. Work around limitations.

Line 3: A tree that cannot sink its roots. It is time to spread out rather than shoot up. Adjust to your surroundings.

Line 2: A seedling in search of sunlight. It is time to reach for the sky. Work your way up.

Line 1: A plant fading for lack of room. It is time to pick up roots. Move to where the environment suits you better.

WOODSMOKE

MIST/FIRE

Mist over Fire. *Think about it.* This is a diagram about things that change into other things . . . like the hardwood turning into smoke, steam, and ash. Having drawn the sign of the Woodsmoke, you are undergoing a personal transformation of epic proportions. The time has come to shed your skin and start down a new course. This is a time of rebirth and renewal. The caterpillar becomes a butterfly. The seed becomes a flower. And you become . . . the new you.

For WORK questions. Renovation! Look for new furniture and fixtures, maybe even a new office . . . but it may not be in the place you think. A change of setting as well as scenery is in the works. Stand by for a sudden news flash. <u>Outcome</u>: You make a radical departure.

For LOVE questions. Changing Nature! A definite role reversal is in your future. An entirely new kind of relationship emerges out of the ashes of the old. Your understanding is reborn and a new commitment is made. A new future stretches out in front of you. <u>Outcome</u>: Go forth together.

For MONEY questions. Revitalization! Nothing works quite the way it used to. The investment strategies that worked in the past no longer apply. And you must adjust your portfolio accordingly. Those who make the turnabout come out tomorrow's winners. <u>Outcome</u>: Something entirely different pays off big this time.

For STRATEGY questions. Transformation! This is a situation in which everything reverses. Things break down into their component parts and return to their natural states in a blinding burst of heat and light. What remains often bears no resemblance to its former self. But this is the changing nature of things. So you have no choice but to . . . <u>Outcome</u>: Take on a new identity, and adopt a fresh outlook.

BONUS ANSWERS FOR CHANGING LINES

Line 6: Lucky you have a thick hide . . . or else you might feel these barbs. Somebody's jiving you—and you're laughing right back.

Line 5: A skin becomes a hide. Thus, one thing serves two purposes. You, too, will be asked to perform double duty in the days ahead.

Line 4: Fly by the seat of your pants. But make sure you keep your barn door shut.

Line 3: Caught by the hair of your chinny-chin-chin. But by an equally slim margin, you manage to slip away like a greased pig.

Line 2: By the skin of your teeth, you get by. And good for you! You come in under the wire.

Line 1: Lucky you have a thick skin. Or else all these changes might just get to you. Roll with these punches. Come out a winner.

THE LINGERING FEELING

MIST/MOUNTAIN

Mist over Mountain. *Think about it.* This is a diagram about mutual attraction . . . like the mountain drawing down the mist . . . like the mist clinging to the mountain. Having drawn the sign of The Lingering Feeling, it's clear that you are mutually attracted to someone or something. And it's a persistent or recurring—perhaps constantly renewing—kind of feeling. You are hopelessly, helplessly drawn . . . almost as if you have no choice in the matter. Yet—ironically enough—it may also seem like the most difficult choice you've ever made. Good luck.

For WORK questions. Merger! Two business interests come together on the cusp of a shared idea. But is it just a temporary thing? Or the makings of a permanent fling? It's not quite clear. And only time will tell. But this one certainly looks like a sure thing. <u>Outcome</u>: All together now . . .

For LOVE questions. Sudden Attraction! The two of you fit together like a pair of bookends—but not necessarily cheek to cheek or back to back. Whether you are well matched or unevenly paired would almost seem irrelevant. And that's why we have to suspect it's the real thing. <u>Outcome</u>: Here's someone you could learn to live with.

For MONEY questions. Mutual Attraction! You and your money are made for each other. You can't get enough of it. And it can't seem to let go of you. (At least you'll have no problem falling asleep at night . . . one thousand and one . . . one thousand and two . . .) <u>Outcome</u>: May the two of you live happily ever after.

For STRATEGY questions. The Feeling is Mutual! This is a situation where you gravitate to each other. Sometimes a shared interest is enough, but this is neither necessary nor sufficient. It takes something deeper. And you either feel it or you don't. There's nothing you can do about it. And yet there is sometimes a moment of doubt. <u>Outcome</u>: When your heart skips a beat, follow it up.

BONUS ANSWERS FOR CHANGING LINES

Line 6: Let's quit pretending! It's time to fess up to the facts of life— whatever they may be.

Line 5: What do you plan to do about it? You will surely find your way as long as you feel for it, rather than predefine it.

Line 4: What do your extra senses say? These are the signals you can naturally trust. Go always with your hunches.

Line 3: What signals are you receiving? When the signs are lighted as brightly as this, you have no choice but to obey.

Line 2: What are you feeling? Trust especially in the thoughts that come to you from nowhere and make no logical sense.

Line 1: Who are you fooling? If this isn't the real thing, then what is?

THE GREAT NEBULA

MIST/MIST

Mist over Mist. *Think about it.* This is a diagram about great satisfaction . . . like the swirling stardust within the mist of the Universe itself. Having drawn the sign of The Great Nebula, you are about to delight in the true meaning of life. To say anything else would spoil the surprise. But know this: A most pleasant moment is on its way to you. Something very special occurs.

For WORK questions. Satisfaction! Congratulations on a job well done, a mission accomplished, a project completed, a deadline reached, a goal achieved. . . . Sit back and take a great big breath, my friend. This is what it feels like to accomplish. <u>Outcome</u>: Way to go!

For LOVE questions. Pleasure! Best wishes, my friends. You have truly outdone yourselves this time—and no wishbones about it. A little bundle of joy is winging its way. Delight in its arrival. <u>Outcome</u>: The spittin' image.

For MONEY questions. Delight! Well, they say you can't take it with you, but if you died right now, you'd have a big smile on your face. I don't know what has caused this manna from heaven to fall into your wallet, but don't knock it! Go on, my friend, it's special moments like this that were made for the Gold Card. <u>Outcome</u>: Have a ball.

For STRATEGY questions. Joy! Joy! Joy! This is the kind of situation that should come along every day—or should it? All you really have to do is sit back and drink in the moment. <u>Outcome</u>: It just doesn't get any better than this.

BONUS ANSWERS FOR CHANGING LINES

Line 6: Sing from the rooftops.
Line 5: Sit back and enjoy it.
Line 4: Laugh all the way to the bank.
Line 3: Coo in your sleep.
Line 2: Whistle while you work.
Line 1: Dance in the streets.

Appendix

HOW TO GET YOUR MONEY'S WORTH
(FROM I CHING IN TEN MINUTES)

There are two basic ways to use this book. One way is to start with Reading #1 and go from there on a guided tour. The second option is to start with Reading #16 and use the Master Answer section to do your own thing.

This Appendix offers a few additional and fun things you can do with *I Ching in Ten Minutes*. Some advanced techniques are also covered here.

Thought-for-the-Day-Readings. One of the easiest things to do with *I Ching in Ten Minutes* is to cast a six-line diagram in order to get a thought for the day. Just ask something like, What guidance is there for me today? Toss your coins or count your sticks. (See Reading #16 for how to do this.) Look up your hexagram in Reading #15's answers. Or look in the Master Answer section and read what it has to say.

For Parties. Several of the Readings included in *I Ching in Ten Minutes* can be used right off the shelf to conduct readings for your friends. At your next party, try out: Reading #3, "What's My Sign?"; Reading #7, "Where Do I Stand?"; Reading #10, "What Path Am I On?"; and (great for overnights) Reading #11, "Are We Compatible?"

Mutual Destiny Readings. If you want to see the combined result of any two things working together (such as you and your employer or you and your love) construct an I Ching trigram for each of the two people (or things) involved and then combine them into a single hexagram. Then look up your hexagram in the Master Answer section. (Also see Reading #9.)

Past, Present, and Future Readings. To trace any relationship or developing situation over a period of time, cast three hexagrams — one for the past, one for the present, and one for the future. Look up your hexagrams in the Master Answer section. This will give you a sweeping overview of the situation.

You can also "reset" these time frames to any period you choose. For example, you could do a "yesterday," "today," and "tomorrow" Reading. Or, "last year," "this year," and "next year." Just make sure you decide in advance what time frame you will be using.

There's no reason why you have to limit this Reading to three hexagrams. How about a full-year forecast? Just throw twelve hexagrams, one for each month.

Brainstorming Sessions. Need to get some fresh ideas on a subject? Cast a few six-liners to get some new perspectives. Then, test your own ideas, by asking about each of them in turn. Construct hexagrams for each thought, and interpret the results. You can go back and forth like this all night . . . bouncing ideas off of the I Ching.

Choosing Lucky Numbers. Since the I Ching diagrams can be read literally as numbers, you can use them to identify your winning combinations. Reading #14 presents an easy way to select lucky numbers. Hear are a couple other ways to do it.

For games of chance that use the numbers ranging from 0 to 63, the I Ching hexagrams are a natural. Just cast one six-line diagram for every number you need to pick, then translate your diagrams into numbers.

The process involves some basic arithmetic. The premise is that each solid line in your diagram has a different numerical value, depending upon its position. But if a line is broken, it has no value at all. It doesn't count.

First, cast your hexagram. Let's say you get this one:

6th line solid	=	1
5th line if solid	=	2
4th line solid	=	4
3rd line if solid	=	8
2nd line solid	=	16
bottom line solid	=	32

Broken lines in any position = 0

In this example, the botom line is solid, so—looking across to the numbers on the right—it has a value of 32. The second line also is solid, so it has a value of 16. But the third line is broken, so it has no value at all. This particular hexagram adds up to: 32+16+0+4+0+1 = 53. So 53 is your first lucky number.

In cases where your game involves fewer than 63 numbers, you can still use this method. For any numbers that are higher than your field of play, just "reduce" them, by adding the digits together.

Say, your game has only 48 numbers. For any diagrams you draw that has a value higher than 48, just add its digits together to get a smaller number. In the example above—where the outcome was 53—you would now add 5+3 to get 8 as a lucky number. If you get a diagram that adds up to 0, skip it. Keep casting hexagrams until you get enough numbers to play.

For games that involve 31 numbers you can cast five-line I Ching diagrams, using these values for the lines:

▬▬▬▬▬▬	5th line solid	= 1
▬▬▬▬▬▬	4th line solid	= 2
▬▬▬▬▬▬	3rd line solid	= 4
▬▬▬▬▬▬	2nd line solid	= 8
▬▬▬▬▬▬	bottom line solid	= 16
Broken lines in any position		= 0

If your game has more than 63 numbers, I suggest that you switch to another game, since you are dealing with impossible odds! But to do the calculation, just add a seventh line to your hexagram. Solid lines on the bottom of the diagram will now have a value of 64. Solid lines in the second position will now be worth 32. And so on (16, 8, 4, 2, 1).

Traditional Stick Counting. *I Ching in Ten Minutes* presents two very modern, very simple, and very accurate ways of using sticks to consult the I Ching. The methods described in Reading #16 will in fact produce nearly identical results to the much more complex and ancient technique for counting sticks.

However, some say that the old ways help them to establish a more meditative mood, which results in a better Reading. So if you would like to count sticks like the ancients, here's how:

First, you'll need 50 sticks of some kind, each between eight and 12 inches long. (Traditional sticks are made from the stalks of the Chinese herb plant yarrow. You could make do with any willowy twig. But virtually any kind of stick will work. Be creative!)

Take your bundle of sticks in hand—light your incense, ring your bell, say your prayers, face the proper direction (let's say West), and wave your sticks three times through the rising smoke. Write your question down on a slip of paper, and concentrate on it as you do the following:

First, <u>remove one stick</u> from your bundle and set it aside completely. You no longer need it.

1. Divide the remaining sticks into two bundles—LEFT and RIGHT.
2. RIGHT bundle: Remove one stick. Hold onto it.
3. LEFT bundle: Count off the sticks **by fours**. Hold onto the last group of one to four sticks.
4. RIGHT bundle: Count off the sticks **by fours**. Hold onto the last group of one to four sticks.
5. Recombine all the sticks you have <u>not</u> held onto.
6. Repeat steps 1–5.
7. Repeat steps 1–4.
8. Count the number of sticks you have hung onto.
9. Translate this number into a line:

Now repeat this process five more times to get your six-line hexagram. Stack each new line on top of the one you cast before. Look up your hexagram in the Master Answer section.

The method described here is a reinterpretation of traditional sources. Thanks once again to Michael McCormick.

I Ching Numerology. Yet another way to construct an I Ching hexagram is to add up some numbers. First, "add up" the numerals in today's date. If this is 12/31/1999: add 1+2+3+1+1+9+9+9 = 35. Then add again: 3+5 = 8. Eight is your number. If you end up with a 9, convert it to a 1. This first step will give you the I Ching three-line diagram for the date on which you are asking the question:

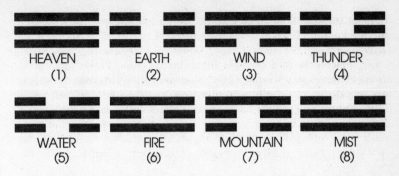

HEAVEN	EARTH	WIND	THUNDER
(1)	(2)	(3)	(4)

WATER	FIRE	MOUNTAIN	MIST
(5)	(6)	(7)	(8)

Next complete a second step to see what the prospects are for a particular person, place, or thing. For example, to find out whether you will be fortunate in your new house, add up the numerals in the address just like you added up the date in Step 1. Or to learn about employment prospects, add up your Social Security number. To learn how your trip will go, add up your driver's license number or your passport number. To find out what kind of news you can expect to hear, add up your phone number. You get the idea—anything with a number is fair game.

For things that don't have a number, convert letters to numerals by using this chart:

1	2	3	4	5	6	7	8
A	B	C	D	E	F	G	H
I/J	K	L	M	N	O	P	Q
R/S	T	U	V	W	X	Y	Z

If, for example, the name of the company in question is Zebra, you would convert each letter to its number and add: $8+5+2+1+1 = 17$. Then, adding again: $1+7 = 8$. In this case "8" is your answer. Use the #8 trigram from the table and place it on top of the trigram for the date in question. Then consult the Master Answer section for the resulting hexagram you have thus created (Mist/Mist in the example).

This numerological method is a combination of various traditions both Western and Eastern, including the Chinese school of thought known as Plum Blossom numerology, which dates to about A.D. 1000.

If you like working with numbers, don't miss Readings #3, #6, #10, and #11, which use additional numerology techniques.

Using stones. Besides coins and sticks, other tools can be used for conducting I Ching Readings. For example, you could use 16 stones of different colors.

In this scenario, let's say black stones are equal to a broken line, white stones are equal to a solid line, grey stones are solid changing to broken, and speckled stones are broken changing to solid. To assemble your I Ching stones, you'll need to find seven black stones, five white stones, three gray stones, and one speckled stone—all of about the same shape and size. Beach pebbles come to mind. But feel free to develop your own color scheme or substitute other objects like shells, pottery shards, or beads.

To draw your diagram, just put your "stones" in a bowl or a bag and draw one out at random for each line. Consult your color scheme and jot down your line. Return each stone to the container before you draw again.

This method—as well as the stick selection method in the Extra Credit section of Reading #16—comes from Larry Schoenholtz's book, *New Directions in the I Ching*, University Books, 1975. Thanks to Greg Whincup for rediscovering it.

Meditation on the Trigrams. Though few and simple, the I Ching trigrams (see Reading #8) provide much food for thought. Try drawing and repeating them once a day for a while—untill you can picture them in your head and recall their manes. Then, whenever you need a little boost of inspiration, run over them in your mind. It works every time.

Meditation on the Hexagrams. After you have learned to meditate on the trigrams, see if you can start "flipping through" the hexagrams in your head. It's really not as hard as it sounds, as long as you think of the hexagrams as one trigram on top of another: Heaven over Heaven, Heaven over Earth, Heaven over Wind, etc. To complete your meditation just turn the lights down low and run through the entire sequence of 64 combinations in your head. (If you need some help, flip through the Master Answer section and look at each hexagram in turn while you say its name. . .Earth over Heaven, Earth over Earth, Earth over Wind, and so forth.) Surprisingly enough, this simple process will rapidly improve your ability to relate to the diagrams. And who knows, it may even be a cure for insomnia!

Index

ALL THE QUESTIONS YOU CAN ASK

With *I Ching in Ten Minutes*, you can ask just about any question that's on your mind. But these are the questions that are actually listed in the book. If you can't find one that exactly matches your needs today, look for the one that's close enough.

* Consult the Extra Credit section of this Reading
** Consult the Extra, Extra Credit!

Which way should I go to find true love? 5

Who can I turn to? 9
Who am I looking for? 3 *
Who can I trust? 9
Will we come closer? 13
Will we drift further apart? 13

CAREER & WORK   READING

Are conditions favorable to ask for a raise? 1
How will my career unfold? 13
How will our meeting go? 11 *
How will this partnership work? 11 *
Is the timing right for making a career move? 1

What are the odds that I will get ahead? 4
What are the prospects for _____? 4
What can I expect from my boss? 8
What changes can I expect at work? 13
What forces are at work on the job? 2

What is my key to success with this job? 14
What is my relationship with this company? 8
What kind of energy surrounds me at school? At work? 2
What role do I play at work? 7
What success will come of this joint venture? 14

What's my situation at work? 10 *
What's the bottom line on this job? 15
Where do I stand in my career? 7
Which way am I headed with this job? 5
Which way should I face to do my best work? 5 **

Which way should I go to locate work? 5
Who can I trust in business dealings? 9

MONEY & FINANCE   READING

Is the timing right for making money? 1
What are the prospects for buying a new car?
   For increasing my income? 4
What changes can I expect with my money? 13

* Consult the Extra Credit section of this Reading
** Consult the Extra, Extra Credit!

STRATEGY & POLITICS   READING

* Consult the Extra Credit section of this Reading
** Consult the Extra, Extra Credit!

PERSONAL DEVELOPMENT   READING

How am I doing today?	7 *
How do I relate to others?	7
How do others see me?	3 **
How should I handle it?	8 *
Is this the right time to act on my instincts?	1
What is my key to success?	14
What forces are at work in my life right now?	2
What role do I play?	7
What's my sign?	3
What's my situation?	10 *
Where do I fit in?	7
Which way am I headed?	5
Who can I lean on?	9

SOUL-SEARCHING   READING

How can I overcome my past?	12
How do I relate? To my environment?	7
How is my spirit progressing?	13 *
How will my soul evolve?	13
Is the force with me?	2
Is this a good time to consult the I Ching?	1
Is this the right time to act on my dreams?	1
What path am I on?	10
What do I have coming to me?	12 *
What does my soul require?	13 *
What have I learned?	12
What kind of energy do I need to tap into?	2
What kind of energy surrounds me right now?	2
What kind of vibrations am I picking up on?	2
What will heal my spirit?	13 *
What's my karma?	12
What's the answer for me?	14
What's the magic word?	15 *
Where will my soul-search lead?	15

* Consult the Extra Credit section of this Reading
** Consult the Extra, Extra Credit!

* Consult the Extra Credit section of this Reading
** Consult the Extra, Extra Credit!

I Ching in Ten Minutes

* Consult the Extra Credit section of this Reading
** Consult the Extra, Extra Credit!

FOR FURTHER INFORMATION

RECOMMENDED READING

If, after using this book, you would like to know more about the I Ching and its fascinating history, theory, and philosophy, there are many good books on the subject. I highly recommend the following:

Greg Whincup: *Rediscovering the I Ching*, Doubleday, 1986.

Barbara G. Walker: *I Ching of the Goddess*, Harper & Row, 1986.

Kerson and Rosemary Huang, *I Ching*, Workman Publishing, 1987.

R. L. Wing, *The I Ching Workbook*, Doubleday, 1979.

Thomas Cleary, *I Ching: The Book of Change*, Shambhala Pocket Editions, 1992.

For those who would like to see something a little more visual than an I Ching hexagram, I recommend the following illustrated books:

Ann Williams and Ralph Metzner, *Images from the I Ching: Visual Meditations from the Book of Change*, Prism Press, 1987.

R. L. Wing, *The Illustrated I Ching*, Doubleday/Dolphin, 1982.

ACKNOWLEDGMENTS

During the writing of this book, a particular sequence of songs was especially important to me. I'd like to thank the following recording artists for helping me understand the I Ching trigrams.

Roger Waters
"Perfect Sense, Part I"
From *Amused to Death*, Columbia, 1992

HEAVEN
Joni Mitchell
"Slouching Towards Bethlehem"
"Night Ride Home"
From *Night Ride Home*, Geffen Records, 1991

EARTH
Bruce Springsteen
"Lucky Town"
"My Beautiful Reward"
From *Lucky Town*, Columbia, 1992

Boyz II Men
"Motown Philly"
From *Cooley High Harmony*, Motown, 1991

WIND
Poison
"Ride the Wind"
"Something to Believe in"
From *Flesh & Blood*, Capitol, 1990

THUNDER
Extreme II
"Decadence Dance"
"Hole Hearted"
From *Pornograffitti*, A&M Records, 1990

———

Red Hot Chili Peppers
"Under the Bridge"
From *Blood Sugar Sex Magik*, Warner Bros., 1991

———

WATER
Sting
"All This Time"
"Mad About You"
From *The Soul Cages*, A&M Records, 1991

FIRE
Slaughter
"Burning Bridges"
"Fly to the Angels"
From *Stick It Live*, Chrysalis Records, 1990

———

The B-52's
"Roam"
From *Cosmic Thing*, Reprise Records, 1989

———

MOUNTAIN
Madonna
"Oh Father"
"Like a Prayer"
From *Like a Prayer*, Sire Records, 1989

MIST
Bruce Springsteen
"With Every Wish"
"Soul Driver"
From *Human Touch*, Columbia, 1992

I Ching in Ten Minutes

Body Count
"C Note"
From *Body Count*, Sire Records, 1992

---

*With special thanks to Turtle for taking me into the woods.
May you live a hundred dog years, pal.*

And to Addie: xxxo

FASCINATING BOOKS
OF SPIRITUALITY
AND PSYCHIC DIVINATION

CLOUD NINE: A DREAMER'S DICTIONARY
by Sandra A. Thomson
77384-8/$6.99 US/$7.99 Can

SECRETS OF SHAMANISM:
TAPPING THE SPIRIT POWER
WITHIN YOU
by Jose Stevens, Ph.D. and Lena S. Stevens
75607-2/$6.50 US/$8.50 Can

THE LOVERS' TAROT
*by Robert Mueller, Ph.D., and Signe E. Echols, M.S.,
with Sandra A. Thomson*
76886-0/$11.00 US/$13.00 Can

REASON TO BELIEVE: A PRACTICAL
GUIDE TO PSYCHIC PHENOMENA
by Michael Clark
78474-2/$5.99 US/$7.99 Can

SPIRITUAL TAROT: SEVENTY-EIGHT
PATHS TO PERSONAL DEVELOPMENT
*by Signe E. Echols, M.S., Robert Mueller, Ph.D.,
and Sandra A. Thomson*
78206-5/$12.00 US/$16.00 Can